REINVENTING CHRISTIAN DOCTRINE

REINVENTING CHRISTIAN DOCTRINE

Retrieving the Law-Gospel Distinction

Maarten Wisse

LONDON • NEW YORK • OXFORD • NEW DELHI • SYDNEY

T&T CLARK

Bloomsbury Publishing Plc

50 Bedford Square, London, WC1B 3DP, UK
1385 Broadway, New York, NY 10018, USA
29 Earlsfort Terrace, Dublin 2, Ireland

BLOOMSBURY, T&T CLARK and the T&T Clark logo are trademarks of
Bloomsbury Publishing Plc

First published in Great Britain 2023
Paperback edition published 2024

Copyright © Maarten Wisse, 2023

Maarten Wisse has asserted his right under the Copyright, Designs and Patents Act, 1988, to be identified as Author of this work.

For legal purposes the Acknowledgements on p. x constitute an extension of this copyright page.

Cover image: Detail of the pulpit, St. Stephen's Church, Tangermünde, Germany © Maarten Wisse

This work is published open access subject to a Creative Commons Attribution-NonCommercial-NoDerivatives 4.0 International licence (CC BY-NC-ND 4.0, https://creativecommons.org/licenses/by-nc-nd/4.0/). You may re-use, distribute, and reproduce this work in any medium for non-commercial purposes, provided you give attribution to the copyright holder and the publisher and provide a link to the Creative Commons licence.

Bloomsbury Publishing Plc does not have any control over, or responsibility for, any third-party websites referred to or in this book. All internet addresses given in this book were correct at the time of going to press. The author and publisher regret any inconvenience caused if addresses have changed or sites have ceased to exist, but can accept no responsibility for any such changes.

A catalogue record for this book is available from the British Library.

A catalog record for this book is available from the Library of Congress.

ISBN: HB: 978-0-5677-0430-6
PB: 978-0-5677-0431-3
ePDF: 978-0-5677-0432-0
ePUB: 978-0-5677-0433-7

Typeset by Newgen KnowledgeWorks Pvt. Ltd., Chennai, India

To find out more about our authors and books visit www.bloomsbury.com and sign up for our newsletters.

*To the memory of Christoph Schwöbel (1955–2021)
For teaching me the difference between Law and Gospel*

Iam vero Evangelium stricte dictum, ut à lege distinguitur, directe & per se non praescribit nobis officium nostrum, aut quid nos facere debeamus, dicendo, hoc fac, aut crede, aut confide … Sed refert, nuntiat, significat nobis, quid Christus pro nobis fecerit, quidque Deus in Christo promittat, quid facere velit, & facturus sit.

– Gisbertus Voetius, *Selectae disputationes theologicae* (Ultrajecti: Johannes à Waesberge, 1648–69), IV, 26

CONTENTS

Acknowledgements x

Chapter 1
RETRIEVING THE LAW-GOSPEL DISTINCTION FOR THE TASK OF
DOGMATICS 1
   1.1 Introduction 1
   1.2 Reinventing Christian dogmatics 3
   1.3 Dogmatics from the perspective of the Law-Gospel distinction 4
   1.4 Dogmatics as a 'second act' 7
   1.5 Christology as the root of dogmatics 8
   1.6 Christology and soteriology are intertwined 11
   1.7 Does the Law do away with the Gospel? 13
   1.8 Overview 16

Chapter 2
LAW AND GOSPEL AS A HEURISTIC LENS 19
   2.1 Introduction 19
   2.2 Law and Gospel: A working definition 20
   2.3 The history of the distinction 21
       2.3.1 Looking back: Augustine 22
       2.3.2 The medieval tradition: Peter Lombard and Thomas Aquinas 26
       2.3.3 The key source of the distinction: Melanchthon 26
       2.3.4 The exception: Calvin 30
       2.3.5 The rule: Reformed scholasticism 36
       2.3.6 The twentieth century: Barth 38
   2.4 Towards a new understanding of Law and Gospel 42

Chapter 3
SCRIPTURE USE IN AUGUSTINE AND THE REFORMATION 47
   3.1 Introduction 47
   3.2 Christocentrism 48
   3.3 Augustine on Law and Gospel, 'nature' and 'grace' 51
       3.3.1 Sermon 141 53
       3.3.2 Sermon 229G 56
   3.4 The Johannine prologue in the Reformation 59
   3.5 The problem in a nutshell 61
   3.6 Radical receptions of the Johannine prologue 65
       3.6.1 Michael Servetus 65

	3.6.2 Sebastian Franck	67
	3.6.3 Melchior Hoffman and Menno Simons	71
	3.6.4 Martin Bucer and John Calvin	72
	3.6.5 Martin Luther	74
3.7	Conclusion	77

Chapter 4
CHRISTOCENTRISM IN KARL BARTH, THE GOSPEL OF JOHN AND THE POSSIBILITY OF NATURAL THEOLOGY 79

4.1	Introduction	79
4.2	Barth as an experimental theologian	80
4.3	The Barmen Declaration	84
4.4	A historical deconstruction of Barth's reading of Barmen in *Church Dogmatics* II/1	89
4.5	'The Word of God as the task of theology' (1922)	91
4.6	'The first commandment as theological axiom' (1933)	98
4.7	'Three basic patterns of theology' (1936)	105
4.8	Christocentrism in the *Church Dogmatics* I/2	110
4.9	Barth and the Johannine tradition	113

Chapter 5
CONTRA ET PRO *SOLA SCRIPTURA* 115

5.1	Introduction	115
5.2	What do I mean by *sola scriptura*?	116
5.3	It's dogmatics and preaching, stupid!	120
5.4	The *sola scriptura* makes theologians lazy	122
5.5	Scripture between Law and Gospel	124
5.6	Pro *sola scriptura*	127
5.7	Consequences of this step	128

Chapter 6
IN DEFENCE OF DOUBLE PREDESTINATION 131

6.1	From Law and Gospel to predestination and the other way around	131
6.2	Why predestination matters today	132
6.3	Definition of terms	134
6.4	Three basic options in soteriology	136
	6.4.1 Hard universalism	136
	6.4.2 Soft universalism	142
6.5	Understanding double predestination	144
6.6	Innovating double predestination	145
6.7	Predestination and assurance of faith	147

Chapter 7
ATONEMENT: SOCINUS AND OWEN IN CONVERSATION 151
   7.1 Two theses 151
   7.2 Socinus' critique of substitutionary atonement 152
   7.3 John Owen's reply 153
   7.4 Owen's use of the Bible 154
   7.5 Anthropology as an argument 155
   7.6 How Socinus and Owen share the same concern 157
   7.7 Diagnosing the Fall 158
   7.8 God as the lord of Florence 160
   7.9 God, Law and Gospel 162

Chapter 8
HOLY SUPPER: RETRIEVING ABRAHAM KUYPER 165
   8.1 Introduction 165
   8.2 Abraham Kuyper on the Lord's Supper 168
   8.3 Comparison and further analysis 170
   8.4 Preliminary conclusion 176
   8.5 In search of a new paradigm 177
   8.6 A Zwinglian point of view? 180
   8.7 Extra calvinisticum? 182

Chapter 9
LAW AND GOSPEL AS A KEY TO THE THEOLOGY OF THE RELIGIONS 185
   9.1 Introduction 185
   9.2 Religions as sources of knowledge and truth 186
   9.3 The Law and Gospel distinction as a critical instrument in theology 189
   9.4 Religion as truth and the nature of the Gospel as promise 194

Bibliography 199
Biblical Index 211
General Index 212

ACKNOWLEDGEMENTS

Books tend to take a long time to complete, at least for me. This book is no exception. It began to take shape during my stay in Germany from 2004 to 2006, when I was working on a monograph on Augustine's Trinitarian theology. Along the way, I discovered that Augustine's theology is characterized by a certain duality that I missed in contemporary theology and even in contemporary interpretations of Augustine. I increasingly noticed how important that duality really was to my own way of doing theology, and this realization led to a growing curiosity as to what that duality might be and how it could become key for doing systematic theology in the here and now. Step by step, I learned to see what this intuition offered, and it took a long time, alongside an academic career that is about so much more than just doing research, to flesh out in greater detail what it means to do theology in terms of 'Law' and 'Gospel', as I gradually learned to call it.

Many people have provided crucial insights along the way, sometimes also by proposing them in ways radically different from how I have eventually come to use them. In all sorts of ways, I owe this book to my systematic-theological training at Heidelberg and Tübingen under the supervision of Christoph Schwöbel. Before this book was published, Christoph suddenly passed away. This book is dedicated to his memory. Although he hesitated to use the Law-Gospel distinction as key to systematic theology, it was never far from his Lutheran approach to theology, and so I learned from him in many more respects than I first realized. A second important intellectual environment for the writing of this book was the Faculty of Theology, now the Faculty of Religion and Theology, at the Vrije Universiteit Amsterdam. When I arrived there in 2009, I was still working on my Augustine monograph, but the deep interest of the systematic theologians there – and of Kees van der Kooi in particular – in the relationship between the use of Scripture and systematic theology guided me to a combination of reception studies and systematic theology, which is clearly visible in some of the chapters of this book. In this way, I learned to combine the hermeneutical approach of my PhD research with the systematic-theological work for my Augustine monograph. This could not have happened without the wider circle of systematic theologians at the Vrije Universiteit at that time: Gijsbert van den Brink, Martien Brinkman, Eddy van der Borght, Katja Tolstaya, Wim van Vlastuin, Fernando Enns, Henk Bakker, Teun van der Leer and others. I would also like to thank Mirjam van Veen and Jesse Spohnholz – colleagues from the Historical Theology Department – for very stimulating conversations on Reformation history and the radical Reformation in particular.

I completed work on the book at my new institution, the Protestant Theological University. While it may be housed in the same Vrije Universiteit building, it was a new intellectual environment nonetheless, with new colleagues and new things to learn from them. Here, I would like to express my thanks to Rinse Reeling Brouwer, Edward van 't Slot, Wim Moehn, Klaas-Willem de Jong, Arjan Plaisier, Klaas Bom, Benno van der Toren, Heleen Zorgdrager and Rick Benjamins. A new conversation with colleagues working in the area of Christian ethics – Pieter Vos, Petruschka Schaafsma, Rob Compaijen and Theo Boer – brought to the fore fresh insights that proved relevant to the way in which the Law-Gospel distinction could be used in systematic theology.

For their comments on an earlier draft of Chapter 4, I would like to thank my former students Simon van der Linden and Marc Jongma, as well as my colleagues Rinse Reeling Brouwer, Edward van 't Slot and Arjan Plaisier. I would also like to thank Bart Kamphuis, Hans Burger, Arnold Huijgen and other members of the BEST research group for their contributions to Chapter 5. I am indebted to Oliver Crisp, Dolf te Velde and Raymond R. Hausoul, who commented on an earlier version of Chapter 6. I also express my thanks to Kyle Dieleman, Albert Gootjes and Raymond E. Blacketer for working with me to correct my English. Writing academic English is no easy task and will always remain a fragile endeavour, but you helped me to express myself as clearly as possible in a language that is not my own.

This is also the place to thank the publishers for their permission to republish earlier papers as partial book chapters, most in an updated and expanded form. The following chapters were published earlier:

- Parts of Chapter 1 appeared in an earlier form as: 'Retrieving the Law and Gospel Distinction for the Task of Dogmatics', *Neue Zeitschrift für Systematische Theologie und Religionsphilosophie* 61.3 (2019), 297–315.
- A shorter version of the discussion of the Reformation in Chapter 3 was published in German as: ' "… welches alle Menschen erleuchtet"? Die Krise der Europäischen Identität im Spiegel der frühmodernen Rezeption des Johannesprologs', *Neue Zeitschrift für Systematische Theologie und Religionsphilosophie* 55.1 (2013), 1–19.
- Chapter 5 was published as: 'Contra et Pro Sola Scriptura', in *Sola Scriptura: Biblical and Theological Perspectives on Scripture, Authority and Hermeneutics*, ed. Hans Burger and Arnold Huijgen, Studies in Reformed Theology, 32 (Leiden; Boston, MA: Brill, 2017), pp. 19–37.
- An earlier version of Chapter 7 appeared as: 'The Law and Gospel Distinction as a Frame of Reference for Communicative Rationality: Socinus and Owen on Atonement', in *Rationalität Im Gespräch*, ed. Markus Mühling and Martin Wendte, Marburger Theologische Studien, 126 (Leipzig: Evangelischer Verlagsanstalt, 2016), pp. 267–77.
- An earlier and shorter version of Chapter 8 was published as: 'Christ's Presence through the Spirit in the Holy Supper: Retrieving Abraham Kuyper', in *The Spirit Is Moving: New Pathways in Pneumatology*, ed. Gijsbert van den Brink, Eveline van Staalduine and Maarten Wisse, Studies in Reformed Theology, 38 (Leiden: Brill, 2019), pp. 331–45.
- Chapter 9 was published in German as: 'Das Gesetz als Kriterium der systematischen Theologie? Überlegungen zur Konzeption einer Theologie der Religionen', *Zeitschrift für Dialektische Theologie* 34.2 (2018), 99–113.

Chapter 1

RETRIEVING THE LAW-GOSPEL DISTINCTION FOR THE TASK OF DOGMATICS

1.1 Introduction

Modern dogmatics is deeply interested in knowledge about God. In traditional Protestant dogmatics, this interest manifested itself in the attempt to summarize what the Bible has to say about the reality of God and God's acts in creation and redemption. As such, dogmatics is about propositions: it is about who God is, and what God's attributes and God's works are. In the twentieth century, this way of doing dogmatics was subjected to criticism from several different angles. Particularly well known in the Anglo-Saxon world is George Lindbeck's critique of propositional approaches to dogmatics.[1] As a pupil of Hans Frei, Lindbeck formed part of the post-war continental dogmatic tradition which was heavily influenced by the theology of Karl Barth. Barth himself had already distanced himself from dogmatics as a system derived from an idealistic philosophical principle or as a biblicist summary of the message of Scripture. In his mature theology, Barth sought to develop a dogmatics based instead on the Christological dogma (see Chapter 4). In doing so, he established a very close relationship between who God is and what God does. God's being is in God's acts.[2] Although Barth was very much concerned about the reality-depicting status of dogmatics, he still understood dogmatics to be aimed at a description of this reality of God in God's acts. Even when we cannot speak about God as we ought, we must and do speak.[3] The reality of God which is being represented in the language of faith may be a dynamicized reality, but it nevertheless remains a description of reality. In this regard, Lindbeck went one step further when he understood dogmatics as an analysis of the grammar

---

1. George A. Lindbeck, *The Nature of Doctrine: Religion and Theology in a Postliberal Age* (Philadelphia, PA: Westminster, 1984).

2. Cf. Colin E. Gunton, *Becoming and Being: The Doctrine of God in Charles Hartshorne and Karl Barth* (Oxford: Oxford University Press, 1978); Eberhard Jüngel, *The Doctrine of the Trinity: God's Being Is in Becoming* (Grand Rapids, MI: Eerdmans, 1976).

3. Karl Barth, 'Das Wort Gottes als Aufgabe der Theologie', in *Vorträge und kleinere Arbeiten 1922–1925*, ed. Holger Finze-Michaelsen, Karl Barth-Gesamtausgabe 19 (Zürich: Theologischer Verlag, 1990), 151.

of the community of faith. Others, including Don Cupitt in Britain[4] and Harry Kuitert in the Netherlands,[5] went so far as to deny the reality-depicting character of theological expressions altogether. All of these proposals from the twentieth century represented reactions to the propositional character of dogmatics and of theology in general.

In contemporary systematic theology, the approach to dogmatic practice as a descriptive endeavour is nuanced. John Webster, for example, has shown a strong interest in dogmatics as the description of the reality of God: 'Christian dogmatic language about the divine attributes explicates the nature of the triune God by offering an analytical depiction of God's identity.'[6] This description takes the form of a doxology and includes a profound awareness of the mystery of the Triune God that we describe, but is still motivated by a deep longing for truth and a strong bond to the way in which Scripture as revelation speaks about God and God's acts.[7]

Kevin Vanhoozer's work shows a similar nuance in the way in which the representative task of dogmatics is integrated with other functions. On the one hand, Vanhoozer pleads for taking the propositional aspect of faith and dogmatics most seriously. Dogmatics is not only a story or the grammar of the community of faith but refers to the reality of God and to our reality.[8] At the beginning of a recent chapter on the task of dogmatics, Vanhoozer defined 'dogmatics' as 'the church's attempt to employ its own resources (e.g., Scripture, tradition) to issue binding statements concerning who God *is* and what God *is doing*'.[9] On the other hand, Vanhoozer is well aware of the limitations of a merely propositional account of dogmatics. This is why he uses the notion of drama.[10] The drama of God's acts in history issues a call to us to enter this drama and to respond to it in faith: 'Stated even more succinctly: dogmatics says *what is* "in Christ". As we will see, however, saying what is in Christ cannot be abstracted from having the mind of Christ and walking in the way of Christ.'[11] Believers are included in the drama and must live

---

4. Don Cupitt, *Taking Leave of God* (New York: Crossroad, 1981).

5. Harry M. Kuitert, *The Necessity of Faith: Or, Without Faith You're as Good as Dead* (Grand Rapids, MI: Eerdmans, 1976).

6. John Webster, *Confessing God: Essays in Christian Dogmatics II* (London: T&T Clark, 2005), 87.

7. E.g. John Webster, 'Principles of Systematic Theology', *International Journal of Systematic Theology* 11, no. 1 (1 January 2009): 56–71, https://doi.org/10.1111/j.1468-240 0.2008.00423.x.

8. Kevin J. Vanhoozer, *The Drama of Doctrine: A Canonical-Linguistic Approach to Christian Theology* (Philadelphia, PA: Westminster John Knox, 2005), 276–81.

9. Kevin J. Vanhoozer, 'Analytics, Poetics, and the Mission of Dogmatic Discourse', in *The Task of Dogmatics: Explorations in Theological Method*, ed. Oliver Crisp and Fred Sanders (Grand Rapids, MI: Zondervan, 2017), 23; original emphasis.

10. Vanhoozer, *The Drama of Doctrine*, 63–9.

11. Vanhoozer, 'Analytics, Poetics, and the Mission of Dogmatic Discourse', 23; original emphasis.

in a way that fits with what God does in Jesus Christ through the Spirit. But even then, the primary function of dogmatics still is to describe the drama or, to use Vanhoozer's metaphor, to prepare for the re-enactment of the drama of the reality of God and God's acts in history.[12] From this narration of the drama follows the call. Put in terms of the transcendentals, we might say: Truth has primacy. From truth follows goodness, follows ethics, as is paradigmatically the case in Barth's dogmatics.

How widespread the tendency towards a descriptive approach to dogmatics really is can be demonstrated by pointing out how even Sarah Coakley describes 'systematic theology' as 'an integrated presentation of Christian truth, however perceived ... However briefly, or lengthily ... it is explicated, "systematic theology" must attempt to provide a coherent, and alluring, vision of the Christian faith'.[13] In the rest of her book, Coakley shows herself to be profoundly aware of the dangers inherent in a descriptive approach to dogmatics.[14] For this reason, she proposes to embed the descriptive task of dogmatics in the practice of contemplation. That dogmatics has a descriptive aim, however, remains unquestioned.

1.2 Reinventing Christian dogmatics

In this book, I offer an alternative to the primary interest of contemporary dogmatics in its descriptive function by exploring the idea of dogmatics as a dual discourse: one verdictive and critical, the other commissive and positive. In doing so, I place myself in the twentieth-century trajectory regarding theological language as more than merely descriptive language. I was trained in this at the University of Utrecht, where every student of theology was raised in the tradition of J. L. Austin's *How to Do Things with Words* and learned that language is not just propositional but has a range of functions that must be distinguished. Vincent Brümmer's version of Austin's illocutionary theory of language had a lasting influence on my theological development, both consciously and unconsciously.[15]

Austin and Brümmer follow Wittgenstein in construing the meaning of language as its use. Modifying Austin's proposal, Brümmer distinguishes between four basic illocutionary acts, purposes of language: 'constatives' (Austin's 'propositions'), 'prescriptives', 'expressives' and 'commissives'. In twentieth-century

---

12. Vanhoozer, *The Drama of Doctrine*, 243–7.

13. Sarah Coakley, *God, Sexuality and the Self: An Essay 'on the Trinity'* (Cambridge: Cambridge University Press, 2013), 41.

14. Ibid., chapter 1.

15. Vincent Brümmer, *Theology and Philosophical Inquiry* (London: Macmillan, 1981), chapter 2. My first academic publication was based on my master's thesis and discussed the meaning of the authority of the Bible in terms of Brümmer's account of illocutionary theory, combining it with Jóseph M. Bocheński's logical analysis of authority: Maarten Wisse, 'The Meaning of the Authority of the Bible', *Religious Studies* 36 (2000): 473–87.

philosophical theology, most of the discussion surrounding the implications of illocutionary theory for theological language has centred around the role of constatives/propositions versus expressives. If we were to describe the above developments in twentieth-century dogmatics using Austin's theory of illocutions, we could say that traditional dogmatics is primarily interested in accounts of faith as propositions, liberal dogmatics in expressives and the newer dogmatics in a richer understanding of propositions, qualified by the broader context of doxology (expressives) or drama (propositions in narratives).

1.3 Dogmatics from the perspective of the Law-Gospel distinction

Over the years, I learned to think about the duality of theological discourse in new ways. Being trained not only in Anglo-Saxon philosophical theology but also in the history of ideas, the history of Reformed scholasticism, the early Church and modern systematic theology, I came to view this duality as a postmodern version of the classical Reformational Law-Gospel distinction, although I initially discovered it in the theology of Augustine (see Chapter 2). Historically, the Law-Gospel distinction goes back to Luther, and many still see it as a particularly Lutheran distinction. During the past several decades, and especially in the United States, scholars have rightly argued for its appropriate place within the Reformed tradition as well.[16] As I said, however, it goes as far back as Augustine and even beyond him to the theology of Paul.

By rethinking theological discourse in terms of the Law-Gospel distinction, I aim to shift the attention from propositions and expressives to the role of prescriptives (Law) and commissives (Gospel). As such, I do not want to deny the role of propositions and expressives in religious discourse, but I do want to find a new place for them and thus shift the attention of theologians away from the question of realism to 'new' and at the same time 'old' functions of religious language. In doing so, I hope to overcome the downside to the influence of Enlightenment thought on Christian theology. Modernity, characterized as it is by an epistemological interest in the reliability of knowledge claims, tends to reduce theological discourse to a source of knowledge. As I have illustrated above, it is true that this reduction of theological discourse to propositions was subjected to various kinds of criticism in the twentieth century. However, much theology remains determined by this epistemological paradigm, even when postmodern

---

16. R. Scott Clark, 'Law and Gospel in Early Reformed Orthodoxy: Hermeneutical Conservatism in Olevianus' Commentary on Romans', in *Church and School in Early Modern Protestantism: Studies in Honor of Richard A. Muller on the Maturation of a Theological Tradition*, ed. Jordan J. Ballor, David S. Sytsma and Jason Zuidema, Studies in the History of Christian Traditions 170 (Leiden: Brill, 2013), 307–20; Michael S. Horton, 'Calvin and the Law-Gospel Hermeneutic', *Pro Ecclesia* 6, no. 1 (2002): 27–42; I. John Hesselink, *Calvin's Concept of the Law* (Allison Park, PA: Pickwick, 1992).

theologies deny the possibility of epistemological access to God and the world. For, in denying this access, they nevertheless remain determined by the modern reduction.[17]

In this book, I propose to look at the entire task of dogmatics from the perspective of Law and Gospel in a more encompassing and conscious way than the Christian tradition has commonly done. Of course, I would like to do so in a new context, informed in various ways by influences from the Enlightenment and postmodernity.

Before I introduce the overall argument of this book and make a concise case for its central thesis, I would like to quote the description of the Law-Gospel distinction from the Dutch seventeenth-century theologian Gisbertus Voetius (1589–1676) in order to give an impression of what that distinction amounts to:

> The Gospel in the strict sense, however, insofar as it is distinguished from the law, does not directly and in itself prescribe to us our plight, nor what we have to do, saying, 'Do this', or, 'Believe this', or, 'Have faith' ... But it refers to, witnesses of, and signifies to us what Christ has done for us, what God promises to us in Christ, what he wants to do, and what he will do.[18]

While Chapter 2 will be devoted in its entirety to an account of the history and significance of the Law-Gospel distinction, here it suffices to note that Voetius distinguishes very sharply between the two main discourses in theology. Although he certainly acknowledges that commands and promises are present in both the Old and the New Testament, he nevertheless distinguishes between them as the two fundamental ways in which God communicates with us. The distinction aims to safeguard both the commands and the promises. As a follower of the Puritans in the Dutch context, Voetius certainly would not want to do away with the Law. Nevertheless, he is equally concerned to ensure that the Gospel, in the strict sense of the term, remains free from any prescriptive element. The Gospel does not even demand faith from us. This shows the depth of Voetius' concern to keep the Gospel free as God's promise, neither dependent on nor bound to our human response.

From the perspective of the Law-Gospel distinction, an objection obtains here against the way in which dogmatics is often practiced, namely as a description of the reality of God and God's acts (see above). If dogmatics is primarily interested

---

17. For a more extensive account of this point, see Maarten Wisse, *Trinitarian Theology beyond Participation: Augustine's de Trinitate and Contemporary Theology*, T&T Clark Studies in Systematic Theology 11 (London: T&T Clark International, 2011), chapter 1.

18. Gisbertus Voetius, *Selectae disputationes theologicae* (Ultrajecti: Johannes à Waesberge, 1648-69), IV, 26: 'Iam vero Evangelium stricte dictum, ut à lege distinguitur, directe & per se non praescribit nobis officium nostrum, aut quid nos facere debeamus, dicendo, hoc fac, aut crede, aut confide; ... Sed refert, nuntiat, significat nobis, quid Christus pro nobis fecerit, quidque Deus in Christo promittat, quid facere velit, & facturus sit.'

in the description of God's being and acts, the implication is that it is first of all a description of God's saving acts towards us. The way in which dogmatics speaks about God and God's acts in history is determined by the Gospel and the Gospel alone. Precisely as a description of the Triune God's acts, it takes its point of departure in the Gospel.

That this is indeed the effect of seeing dogmatics primarily as a description of God's being and acts can be illustrated from the way in which modern dogmatics typically views God's saving acts towards Israel. Usually, they are understood as a foreshadowing of God's saving acts in Jesus Christ. What God does in God's covenant with Israel is now fundamentally of the same kind as what God does in Jesus Christ. This can be demonstrated with the examples of Barth, for whom Israel is fundamentally a parallel to God's covenant in Jesus Christ,[19] or Hendrikus Berkhof,[20] or Abraham van de Beek and his theology of Israel.[21] In their work, the basic Law-Gospel distinction has disappeared, partly consciously, partly unconsciously.

With the disappearance of this distinction, however, a conflict emerges between the Gospel as a claim to the truth about God and about God's acts in history on the one hand, and the nature of the Gospel as a promise and invitation on the other. This conflict becomes clear when the classical Law-Gospel distinction is translated into illocutionary terms. According to Vincent Brümmer, every 'constative' hides an implicit, secondary prescriptive illocution: every time we confront a conversation partner with a knowledge claim, it involves a latent call to accept the claim as true.[22] And so, if the primary task of dogmatics is the representation of the Gospel and God's acts in Israel and the nations, this has the important consequence that we are invited and, given good grounds, also intellectually obliged to accept this representation as true and as corresponding to the reality of God and God's acts. Many dogmatic controversies seem to revolve around this dynamic; they are about the question of whether that which is being claimed is true. The same applies to many debates between believers and non-believers, namely whether or not that which Christians claim to know about God on the basis of revelation is true or not. And if it is true, and you do not accept it, you are either intellectually substandard or discredited. From the perspective of the Law-Gospel distinction, this turns the Gospel into a Law. If the content of the Gospel is a representation of the reality of God and God's acts in the world, then it is not primarily good news, but first of all a claim to truth that is not as such available to all, but only to those who accept a certain revelation as true.

---

19. Karl Barth, *Church Dogmatics*, trans. Geoffrey William Bromiley and Thomas F. Torrance (Edinburgh: T&T Clark, 1975), II/2 and III/1.

20. Hendrikus Berkhof, *Christian Faith: An Introduction to the Study of the Faith* (Eugene, OR: Wipf and Stock, 1999), sec. 30.

21. Abraham van de Beek, *De kring om de Messias: Israël als volk van de lijdende Heer: Spreken over God 1,2* (Zoetermeer: Meinema, 2002).

22. Brümmer, *Theology and Philosophical Inquiry*, 26–33.

This is one of the reasons why I would like to propose to learn to speak twice in dogmatics. The task of dogmatics is not primarily to describe the reality of God and his acts. Quite the contrary, it intends to protect the mystery of this reality by moving back and forth, maintaining a balance, between the prescriptives (or rather, verdictives) of the Law and the commissives of the Gospel.

This back-and-forth movement between the commissives of the Gospel and the verdictives of the Law includes references to reality or, perhaps more accurately, is concerned with the reality of the mystery of God and God's acts. In this sense, I try to overcome the divide between a propositional and a non-propositional understanding of dogmatics. My proposal can be elucidated once again in terms of the theory of illocutions as understood by Brümmer. Every commissive, so Brümmer argues, always includes one or more implicit constatives.[23] I cannot believe someone who offers me one hundred dollars for nothing, if I do not believe that this person actually has one hundred dollars. Nevertheless, this person's intention is not to claim that he has one hundred dollars. The speaker's intention is to communicate to me his sincere intention to give me those one hundred dollars, provided that I am willing to accept them. It is indeed true that every commissive implies the need for a response from the conversation partner, but this response does not take the form of an obligation.[24] It is an invitation to which the conversation partner is free to respond.

1.4 Dogmatics as a 'second act'

In light of the above, we can raise the question of the proper place for dogmatics, its locus vis-à-vis the community of faith. If the Gospel is about a promise, the question arises as to the extent to which dogmatics is called to proclaim this promise, or, if the Law is about verdictives, the extent to which dogmatics is called to proclaim those verdictives. Contrary to recent claims, it is not obvious that dogmatics as a discipline belongs to the community of faith and that it should join this community in a confession of faith or an affirmation of its truth claims. As far as I can see, dogmatics is not primarily intended as a witness to God's promises (cf. below). In this regard, I would like to distinguish the task of dogmatics from the task of the proclamation of the Gospel within the community of faith.

---

23. Ibid.

24. It is now increasingly common in 'theologies of the gift' to emphasize that there is no gift without a response. However, this does not undo the fact that these responses can be of different kinds. Even a gift which is refused remains a gift on the part of the giver. Cf. e.g. Louis-Marie Chauvet, *Symbol and Sacrament: A Sacramental Reinterpretation of Christian Existence*, trans. Patrick Madigan (Collegeville, MI: Liturgical, 1995), 108; Risto Saarinen, *God and the Gift: An Ecumenical Theology of Giving* (Collegeville, MI: Liturgical, 2005), 9, 106; John M. G. Barclay, *Paul and the Gift* (Grand Rapids, MI: Eerdmans, 2017), chapter 1.

In my understanding, the task of dogmatics is to bring the witness to the reality of God's coming into the world for our salvation critically into a balance with the verdictives of the Law. Although the Law does command, insofar as it commands regarding speech about God and his acts, it primarily speaks negatively, verdictively, as 'thou shall not make any Gods before me'. This is why, from an illocutionary point of view, the Law does not so much contain prescriptives as verdictives. But then, in a complex relationship with these verdictives, it links up the verdictives with prescriptives that concretely and positively aim at appropriate human behaviour towards other humans, requiring the performance of righteousness.

This point may be deserving of further explanation, since the verdictive nature of the Law has ramifications for the task of dogmatics. If the *proprium* of the Gospel is promise, these promises witness to the reality of God and God's acts in history, not primarily in order to claim them to be true but in order to invite us to entrust ourselves to them for our salvation. Dogmatic inquiry into the truth of the Gospel, however, is not so much an inquiry into the truth about God and God's acts themselves but is rather a balancing out of these truths in the face of the verdictives of the Law. The Law does not prescribe or claim that much, precisely because it is composed of verdictives rather than prescriptives. Rather, it delimits the possible implications that we may draw from the promises of the Gospel by saying: Do not act like this.

As I have said, my contention is that dogmatics must be distinguished from the primary role of the Christ-confessing community of faith. The concrete reality of God is witnessed to in the community of faith, but it is also actually present in Word and Sacrament. Implicitly, dogmatics has often had a place in faith communities as a basis, as the foundation. First, dogmatics had to define clearly, on the basis of Scripture, what the community of faith had to believe, and then the community of faith would follow along the lines of that definition. This, I believe, positions dogmatics falsely vis-à-vis the community of faith. It is not the theologian who knows the truth about God and the world, but it is the ordinary believer who participates in the community of faith and, as such, partakes in the reality of salvation. The task of the doctrinal theologian follows upon that practice of faith, critically reflecting on that faith in the light of Scripture and the Christian tradition, but in particular putting the community's appropriation of the reality of God to the test of the verdictives of the Law. Theology is, as Gustavo Gutiérrez famously stated, a second act.[25]

1.5 Christology as the root of dogmatics

In the remainder of this chapter, I will make a concise attempt to substantiate this proposal for doing dogmatics in terms of the Law-Gospel distinction. The

---

25. Gustavo Gutiérrez, *Theology of Liberation: History, Politics, and Salvation*, trans. John Eagleson, rev. edn with a new introduction (Maryknoll, NY: Orbis, 2009), xxxii–xxxvi.

claims made below will be elaborated in greater detail in subsequent chapters. My proposal seeks to serve two aims. On the one hand, this new paradigm for doing dogmatics must be successful in elucidating how doctrinal reflection works in the history of Christian theology. On the other hand, the new paradigm must provide a constructive frame of reference for doing dogmatics in the present. The first locus in terms of which I will elucidate the explanatory power of the Law-Gospel distinction is Christology. This is not a coincidence, because, as I will argue below, I follow Augustine's claim that Christology is the root of dogmatics.

Above, I suggested that theology critically reflects on the balance between Law and Gospel from the way in which the community of faith appropriates the message of salvation in Christ. The balance between the commissive nature of the Gospel and the verdictive nature of the Law is necessary because, seen from the perspective of the dynamics between Law and Gospel, the way in which salvation is appropriated by the community of faith is far from being obvious or obviously right. The community of faith operates within the tension between the appropriation of salvation by virtue of Christ's incarnation and work on earth on the one hand, and the distinction between God and the world as prescribed by the Law on the other. This relates to the very drastic and far-reaching character of the Gospel. Something happens in the Christian faith that is anything but self-evident in such monotheistic religions as Judaism, Christianity and Islam. This is all the more clear for Judaism and Islam, insofar as they distinguish themselves from Christianity. In Christianity, the divine condescends radically to the created order, although, from a monotheistic perspective, this world must be seen as fundamentally distinct from God. This tension constantly puts to the test the truth and validity of the community of faith's appeal to this condescension of God into the created order and the community's celebration of it in confession and Christian life. It does so in terms of the monotheistic fundamental conviction that God and the world must be distinguished. The community of faith is constantly in danger of interpreting God's condescension into the created order in a way that breaches the verdictives of the Law and appropriates God in a manner that makes God its own (see Chapter 3).

My claim is twofold: historical and descriptive on the one hand, dogmatic and normative on the other. For one, my contention is that classical pre-modern dogmatics can be understood in terms of this tension, and even better so than as an endeavour which aspires to represent the reality of God and God's salvific acts in the world with human words. In addition, but still on the historical level, I would like to propose that the classical pre-modern dogmatic appeal to Scripture is better understood in terms of moving back and forth within this tension between Law and Gospel than as a summarizing redescription of the truth of Scripture's teaching.[26] Finally, my proposal is that contemporary dogmatics can be

---

26. Maarten Wisse, 'Doing Theology through Reception Studies: Towards a Post-postmodern Theological Hermeneutics', *Nederduits Gereformeerd Theologisch Tijdschrift* 53, no. Supplement 3 (2012): 239–49, https://doi.org/10.5952/53-0-237.

fruitfully understood normatively as having to critically engage the claims of the contemporary communities of faith as operating within this tension between Law and Gospel.

I will illustrate the historical claim, while gradually shifting into dogmatics. When we seek to understand the task of dogmatics in terms of how classical premodern dogmatics took up this task, the tension between the appeal to God's incarnational acts in history and the demands of the Law is tremendously helpful indeed. From this perspective, it is entirely natural for Christology to be the birthplace of dogma. It is typical for modern contemporary dogmatics to suggest that the key decisions in theology are taken in the concept of God, as suggested by Christoph Schwöbel, for example.[27] From his perspective, dogmatics orients itself towards the understanding of the reality of God and the world.[28] However, in the *Enchiridion*, we find Augustine claiming that every dogmatic decision can be traced back to a decision made in Christology.[29] From my perspective, then, the long process of reflection on Christology is not so much to be understood as an attempt to grasp the nature of the Christ-event, but rather as an attempt to bring the drastic implications of the Christ-event, to which the New Testament witnesses in at times very drastic terms, into a balance with the conditions for responsible God-talk in the Old Testament. The same can be argued for the doctrine of the Trinity.

If we put this in terms of the interpretation of Scripture in theology, we see the same pattern (see Chapter 3). Against the background of the Law-Gospel distinction, we can understand that the classical reading – by Calvin, for example – of Jn 1.14 (i.e. the Word has become flesh) as a two-nature Christology is not so much to be understood as the best possible account of what John aims to say. Quite the contrary, as Michael Servetus already understood quite well in the sixteenth century. It should rather be understood as moderating the potentially drastic implications of this witness to the Christ-event in view of the verdictives of the Law. God cannot become human and humans cannot become God because God is in heaven and we are on earth.

Both Christology and the Trinity, in their mature, classical Nicene-Constantinopolitan and Chalcedonian forms, can hardly be understood as coherent descriptions of the reality of the Triune God and Christ. Augustine's mantra in *De Trinitate*, 'The Father is God, the Son is God and the Holy Spirit is God, nevertheless not three Gods, but one God', is more like a circle around a mystery than a description of a matter of fact.[30] Karen Kilby has argued that

27. Christoph Schwöbel, 'Einleitung', in *Gott, Götter, Götzen: XIV. Europäischer Kongress für Theologie (11.–15. September 2011 in Zürich)*, ed. Christoph Schwöbel (Leipzig: Evangelischer Verlagsanstalt, 2013), 11–20.

28. Christoph Schwöbel, 'Die Trinitätslehre als Rahmentheorie des christlichen Glaubens. Vier Thesen zur Bedeutung der Trinität in der christlichen Dogmatik', in *Gott in Beziehung: Studien zur Dogmatik* (Tübingen: Mohr Siebeck, 2002), 25–51.

29. Augustinus, *Enchiridion, de Fide, Spe et Charitate*, I, 6.

30. Wisse, *Trinitarian Theology*, chapter 2.

pretty much the same can be said about Thomas Aquinas' doctrine of the Trinity.[31] If we ask Augustine: 'Why three?' he will answer: 'Because this is what the New Testament teaches us.' If we ask: 'Why one?' he, quoting Deuteronomy, will reply: 'Because the Lord, the Lord, is one.' From the perspective of dogmatics as a description of God and his acts, the mystery-character of the Trinity is a problem. In fact, it was one of the main reasons for the development of a social view of the Trinity. From the perspective of dogmatics as a balance between Law and Gospel, it is a virtue. The reality of God and God's acts is not as such directly the object of dogmatic production of knowledge but rather the point of departure from which, in proclamation and the practice of faith, questions of balance emerge that give rise to dogmatic reflection.

1.6 Christology and soteriology are intertwined

Keeping the balance between Law and Gospel extends far beyond the seemingly abstract questions of Christology and Trinity. My perspective on classical dogmatics can make the most of the fact that these were never abstract questions anyway, since they, as potentially imbalanced ways of speaking about God, could represent dangerous ways of speaking about salvation. In Christology, the totality of our salvation is at stake, as illustrated, for example, in Athanasius' well-known deification phrase: God became human, so that we could become divine.[32] Here too, the distinction within a two-nature Christology precludes the soteriological statement from transgressing the boundary between God and creation. It is precisely because in this condescension the integrity of God is retained in the face of the human, assumed nature of Christ that also in our becoming divine the entirety of our human nature is safeguarded. This is why the tradition, including Athanasius, speaks about deification as a matter of adoption and not as a matter of nature.[33] And this is precisely the point where, in Reformation times, the heart of the controversy between the mainstream Reformation and the radical Reformation must be located. The Christology of such Anabaptists as Menno Simons, and, even more radically, of Michael Servetus, was accompanied by a radical soteriology in which the distinction between God and the world became problematic.

The Reformation also shows that the concern for the integrity of the divine and human natures is not just relevant with regard to its implications for the degree to which humans are thought to become divine but also with regard to the extent to which Christ's incarnation and death on the cross do away with the requirement to keep the Law, especially the second table. Luther discovered the

---

31. Karen Kilby, 'Aquinas, the Trinity and the Limits of Understanding', *International Journal of Systematic Theology* 7, no. 4 (1 October 2005): 414–27, https://doi.org/10.1111/j.1468-2400.2005.00175.x.

32. Athanasius, *De incarnatione verbi*, 54, 3.

33. Athanasius, *Contra Arianos*, I, 45.

depth of the incarnation anew, and he did so in particular with an eye for our redemption. This rediscovery was centred around the insight that our salvation is accomplished entirely by God, without any role for us. For Luther, this was not a matter of bypassing the justice that the Law requires of us. Quite the contrary, God alone can establish justice, and so we glorify God and fulfil his Law in particular by ascribing our redemption to God and to God alone.[34]

But in the meantime a door had been opened threatening to disturb the delicate balance between Law and Gospel, for if we are justified because of God's work for us in Christ alone, do we still have to do good works? What about the concrete obedience and righteousness required by the Law? At this point, Luther and friends had to find their way between the pitfalls of antinomianism and works righteousness. They were considerably helped in this by the drastic responses to these questions that came from the camp of the Anabaptists and others. The history of Protestantism and evangelicalism shows us that the practical question of the balance between justification and sanctification still requires attention, even when it seems defined clearly in dogmatic terms. The conflict arising from Faustus Socinus' critique of the Reformation doctrine of atonement is a good example of this (see Chapter 7). In his time, Socinus challenged a balance that had only been reached with considerable difficulty, namely the balance between the insight that we are saved only through the grace of God (Gospel) and the conviction that concrete obedience to the Law is demanded from us by God (Law). Socinus criticized this balance because, within the context of the Reformation, he was not convinced by the suggestion that the radical forgiveness of which the Gospel speaks according to its Reformation understanding indeed leads to the concrete practice of righteousness of which the same Gospel likewise speaks. This is why he rejected a satisfaction theory of atonement: You can only perform righteousness yourself, and if you do not, you need to repent and do better in the future. Jesus can be your example and inspiration, but it is you who must do it. To suggest otherwise is, in Socinus' estimation, to promote cheap grace.

Of course, such an argument requires a reorganization of the message of Scripture to support this thesis. A major part of Socinus' *De Jesu Christo servatore* is dedicated to that project. It is not that Socinus manages to offer a better summary of the message of Scripture than the mainstream Reformation has done. Rather, he prioritizes the proofs from Scripture in a different way. The concrete justice required of us in the Old Testament prevails over the grace received according to the New Testament. On their part, John Owen and all other seventeenth-century critics of Socinus emphasize that human beings cannot fulfil the requirements of the Law on their own. This is why we can only be saved by what God does for us. Nevertheless, Owen shared Socinus' concern with regard to the requirement of concrete righteousness. As a Puritan, his deepest desire was to combine the

---

34. See Martin Luther, 'Large Catechism', in *Triglot Concordia: The Symbolical Books of the Ev. Lutheran Church*, trans. F. Bente and W. H. T. Dau (St. Louis, MO: Concordia, 1921), 580–94, on the first commandment.

message of communion with God through the saving work of Christ with the concrete fulfilment of the Law as required under the Old Testament. This is why the Puritans and their Dutch followers from the so-called Further Reformation (*Nadere Reformatie*) were so intent in their pursuit of practical piety, including strict Sunday observance as a sharpening of the interpretation of the fourth commandment. It is true that the Gospel preaches redemption through the work of Christ, but this redemption does not – and this is the point where the debate goes on – do away with the requirements of the Law.

1.7 Does the Law do away with the Gospel?

Up to now, I have argued that the history of dogma (and the history of Reformed theology in particular), as well as the normative task of dogmatics, should be understood in terms of the dynamics between Law and Gospel. In the preceding sections, I took the function of the Gospel to be to point especially to what God does for us in Christ, and that of the Law to protect the mystery of the Gospel by ensuring that, in our understanding of what God does in Christ, God's work and the work of humans are not confused. In this regard, the application of the Law to the witness of the Gospel serves to underline the limits that an Augustinian doctrine of grace poses to the understanding of the Gospel. Accordingly, dogmatics can be understood as a prophetic critique of the domestication of the mystery of God and the salvation that meets us in Christ.[35] In this section, I will detail why dogmatics is not only prophetic in nature (in the technical sense, 'elenctic') but also a constructive (or 'irenic') discipline. For if dogmatics is to be elenctic, it must also testify to what God does for us in Christ. Dogmatics cannot simply be a prophetic criticism on anything. It is primarily prophetic criticism of the understanding of the subject of Christian theology, that is, God's revelation in creation and in Jesus Christ.

In other words, if, with the help of the Law-Gospel distinction, the Law really needs to protect the mystery of God and its revelation in Christ for what it is, then it cannot nullify the Gospel and certainly cannot be without the Gospel. Even in the Reformation it was understood that the Gospel, in its deepest sense, is the fulfilment of the Law, so that the requirements of the Law cannot be met except through faith in the Gospel.[36] And so, true theology cannot just criticize the Gospel, but it must at the same time also be a witness to it. From the foregoing, one

---

35. Maarten Wisse, 'De integratie van theologie en religiewetenschap in Stefan Paas' Vreemdelingen en priesters: De Utrechtse theologische faculteit in de jaren '90', *Soteria* 35, no. 1 (2018): 19–31.

36. Eilert Herms, *Phänomene des Glaubens: Beiträge zur Fundamentaltheologie* (Tübingen: Mohr Siebeck, 2006), 379–80; Martin Luther, 'Von der Freiheit eines Christenmenschen', in *Weimarer Ausgabe* (WA), VII, 20–38, VII, 26. All references to 'WA' are to Martin Luther, *D. Martin Luthers Werke* (Weimar, 1883–2009).

might mistakenly infer that the task of dogmatics is to keep the Gospel as small as possible. This way, the Gospel is protected as well as it might be. If salvation in Christ does not go out too far into this world, its mystery-character will be sufficiently protected. It is as if, to use the language of Jesus' parable, we have buried our precious talent in the ground so as not to lose it.[37]

The question is also whether the Gospel can actually exist in our history without becoming our possession. Our postmodern context makes us more than ever aware of the power dynamics in which every religious claim is embedded. Is not the prophetic power of the Law so strong that there is no place for the Gospel? Is there a church that does not claim to have the truth? What preacher can ultimately avoid the idea that she or he speaks on behalf of God, when in fact these are simply ordinary human words completely determined by a particular time and place?

However, dogmatics can never only be elenctic. If dogmatics does become merely elenctic, we will always only be critiquing forms of faith. Our theology will become so negative that we will not be able to say anything about the mystery of God. Every discourse bearing witness to God or any rite presenting God will be pulled down by merciless deconstruction. While such critique may have the appearance of holiness, before we realize it, every image of God ends up being weakened, and ultimately only the image of oneself remains. If we practice theology this way, we are simply a god on the throne of our own criticism and will find ourselves in deadly loneliness.[38]

We can make this point not only from a theological but also from a philosophical point of view, since it is one that the Marxist philosopher Terry Eagleton already made in the context of Derrida's philosophy of deconstruction.[39] When deconstruction becomes all-encompassing, trivialization and 'tribalization' lie in wait around the corner.[40] In the end, if everyone has their own truth which is in their own interest, why bother? As such, there will no longer be any reason to strive for truth and justice. All truths would be equally false. Derrida's interest in notions such as justice, the future and the messianic shows that he is aware of this risk and tries to avoid it.[41]

For Christian theology to survive, there must be a narrow path on which the prophetic power of the Law is not annulled by the Gospel, while the Gospel is at the same time not deprived of its power by the Law. The Gospel, after all, makes possible what the Law requires. For dogmatics this again requires clear insight

---

37. Mt. 25.18.

38. For a more extensive and technical discussion with reference to Augustine, see Wisse, *Trinitarian Theology*, chapter 1.

39. Terry Eagleton, 'Marxism without Marxism', in *Ghostly Demarcations: A Symposium on Jacques Derrida's Spectres of Marx*, ed. Michael Sprinker (London: Verso, 1999), 83–7.

40. Cf. Tom Jacobs, 'Kritiek van de zuivere verlichting: naar een dialectiek van de universaliteit' (Katholieke Universiteit Leuven, 2010).

41. Jacques Derrida and Maurizio Ferraris, *A Taste for the Secret* (Cambridge: Polity, 2002), 19–21.

into its limited place in relation to the religious community.[42] Likewise important is the role of dogmatics as a second act. The necessary precondition for dogmatics is the concrete and actual presence of God in Christ in the midst of the Christian community. Dogmatics does not provide formulations that act as the foundation on which the church of Christ can be built. It always lags behind, not only actually, but also in principle. Christ is not truly present in dogmatics, but rather in the signs of bread and wine (see Chapter 8).[43] Right teaching is not a guarantee for the presence of the Lord, but the presence of the Lord is the condition for true doctrine. The Lord is already there, and dogmatics must continually be careful not to step on the Lord's feet.

Therefore, any work of dogmatics is embedded in and relates to the concrete confessing practices of the Christian community, and it cannot do away with that community, not even if it would like to. At the same time, the Christian community in which the Lord is present is a broken one. Therefore, Christians, and theologians in particular, are called to bring the Christian community back to its service to the Gospel.[44] In part, they do so by continually exploring the mystery of the salvation that God accomplishes in Christ.[45] This is especially true because the length and breadth of that Gospel constantly escape the community of faith and its servants.

The presence of Christ in the Christian community is a gift and something that is continually freely given us by God. Thus, this presence remains in the hands of God alone. The Gospel is therefore the fulfilment of the Law without jeopardizing the Law. The task of dogmatics is not to make sure that God is present. God is present in the church, in the world and in our hearts, and this is not a product of our own efforts. The Law and the Gospel embrace each other in God who is justice and peace. The task given to us is to do justice. That righteousness is always one that approaches us from the outside, not one we can decide for ourselves or can bring about ourselves. If we claim to do righteousness and our fellow human beings suffer, it is not righteousness. Justice is a public secret; it is a fundamentally communal effort. This is why it is never just ours. Justice comes to us. It is an

---

42. Cf. Maarten Wisse, *Scripture between Identity and Creativity: A Hermeneutical Theory Building upon Four Interpretations of Job*, Ars Disputandi Supplement Series 1 (Utrecht: Ars Disputandi, 2003), 188, http://dspace.library.uu.nl/handle/1874/294105-196; Maarten Wisse, 'Towards a Theological Account of Theology: Reconceptualizing Church History and Systematic Theology', in *Orthodoxy, Process and Product*, ed. Mathijs Lamberigts, Lieven Boeve and Terrence Merrigan, BETL 227 (Leuven: Peeters, 2009), 351–74.

43. Cf. Dorothea Haspelmath-Finatti, *Theologia Prima: Liturgische Theologie für den evangelischen Gottesdienst* (Göttingen: Vandenhoeck & Ruprecht, 2014), 13.

44. Cf. Jan Martijn Abrahamse, *Ordained Ministry in Free Church Perspective: Retrieving Robert Browne (c. 1550–1633) for Contemporary Ecclesiology*, Studies in Reformed Theology 41 (Leiden: Brill, 2020), chapter 5.

45. Cf. Maarten Wisse, 'Christus in het midden: Identiteit en pluraliteit in het reformatorisch onderwijs', in *De multiculturele Refo-school*, ed. John Exalto, Biblebelt Studies 3 (Apeldoorn: Labarum Academic, 2017), 215–38.

encounter. That is why the Law also points us to a righteousness that appears to us in Jesus Christ and transforms us, a righteousness from which we live and to which we witness. But it also is and will always remain a righteousness from God, which is why it is our salvation.

1.8 Overview

Chapter 2 introduces the reader to the key distinction running throughout the book – the Law-Gospel distinction. It traces the history of its development, outlining a series of key shifts that the distinction underwent, connected to the historical and theological context of which it was a part. It also sets out to undertake a twenty-first-century retrieval of the distinction by pointing out the conditions under which I raise it and what this means for the way I use the distinction.

Chapter 3 proceeds to the application of the distinction to the use of Scripture in the history of theology, showing how the actual use of Scripture in the theology of Augustine and the Reformation can be understood in a helpful and convincing manner in terms of the Law-Gospel distinction. The historical survey will demonstrate that the steps which Augustine and various Reformers take in their interpretation of Scripture are not so much prompted by the 'neutral' aim of describing what Scripture says about God. They should rather be understood in terms of balancing out God's salvific acts in Christ against human abuses of participation in this salvation.

Chapter 4 undertakes a similar enterprise, although it now analyses the development of the theology of Karl Barth as the father of Christocentrism. Examining his reception of the Gospel of John through a series of articles from the 1920s onwards, it will show how Barth explored a range of different options for doing dogmatics before he arrived at his mature Christocentric approach. By pursuing these various options further, I open up Barth's work to an approach in terms of the dynamics between Law and Gospel and aim to show that it actually fulfils Barth's own aims better than his mature Christocentrism does.

Chapter 5 presents the first of a range of dogmatic topics that are now approached from a new perspective through the Law-Gospel distinction. The first of these is the doctrine of Scripture. While Chapter 3 already shows that the actual use of Scripture in theology in the Reformed tradition can be convincingly described as operating through this distinction, the doctrine of Scripture itself has never actually been examined on its basis. That examination is now done in this fifth chapter, leading to a critical analysis of the Reformation *Sola Scriptura* maxim. However, it will also be demonstrated how a theology that understands itself as operating within the dynamics between Law and Gospel at the same time requires the *Sola Scriptura* maxim, albeit understood in a much more critical way.

Chapter 6 provides a novel defence of the Reformed doctrine of double predestination, thereby leading the dynamics between Law and Gospel back to where it all started, namely the doctrine of grace and the distinction between God and human actions. Moving beyond the traditional doctrine of double predestination, this chapter understands predestination in terms of the power dynamics discovered in postmodernity, arguing that this doctrine aims to keep our ultimate destiny out of our own hands, denying us a position of absolute power over our fate.

Chapter 7 presents a conversation between two theologians from the sixteenth and seventeenth centuries with sharply opposing views on the doctrine of the atonement. In this conversation, Faustus Socinus argues against the notion of substitutionary atonement, while John Owen counters that substitutionary atonement is necessary because God cannot leave sin unpunished. In spite of their strong disagreement, the two will be shown to share the same concern, although they offer strikingly different solutions. What they share is the concern about what believers' appropriation of salvation in Christ means for their concrete practice of justice as renewed human beings. In order to avoid cheap grace, Socinus denies substitution altogether, whereas Own aims to strengthen the believer's piety through dependence on the grace of God. While Socinus and Owen differ markedly in their understanding of atonement, their theological concerns can be understood very well in terms of the dynamics between Law and Gospel.

Chapter 8 puts to the test a theology that aims to work on the basis of the Law-Gospel distinction in terms of a retrieval of Abraham Kuyper's understanding of the Lord's Supper. A theology based on the Law-Gospel distinction tends to lead to a strong emphasis on the difference between God and the world, and thus to a critique of mediations between God and the world. At least this has historically been so in the Reformed tradition. Kuyper is a notable example of this. I will argue that he provides various avenues for moving a contemporary account of the Lord's Supper ahead in favour of the mediation of salvation through the sacraments, including a robust account of real presence.

Chapter 9 offers an account of a theology of the religions in terms of the dynamics between Law and Gospel. In this chapter, I engage in a conversation with current developments in the theology of the religions emphasizing the importance of the particularity of religious traditions. Building on these developments, I argue that such an emphasis on particularity is at odds with the current tendency towards a Trinitarian or Christocentric account of Christian theology, because such accounts turn the Gospel into a Law. A theology of the religions that operates within the context of the Law-Gospel dynamics not only successfully avoids this trap but also strengthens the possibilities for a true dialogue between varying religious traditions.

Chapter 2

LAW AND GOSPEL AS A HEURISTIC LENS

2.1 Introduction

In the previous chapter, which served as the introduction to the book, we posed the following thesis: ever since the Enlightenment, dogmatics has been understood primarily as a description of the reality of God in God's revelation. From the perspective of the Reformational distinction between Law and Gospel, this turns the Gospel into a Law. It renders the Gospel into a claim that requires acceptance, whether through the use of reason or on the basis of blind authority. We, by contrast, have sketched dogmatics as a prophetic message aimed at protecting the mystery of God who came among us in Christ. Through the critical use of the Law, and the first commandment of the Decalogue in particular, dogmatics has the task to protect the Gospel from misappropriation. In Chapter 3, we will show how this approach to dogmatics can be used to examine the role of Scripture in dogmatics in a new way. In Chapter 4, we will then develop our approach to dogmatics in conversation with Karl Barth's Christocentrism. The remaining chapters will be used to illustrate how our approach works when it is applied to a variety of dogmatic loci.

Our approach to dogmatics therefore introduces the Law-Gospel distinction in a new way, while still borrowing from the Reformed tradition's use of it. Thus, my approach to the distinction fits into the recent tradition framing systematic theology as 'retrieval'.[1] The purpose of the present chapter is to show how my use of the Law-Gospel distinction fits within its history in the Christian tradition. In Section 2.2, we will set out a working definition of the distinction to set up our examination of the history of Christianity. In Section 2.3, we will then discuss the history of its use. In doing so, we will concentrate on several crucial shifts that are important to my argument. In their light, I will use Section 2.4 to give an

---

1. The term 'theology of retrieval' was coined by John Webster, 'Theologies of Retrieval', in *The Oxford Handbook of Systematic Theology*, ed. Kathryn Tanner, John Webster and Iain Torrance (Oxford: Oxford University Press, 2007), 583–99. Since its introduction, the term has been appropriated by various authors so that we can now indeed speak of a plurality of theologies of retrieval, as the title of a recent collection of essays has it: Darren Sarisky, ed., *Theologies of Retrieval: An Exploration and Appraisal* (Edinburgh: T&T Clark, 2017).

account of my own use of the distinction, situating it in a postmodern context and indicating how it relates to the various stages outlined.

2.2 Law and Gospel: A working definition

Readers unfamiliar with the Law-Gospel distinction and its interpretation in the history of Christianity may wonder about its meaning. A logical place to start would be the intuition that 'Law' refers to those places in the Bible where laws are found, with the term 'Gospel' referring to the passages where the good news about Jesus is proclaimed. Another ready option would be to understand 'Law' as pointing to the Old Testament and 'Gospel' to the New Testament. Given the wide range of possible meanings, what is that we are actually talking about?

Defining one's terms before using them seems an easy and obvious thing to do, but in this case the matter is more complex than might be assumed on the face of it. Part of the purpose of this book is to 'reinvent' Christian dogmatics by 'retrieving' the Law-Gospel distinction. This implies that the definition of the distinction is part of the argument we are developing. Our definition is, therefore, not theologically neutral but entails much of the theology of Law and Gospel that we are going to develop. The purpose of this chapter is to situate my own use of the distinction in the context of its history. Therefore, the task of defining the terms 'Law' and 'Gospel' prior to our description of their historical use presents us with a kind of chicken-and-egg problem; to know what we are talking about when we describe the history of the concepts, we need to know their meaning. At the same time, we need the history of the distinction to understand what we mean by it.

For this reason, I will preface my historical overview with a working definition to indicate what I mean by Law and Gospel, before refining the definition of these terms in my account of the history of their use. This working definition will also be of partial influence on that historical description, since my own use of the distinction takes its starting point in the work of Philip Melanchthon. As a consequence, my discussion of Augustine and Thomas Aquinas will inevitably have the character of a look back at the distinction's prehistory.

Against one's possible intuition, Melanchthon's distinction between Law and Gospel neither points to a body of legal texts in the Bible over against the four gospels nor refers to the Old and New Testament. On such a definition, almost every single Christian theologian would accept the benefit of such a distinction. Yet, this is not what Melanchthon means when he uses these terms, nor do I use them in that sense. For this reason, I will consistently write 'Law' and 'Gospel' with capital letters. My use of capitals is not so much meant to indicate that they are sacred or God-given, although I agree they are. Rather, it is to prevent the misunderstanding that the terms 'Law' and 'Gospel' refer to concrete bodies of texts.

To make things slightly more complicated, we will see that many Reformed theologians after the Reformation, such as Gisbertus Voetius (1589–1676), actually distinguished two levels of meaning for the terms 'Law' and 'Gospel'. At prima facie level, they accept the 'rough' meaning of the distinction, taking it indeed to mean the Old versus New Testament or, more precisely, the Old and New Covenant. But next to this prima facie level, they also accept a more precise and proper meaning, and this is indeed the one that reflects what I mean when I distinguish between Law and Gospel. With this more precise and proper meaning, following Melanchthon, these Reformed theologians envision the fundamental nature of the Law as a 'commandment' and the Gospel as 'God's free offer or promise of salvation' (in Jesus Christ). On this account, anything in a concrete biblical passage demanding something from us is a Law. And, insofar as a Scripture text points to God's free offer of salvation (in Christ), it is Gospel. Rather than pointing to 'things out there' (e.g. biblical passages, sermons, theological theses) as being either Law or Gospel, the distinction provides a heuristic lens through which one can investigate 'things out there' and assign them (or aspects of them) as belonging to either Law or Gospel, depending on whether they make demands on us or draw us to God's free promise of salvation in Christ.

A natural consequence of this use of the distinction is that we find both Law and Gospel in both the Old and the New Testament. This explains my use of brackets around 'in Jesus Christ' in the definition. Drawing on Hebrews 11, traditional pre-modern Christianity largely shared the conviction that the saints in the Old Testament were saved by faith in Christ, so that the Old Testament, insofar as it points to God's free promise of salvation, points to the Gospel fulfilled in Christ. This theme will return in the historical overview below.

An illuminating example of the way the distinction works can be taken from Exod. 20.2: 'I am the Lord your God, who brought you out of the land of Egypt, out of the house of slavery.' What makes this example so helpful and intriguing is its place right at the beginning of the Decalogue. Could anything be more 'Law' than the Ten Commandments? Traditional theologians, however, typically understood this verse to witness to the Gospel and not the Law.[2] They did so because it contains God's promise that he would be Israel's God, God with us, a promise whose ultimate fulfilment traditional Christian theology sees in Jesus Christ.

2.3 The history of the distinction

Now that we have developed a basic definition of the Law-Gospel distinction, we can take the next step and consider its origins. In what follows, we cannot trace the history of the distinction in all its details. Instead, we will offer a brief discussion of several landmarks from that history and, more importantly, identify a series of crucial shifts between those landmarks in order to illustrate the developments in the history of the distinction. As such, we will attempt to identify the tradition and circumstances within and under which my own proposal for the distinction

---

2. Cf. Gisbertus Voetius, *D. Gysberti Voetii Selectarum Disputationum Fasciculus*, ed. Abraham Kuyper (Amstelodami: Wormser, 1887), 370.

must be situated and understood. The first shift is the one from Augustine's use of grace and works to Luther and Melanchthon's use of the distinction between Law and Gospel. The second is the shift from the Reformation and post-Reformation scholastic use of the distinction between Law and Gospel to Karl Barth's reversal in his reintroduction of the distinction in the form of Gospel and Law. As a third and final step, I will propose my own use of the distinction as influenced by the shift from a modern to a postmodern context, consciously integrating aspects of the previous stages of the distinction's history.

In our search for a starting point to the history of the Law-Gospel distinction, we most often encounter the name of Martin Luther to whom the distinction is commonly attributed.[3] Crucial to Luther's Reformation discovery was his insight that there is a difference between God's justice through which God demands justice from us, and the justice through which God justifies the sinner. This insight became the basis of his entire theology. Even though Luther was the one to discover the distinction between Law and Gospel and used it throughout his work, Melanchthon, as we will see, was actually the one to introduce it into systematic theology through his widely used *Loci Communes*.

In the sixteenth century, theologians did not often provide extensive quotations or citations in their works. This also emerges when we turn to consider the possible sources for the Reformers' distinction. However, in the 1521 edition of his *Loci Communes*, Melanchthon does refer to Augustine's *De spiritu et littera* in his chapter on the distinction between the Old and the New Testament, where he also elaborates on the Law-Gospel distinction.[4] This is reason enough to begin our exploration with Augustine and to consider the extent to which Luther and Melanchthon may have found inspiration there.

2.3.1 Looking back: Augustine

While we do not need to deal with Augustine at length, his contribution is still worth addressing for two reasons.

First, Augustine's theology represents the breeding ground for the present project. I did not discover the significance of the Law-Gospel distinction for doing systematic theology today in Reformation theology, but through my study of Augustine.[5] This recognition immediately introduces yet another complication for

---

3. Cf. Christoph Schwöbel, 'Law and Gospel', in *RPP*, ed. Hans Dieter Betz, 4th edn, vol. 3 (Tübingen: Mohr Siebeck, 2006–13), 862–7.

4. Philippus Melanchthon, 'Loci Theologici [1521]', in *Opera Quae Supersunt Omnia*, ed. Karl Bretschneider and Henricus Ernestus Bindseil, vol. XXI (Braunschweig: Schwetske, 1854), 195.

5. See Maarten Wisse, *Trinitarian Theology beyond Participation: Augustine's de Trinitate and Contemporary Theology*, T&T Clark Studies in Systematic Theology 11 (London: T&T Clark International, 2011), esp. chapters 3, 4 and 6. As the title indicates, the object of study was not Augustine's *De spiritu et littera* but his *De Trinitate*.

the distinction, namely its relationship to the distinction between nature and grace. In my earlier work on Augustine, I was struck by a constant interplay between, on the one hand, the way in which human beings are naturally directed to God and, on the other hand, the role of salvation in Christ as mediated through the church. The one cannot be understood without the other. The way Augustine connects salvation as it is proclaimed by the Christian faith to a natural desire for ultimate happiness (the so-called *desiderium naturale*) is a good example of this interplay.

As such, Augustine construes Christian faith as something closely related to a domain that Christians and non-Christians alike share as creatures, a domain in which God is already present, albeit not yet present 'in Christ'. In this conception, the notion of God as justice and humanity's natural instinct for the good plays a crucial rule. God is the Good itself, given that every human being has a sensitivity for the good, and thus for God. This understanding is in turn related to the conviction that the Decalogue is not something that comes to human beings as something alien to them. Rather, the Decalogue is a reminder of something that is part of our creaturely setup. This is why every human being is born with a natural sensitivity for the Law (as the Decalogue). Augustine then construes the Gospel as the restoration of the original goodness that was given to humanity in creation. This dynamic became for me the basis for reconsidering the classical Reformation distinction and its potential for a renewal of modern theology.

Augustine's thought therefore formed the breeding ground for this book as a whole. It was Augustine who made me see how theology is not so much based on two sources of knowledge, one natural and another revealed, as Christian theology operates on the basis of the interplay between two ways in which God is with us. God is with us through creation, as a knowledge of, direction to and participation in the Good, not only demanding justice from us but also creating us in that fundamental consciousness of and orientation towards the Good God who has created us. This consciousness and orientation is an inalienable aspect of who we are. It is what we are determined to be. And if we fail in living up to it, we are determined to search for a happiness that we have lost. However, in this situation of fallen humanity, which even in that state remains oriented towards the Good God who has created us, God comes to us and is with us in a second way. That is, God is among us with a free message of the Good News of salvation in Jesus Christ, inviting us to respond in order that we might regain our original righteousness. This in a nutshell is the soteriology that Augustine develops in the second half of *De Trinitate*, as I reconstructed it in my previous book. But it is also the basic intuition behind the present book, which is why I mention it here again.

Second, discussing Augustine in this context helps us to trace the various shifts through which the distinction has passed through the history of Christianity, and the significance of these shifts for reconceiving its contemporary potential. We will see that Augustine's insights into the dynamics of Law and Gospel are very closely related to the doctrine of grace. This is quite natural given our definition of the distinction above, since the insight into the fundamental difference between what God demands and promises is explicitly intended to underline an Augustinian doctrine of grace. Luther and Melanchthon seek to rediscover this Augustinian doctrine of grace in a context that they understand to be dominated by works righteousness and by a persistent tendency to confuse what God does for us with what we have to do for God.

Augustine wrote *De spiritu et littera* in 412 or 413 CE, during the first period of the Pelagian controversy, as a reply to a question posed to him by his friend Marcellinus.[6] The central question in the text is whether human beings can attain perfection in this life. Augustine addresses this question by way of an extensive treatment of 2 Cor. 3.6: 'for the letter kills but the Spirit gives life'. Situated as it is in the context of the Pelagian controversy, the question is already related to the distinction between the work of God and the work of humans, which went on to become an important theme in Luther's doctrine of justification.[7]

Augustine explains the biblical passage from which the work derives its title by an appeal to Paul's Epistle to the Romans, in particular Rom. 5.20: ('The law was brought in so that the trespass might increase. But where sin increased, grace increased all the more'; NIV):

> He shows clearly enough that one should rather interpret it as we said above, namely, that the letter of the law, which teaches that we should not sin, kills, if the life-giving Spirit is not present. After all, it leads us to know sin rather than to avoid it and increases sin rather than lessens it, because the transgression of the law is added to the evil desire.[8]

Through a specific reception of Paul in the context of a controversy on the question whether the (Mosaic) law has been given to bring us eternal life by its fulfilment, Augustine hints at what the later tradition will call the Law-Gospel distinction. In Augustine's interpretation, 'law' is a set of concrete commandments, but these commandments are interpreted as 'letter' opposed to 'Spirit', such that 'letter' refers to the function of this law, which is no longer primarily a concrete rule of life, but rather an instrument to bring us to conviction of sin. The law interpreted as 'letter' shows us what we must do but cannot do in our own power. Paul's distinction between letter and Spirit is intended to sort out the role of the Old Testament commandments and their elaboration in contemporary Jewish life for the lives of Christians. Augustine, however, uses the distinction to treat another question, which is one that concerns the possibility of a morally perfect Christian life.

Subsequently, Augustine construes the concept of 'Spirit' to denote God's bestowal of justice on the sinner (as Luther will do centuries later), once again on the basis of a passage in Paul, this time Rom. 3.21-26:

---

6. Augustine, *Answer to the Pelagians*, I, ed. John E. Rotelle, trans. Edmund Hill, Works of Saint Augustine: A Translation for the 21st Century 23 (Hyde Park, NY: New City, 1997), 142.

7. Cf. ibid., 5, 7.

8. Ibid., 5, 8.

> He said, 'The righteousness of God has been revealed.' He did not say: 'The righteousness of human beings or of our own will.' He said: 'The righteousness of God, not that by which God is righteous, but that with which he clothes a human being when he justifies a sinner.' This is testified to by the law and the prophets; to this the law and the prophets bear witness. The law bears witness, because by commanding and threatening and yet justifying no one it indicates clearly enough that human beings are justified by the gift of God through the assistance of the Holy Spirit.[9]

What we also already see here in Augustine is that the law and the prophets, as he calls them, bear witness to both the letter and the Spirit or, to use the Reformation terms, both the Law and the Gospel. A significant number of aspects from the Reformation distinction between Law and Gospel can therefore already be found in *De spiritu et littera*. While Augustine does not name them in that way, he, like the Reformers Luther and Melanchthon, creates two levels of discourse in speaking about 'law'. The first is the prima facie level, where he simply speaks about the law. The second is the deeper level of the function of the law, namely as letter and Spirit. The term 'law' occurs quite often at this stage of Augustine's argument, since it is not until later on in the work that the term 'Gospel' comes to be introduced. In paragraph 13,22, he offers the following summary of the argument he has made in the first part of *De spiritu et littera*:

> Having then weighed and considered these points in accord with the ability that God is pleased to give us, we conclude that human beings are not justified by the commandments that teach us to live well, but only through faith in Jesus Christ, that is, not by the law of works, but by the law of faith, not by the letter, but by the Spirit, not by the merits of actions, but gratuitously by grace.[10]

In the second part of his argument, Augustine then goes on to relate his letter-Spirit distinction to the notion of covenant by way of a discussion of the new covenant in Jeremiah 31. In this context, he maintains that the saints under the Old Testament were saved by the work of Christ. As I have already briefly noted (and will develop at greater length below), this was to be a key point in the Reformation discussion of the Law-Gospel distinction. In terms of the use of Scripture, one might say that Augustine links up Romans, or more broadly the theology of Paul, with the notion of the new covenant from Jeremiah. Together, they are used to substantiate his theology of grace.

Augustine does not use the distinction between works and grace as a hermeneutical key to the interpretation of the Bible as a whole, such that we must ask for every verse in the Bible whether its message is about works or grace, Law or Gospel. This is what the Reformation was to add to his argument. Augustine

---

9. Ibid., 9, 15.
10. Ibid., 13, 22.

rather uses the distinction between letter and Spirit to counter the danger of perfectionism, which may draw on certain biblical passages for support.

2.3.2 The medieval tradition: Peter Lombard and Thomas Aquinas

When on our way to the Reformation we proceed to the Middle Ages, we must ask whether medieval scholastic theology offers a breeding ground for the development of the Law-Gospel distinction, as Luther and Melanchthon were to introduce it later on. This is indeed a distinct possibility. However, at first sight, it seems there is little reason to think so. In medieval scholastic theology, as in Peter Lombard and Thomas Aquinas, for example, the 'Gospel' is identified as 'New Law'.[11] This idea of calling the Gospel a 'new law' did not appeal to the Reformers, and in the first edition of his *Loci Communes* Melanchthon polemicized against the use of these terms.[12]

These forms of resistance do not, however, necessarily mean that the core of the distinction between Law and Gospel was altogether lost during the Middle Ages. If we take Aquinas as an example, we see in the very first article to the *quaestio* on the New Law that he is well aware of the nature of the New Law as grace, referring to Augustine's *De spiritu et littera* to make this point.[13] In the second article, he continues by drawing a sharp distinction between two elements in the New Law. The first element is the work of the Holy Spirit who justifies the sinner, while the second contains the precepts of faith and guidance to the believer. This second element does not justify.[14] Our quick survey thus suggests that what is at stake in the Law-Gospel distinction was not altogether absent from medieval theology, even though its terminology certainly was not clear enough from a Reformation perspective.

2.3.3 The key source of the distinction: Melanchthon

As we have noted, the most likely candidate for the systematization of the Law-Gospel distinction is Luther's friend Philip Melanchthon, who did so in the 1521 edition of his *Loci Communes*, four years after Luther had given the decisive impulse to the Reformation. While Luther himself does use the distinction quite extensively, he did not systematize it.[15] As for Melanchthon, he discusses the

---

11. Petrus Lombardus, *Sententiarum Quattor Libri*, IV, II; Thomas Aquinas, *Summa Theologiae*, I-II, q. 106ff.

12. Melanchthon, 'Loci Theologici [1521]', 143-4; Philipp Melanchthon, *Commonplaces: Loci Communes 1521*, trans. Christian Preus (Saint Louis, MO: Concordia, 2014), 95-6.

13. Aquinas, *Summa*, I-II, q. 106, a. 1.

14. Ibid., I-II, q. 106, a. 2.

15. For a concise account of Luther's view, cf. Ernst Wolf, 'Gesetz V. Gesetz und Evangelium, dogmengeschichtlich', in *Religion in Geschichte und Gegenwart*, ed. Kurt Galling (Tübingen: Mohr Siebeck, 1958); Michael Bünker and Martin Friedrich, eds, *Gesetz*

distinction in no less than three different places in his *Loci*. First, in the locus on the law, he distinguishes between different forms of law.[16] Next, he discusses the relationship between Law and Gospel in the locus on the Gospel.[17] And, finally, the theme reappears in the locus on the relationship between the Old and the New Testament.[18]

Already in this early edition of the *Loci*, we see a number of distinctive features of the use of the Law-Gospel distinction coming to the fore:

> First, there is a distinction between the different types of laws and a discussion of the relationships between them. One crucial distinction here is the one between the Decalogue and the other laws. The Decalogue is seen as the summary, but also as a permanent law of God par excellence, detached from other, contextually determined laws in the Bible.[19]

Second, as the key step Melanchthon draws a sharp distinction between 'Law' as the umbrella term for what God demands of us and 'Gospel' as the umbrella term for what God gives:

> Just as the Law is that by which correct living is commanded and sin is revealed, so the Gospel is the promise of God's grace or mercy, that is, the forgiveness of sin and the testimony of God's kindness toward us. By this testimony our souls are assured of God's kindness.[20]

Third, the terms do not so much apply to parts of the Bible, but – and this is the innovation of the Reformation – the distinction between them is used primarily as a hermeneutical tool for distinguishing between aspects of the way in which God acts towards us:

> Generally speaking, there are two parts of Scripture: Law and Gospel. The Law displays sin, the Gospel grace. The Law shows the disease, the Gospel the cure … But Scripture has not handed down Law and Gospel in such a way that you should think the Gospel is only what Matthew, Mark, Luke, and John wrote, or that the books of Moses are nothing but Law. Rather, the message of the Gospel is spread throughout all the books of the Old and New Testament. And so, too, are promises. Likewise, laws are also spread throughout all the books of the

---

und Evangelium. Eine Studie, auch im Blick auf die entscheidungsfindung in ethischen Fragen, Ergebnis eines Studienprozesses der Gemeinschaft evangelischer Kirchen in Europa (GEKE), Leuenberger Texte 10 (Frankfurt am Main: Otto Lembeck, 2007), 7–11.

16. Melanchthon, 'Loci Theologici [1521]', 116ff; Melanchthon, *Commonplaces*, 61ff.
17. Melanchthon, 'Loci Theologici [1521]', 139ff; Melanchthon, *Commonplaces*, 91ff.
18. Melanchthon, 'Loci Theologici [1521]', 192ff; Melanchthon, *Commonplaces*, 151ff.
19. Melanchthon, 'Loci Theologici [1521]', 120ff; Melanchthon, *Commonplaces*, 66ff.
20. Melanchthon, 'Loci Theologici [1521]', 140; Melanchthon, *Commonplaces*, 92.

Old and New Testament. Nor is the common opinion correct that holds that the distinction between the Law and the Gospel depends on the times of their revelation, though it is true that sometimes the Law is presented and sometimes the Gospel, at various times and in differing order. But as far as human comprehension is concerned, all time is a time of Law and Gospel, just as in all times all men have been justified in the same way – their sin has been revealed by the Law, and grace has been revealed through the promise or through the Gospel.[21]

Thus, the distinction between Law and Gospel has a regulatory function for hermeneutics and in fact for theology as a whole. This also represents the primary innovation that the Reformation made over Augustine. In Augustine, the distinction between the letter and the Spirit is important in the doctrine of grace. Regardless of the significance of the doctrine of grace for Augustine's theology, there are also other building blocks to his thought that are not dominated by it as Reformation theology is. These other leading notions in Augustine's theology also imply that the doctrine of grace is not the only hermeneutical key to the reading of Scripture. It is only in Luther and Melanchthon that the doctrine of grace comes to assume this role.

The above point can be further elucidated. Although Augustine does maintain against Pelagius, as the main theme of *De spiritu et littera*, that human moral perfection remains impossible in this life even with the aid of divine grace, moral perfection nevertheless remains one of the leading notions in his theology. In this, Augustine is primarily informed by Mt. 5.8: 'Blessed are the pure in heart, for they will see God.'[22] Although he would readily admit that we cannot reach moral improvement or do good by our own power, moral improvement nevertheless remains a major theme in his theology. Framed in terms of the doctrine of justification, one could say that Augustine understands justification primarily as internal transformation through the work of the Spirit, rather than in terms of 'forensic' justification as the Reformation would have it. In Luther and Melanchthon's theology, especially in its early stage, the doctrine of grace becomes the primary key to the whole of theology. One might say that with them the doctrine of grace becomes an independent locus, and from that independent locus grace begins to determine all the other loci.

How does this work out in the interpretation of Scripture? Both Law and Gospel, as two ways in which God acts towards us, are in principle positive, although this is only so if they are properly understood. Strictly speaking (although the way in which this works out in the actual practice of biblical interpretation is another matter), any element in Scripture that demands something from us is to be seen as Law and therefore, especially in Luther and Melanchthon's early theology, as something that reminds us of what we *cannot* do rather than what we must do.

---

21. Melanchthon, 'Loci Theologici [1521]', 140; Melanchthon, *Commonplaces*, 91.
22. For a more extensive discussion, see Wisse, *Trinitarian Theology*, chapter 3.

Any promise in Scripture as to what God will do should be taken as Gospel and therefore as something we do not have to do, since God does it for and in us. In the Bible we find Law and Gospel mixed together, but the task of the interpreter is to distinguish them. As the distinction between what God demands from us and what God does for us, the distinction parallels the distinction between *opus hominum* and *opus Dei* and as such mirrors the doctrine of salvation by grace alone.[23]

A fourth aspect of Melanchthon's use of the distinction concerns the place of the Law in the life of the believer. In the first edition of the *Loci Communes*, he opts for a rather radical position on this point. He argues that the Law, and, more precisely, the Decalogue, is no longer binding on the Christian:

> You now understand to what extent we are free from the Decalogue. First, we are free because it cannot damn those who are in Christ even though they are sinners. Then we are also free because those who are in Christ are led by the Spirit to keep the Law. For by the Spirit they keep the Law, love and fear God, apply themselves to their neighbors' needs, and desire the very things the Law used to demand of them. And they would do them even if no Law had been given. Their will, the Spirit, is nothing other than the living Law. In the same way, the fathers who possessed the Spirit of Christ before his.[24]

Of course, Melanchthon is well aware that this has the potential to open the door to debauchery, but he overcomes this danger by emphasizing that the Holy Spirit performs good works in us so that the Christian no longer needs the Decalogue.

In the later Melanchthon, all of the above aspects of his use of the Law-Gospel distinction remain. However, a transformation does manifest itself in the fourth element. Starting with the 1535 edition of the *Loci Communes*, Melanchthon expresses himself much more positively on the role of the Ten Commandments in the believer's life. Later Reformed theologians, as well as many Lutherans, followed him in this, and I will do so as well. This more positive view of the Law in the believer's life (usually referred to as the *usus in renatis*) is closely intertwined with a more positive view of the natural law tradition. Going as far back as Augustine, the Christian tradition has typically maintained that the Law as both the Christian and the Jewish tradition speak of it is not something altogether unknown to others but makes explicit what is known to all of us.[25] In support, that tradition cites Rom. 2.15, where Paul says about the pagans: 'They show that the requirements of the law are written on their hearts.' This explicit Law of God is thus connected to what is called the law of nature (*lex naturalis*) as a reminder due to sin. In the first edition of the *Loci Communes*, Melanchthon had been quite critical of the natural

---

23. Schwöbel, 'Law and Gospel'.

24. Melanchthon, 'Loci Theologici [1521]', 196; Melanchthon, *Commonplaces*, 155.

25. Cf. Rémi Brague, *The Law of God: The Philosophical History of an Idea*, trans. Lydia G. Cochrane, 3rd edn (Chicago: University of Chicago Press, 2008), 217–19.

law tradition,[26] although he did offer his own version of it there.[27] In later editions, however, he returns to the traditional understanding.[28]

There is, of course, much more that could be said about Law and Gospel in Melanchthon, but the above suffices for our purposes. As I have argued, the key step in the theology of the Reformation is the paradigmatic role which the Law-Gospel distinction receives in both hermeneutics and theology as a whole. The question whether it is a human being or God who acts thus becomes decisive for every theological locus and for the interpretation of Scripture. But, even when the first steps towards such paradigmatic use had been taken by Melanchthon, the distinction still awaited actual elaboration and implementation in exegesis and theology. The Law-Gospel distinction does not function in discussions on the ecclesial office, although the shape this discussion receives in the Reformation shows its implicit role in shaping the understanding of office. When it comes to the systematic use of the distinction, Luther and Melanchthon left many possibilities untouched. Once more, the Lutheran tradition has shown a tendency to use the distinction in such a way as to privilege the Gospel over the Law due to the negative connotations it associates with Law. As a result, the Lutheran tradition has been impeded in its systematic use of the distinction for constructive theology.

2.3.4 The exception: Calvin

Calvin's formal view of Law and Gospel is clear from the development of his *Institutes* from 1536 through to its later editions. For the arrangement of the 1536 edition, he followed the structure of Luther's *Large Catechism*. But in departure from Melanchthon, who had been working with the distinction between Law and Gospel in his *Loci* ever since 1521, Calvin pays no attention here to the dynamics of Law and Gospel. He does discuss the role of the Law and even its threefold function (in line with Melanchthon, who uses it in his 1535 edition of the *Loci*, as well as the *Scholia* of 1534[29]), but his 1536 *Institutes* does not include the systematic distinction between Law and Gospel.[30]

In the 1559 edition of the *Institutes*, Calvin does discuss the Law, and he even discusses the Law-Gospel distinction, albeit differently from Melanchthon. At certain places, he seems even to reject the use of the distinction as a hermeneutical

---

26. Melanchthon, 'Loci Theologici [1521]', 116; Melanchthon, *Commonplaces*, 61–2.

27. Melanchthon, 'Loci Theologici [1521]', 116–20; Melanchthon, *Commonplaces*, 62–6.

28. Cf. F. H. Breukelman, *Bijbelse theologie/Dl. IV, 1, De structuur van de heilige leer in de theologie van Calvijn*, ed. Rinse Reeling Brouwer (Kampen: J. H. Kok, 2003), 380, 434–5.

29. Cf. Timothy J. Wengert, *Law and Gospel: Philip Melanchthon's Debate with John Agricola of Eisleben over 'Poenitentia'* (Grand Rapids, MI: Baker, 1997), 177.

30. Calvin does, of course, discuss the Law and the Gospel in a certain sense in the first edition, but he does *not* interpret it as the distinction between what God demands and promises, as Luther and Melanchthon do. Cf. Breukelman, *Bijbelse theologie IV, 1*, 107–9. I owe this reference to my colleague Rinse Reeling Brouwer.

key to the understanding of the Bible and theology as a whole. The relevant issues are treated in book II, chapter 9, where the quotations, given below, all constitute new material that had not appeared in earlier editions of his magnum opus.[31] As the surrounding context in this part of the *Institutes* shows, Calvin's important conversation partners against whom he is developing his arguments are Servetus and the Anabaptists. In section 2 of chapter 9 he offers a definition of the Gospel:

> Now I take the gospel to be the clear manifestation of the mystery of Christ. I recognize, of course, that since Paul calls the gospel 'the doctrine of faith' [I Tim. 4.6], all those promises of free remission of sins which commonly occur in the law, whereby God reconciles men to himself, are counted as parts of it. For he contrasts faith with the terrors that would trouble and vex the conscience if salvation were to be sought in works. From this it follows that the word 'gospel', taken in the broad sense, includes those testimonies of his mercy and fatherly favor which God gave to the patriarchs of old. In a higher sense, however, the word refers, I say, to the proclamation of the grace manifested in Christ.[32]

As we see in this quotation, Calvin allows for the use of the distinction between Law and Gospel as the distinction between what God demands and what God promises, but he prefers another definition of the Gospel, namely as the manifestation of grace in Christ. A little later on, he explicitly argues against those who systematically juxtapose Law and Gospel so as to understand Law as what God demands from us and Gospel as what God offers us in Christ. While he does accept the distinction as such, he only does so as a distinction that is useful in the doctrine of grace, not as a hermeneutical key to the whole of theology:

> Hence, also, we refute those who always erroneously compare the law with the gospel by contrasting the merit of works with the free imputation of righteousness. This is indeed a contrast not at all to be rejected. For Paul often means by the term 'law' the rule of righteous living by which God requires of us what is his own, giving us no hope of life unless we completely obey him, and adding on the other hand a curse if we deviate even in the slightest degree. This Paul does when he contends that we are pleasing to God through grace and are accounted righteous through his pardon, because nowhere is found that observance of the law for which the reward has been promised. Paul therefore justly makes contraries of the righteousness of the law and of that of the gospel [Rom. 3.21 ff.; Gal. 3.10 ff.; etc.]. But the gospel did not so supplant the entire law as to bring forward a different way of salvation. Rather, it confirmed and satisfied whatever the law had promised, and gave substance to the shadows. When Christ says, 'The Law and the Prophets were until John' [Lk. 16.16; cf.

---

31. Calvin, *Institutes (1559)*, ed. John T. McNeill, trans. Ford Lewis Battles (Kentucky: Westminster, 1960), 424–5, 428–9.

32. Calvin, *Institutes (1559)*, II.9.2.

Mt. 11.13], does not subject the patriarchs to the curse that the slaves of the law cannot escape. He means: they had been trained in rudiments only, thus remaining far beneath the height of the gospel teaching. Hence Paul, calling the gospel 'the power of God unto salvation for every believer' [Rom. 1.16], presently adds: 'The Law and the Prophets bear witness to it' [Rom. 3.21]. And at the end of the same letter, although he teaches that 'the preaching of Jesus Christ is the revelation of the mystery kept in silence through times eternal' [Rom. 16.25], qualifies this statement by adding an explanation, teaching that he was 'made known through the prophetic writings' [Rom. 16.26]. From this we infer that, where the whole law is concerned, the gospel differs from it only in clarity of manifestation. Still, because of the inestimable abundance of grace laid open for us in Christ, it is said with good reason that through his advent God's Heavenly Kingdom was erected upon earth [cf. Mt. 12.28].[33]

For Calvin, the distinction between Law and Gospel as a systematic distinction between what God demands and promises is subsumed under a more fundamental distinction between the Old and New Testaments. In this fundamental distinction, the Gospel differs from the Law only in terms of the clarity in which the grace of God in Christ is present.

Although Calvin's intended opponent in these quotations is not entirely clear, the substance of his argument suggests that he may well be lashing out at mainstream Reformation views, and at Melanchthon in particular. Certainly the early Melanchthon seems to be in view, but Calvin's criticism also potentially addresses the later editions of the *Loci Communes*. In the 1559 edition of his own *Institutes*, Calvin adds two chapters on the similarities and differences between the Old and the New Testament. At the beginning of the chapter on the similarities, he establishes the following as his point of departure:

> Now we can clearly see from what has already been said that all men adopted by God into the company of his people since the beginning of the world were covenanted to him by the same law and by the bond of the same doctrine as obtains among us. It is very important to make this point.[34]

Even the most charitable reading of this quotation suggests that Luther or Melanchthon, regardless of their interest in the fundamental difference between Law and Gospel, would never have accepted the relationship between Old and New Covenant to be framed in this way. The problem seems to be that Calvin allows for just a single dynamic in both the Old and the New Covenant, and that he calls this dynamic 'law'!

In spite of a broad research tradition that holds Calvin's view on Law and Gospel to depart from Luther's, recent decades have seen a persistent line of

---

33. Ibid.
34. Ibid., II.10.1.

scholarship arguing that the difference between Luther and Melanchthon's view on Law and Gospel, on the one hand, and Calvin's view, on the other, should not be exaggerated. Prominent authors who have made this argument include I. John Hesselink,[35] Michael Horton[36] and R. Scott Clark.[37]

Several arguments have been brought to the fore in the debate. First, scholars have questioned whether the *Institutes* ought really to have the central role it typically receives, arguing that a broader approach to Calvin's corpus as a whole is required. From there, they have suggested that although Calvin does not emphasize the Law-Gospel distinction in the *Institutes*, he does accept it in other works, and, moreover, that even if he does not mention the distinction in the *Institutes*, he does use other terms and distinctions reflective of it.[38] Second, Hesselink – and, following him, Horton and Clark – has suggested that the distinction between Law and Gospel must be interpreted in salvation-historical terms for Calvin, especially when it comes to the *Institutes* of 1559.[39] Finally, Horton in particular has proposed a straightforward model for interpreting Calvin's use of the terms Law and Gospel. Hesselink, as we will see below, proves to be considerably more careful in integrating various strands of Calvin's discourse on Law and Gospel. But according to Horton, Calvin's use of the terms is perfectly clear, provided that we recognize he is using the pair of terms in two different ways. Horton formulates his position concisely when he writes: 'It is clear that Calvin is affirming the law-gospel antithesis with respect to justification (contra Rome) while also preserving the unity of the covenant of grace with respect to the Old and New Testaments (contra Anabaptists).'[40]

It is important to note that the aforementioned authors are directing their arguments against multiple fronts. One of those fronts is a research tradition that has been dominated by the influence of Karl Barth.[41] As we will see below, Barth had his own reasons for emphasizing the difference between the Lutherans and the Reformed on the point of the Law-Gospel distinction. Another front is related to traditional confessional dividing lines that influence the reading of Law and

---

35. I. John Hesselink, *Calvin's Concept of the Law* (Allison Park, PA: Pickwick, 1992).

36. Michael S. Horton, 'Calvin and the Law-Gospel Hermeneutic', *Pro Ecclesia* 6, no. 1 (2002): 27–42, http://web.archive.org/web/20010411225720/http://alliancenet.org/pub/articles/horton.CalvinLG.html; Michael S. Horton, 'Calvin on Law and Gospel', 1 September 2009, https://wscal.edu/resource-center/calvin-on-law-and-gospel.

37. R. Scott Clark, 'Law and Gospel in Early Reformed Orthodoxy: Hermeneutical Conservatism in Olevianus' Commentary on Romans', in *Church and School in Early Modern Protestantism: Studies in Honor of Richard A. Muller on the Maturation of a Theological Tradition*, ed. Jordan J. Ballor, David S. Sytsma and Jason Zuidema, Studies in the History of Christian Traditions 170 (Leiden: Brill, 2013), 307–20.

38. Horton, 'Calvin and the Law-Gospel Hermeneutic', 27–8.

39. Hesselink, *Calvin's Concept of the Law*, 11, 186.

40. Horton, 'Calvin on Law and Gospel'.

41. Hesselink, *Calvin's Concept of the Law*, 57ff.

Gospel.⁴² Some Lutherans have a strong interest in underlining the difference between Lutherans and Reformed for the distinction between Law and Gospel. A final front pertains to the relationship between Calvin and the Calvinists after him. Combining several of these fronts, one might say that scholars who theologize in a Barthian environment have an interest in reinforcing the difference between Calvin and the Calvinists and favouring Calvin over his namesakes since he can be read more easily as being critical of natural theology.⁴³

Against this background, the scholars who emphasize the continuity between Luther, Melanchthon, Calvin and the Calvinists certainly deserve support. It is indeed true that Calvin must be read in context, including his scholastic context, and that his commentaries and sermons are important sources alongside the *Institutes*. Furthermore, I certainly agree that the distinction between Law and Gospel plays a crucial role in the Reformed tradition. This is especially true of the Reformed tradition immediately after Calvin and up until the time federal theology gained supremacy towards the end of the seventeenth century (see below). Finally, it is also important to be aware of Barth's very specific reasons for emphasizing his Calvinistic inclinations, which nevertheless should not be confused with the historical reality of the sixteenth and seventeenth centuries.

In spite of all this, I do, however, think that there are also reasons not to follow all too quickly in this line of scholarship since it exaggerates the level of continuity between Luther-Melanchthon and Calvin. From the first edition of the *Institutes* (1536) onwards, Calvin had the option of following Melanchthon's use of the distinction in the *Loci*. He indeed did so with regard to the third use of the Law. He did not, however, adopt the systematic use of the distinction as an overarching framework for doing theology and, more importantly, for exegesis.⁴⁴

Furthermore, although it is admittedly important to consider not only the *Institutes* but also the commentaries, one must realize that Calvin in the latter moves back and forth considerably in his expressions with the way the biblical texts make their points.⁴⁵ On this account, it should hardly surprise us to find

42. Ibid., 1–2.

43. Cf. Horton, 'Calvin and the Law-Gospel Hermeneutic', 28; Clark, 'Hermeneutical Conservatism'. Clark's article appears in the Festschrift for Richard Muller, who has spent a major part of his career on debunking the 'Calvin against the Calvinists' myth.

44. For more evidence for the difference between Calvin and Melanchthon on this point, see Breukelman, *Bijbelse theologie IV, 1*, 397.

45. Another interesting albeit entirely different case in point is Krusche's presentation of Calvin's doctrine of the Holy Spirit in creation as the first chapter in his influential study on Calvin's pneumatology. All of the material presented in that chapter comes from the commentaries; no reference whatsoever can be found to the Spirit's role in creation in the *Institutes*. Given that Krusche had a distinctly twentieth-century interest in promoting the role of the Spirit in creation, it is highly significant that he had to resort exclusively to the commentaries to make that point and could not find anything in the *Institutes*. For this point, see Maarten Wisse and Hugo Meijer, 'Pneumatology: Tradition and Renewal', in *Brill Companion to Reformed Orthodoxy*, ed. Herman J. Selderhuis (Leiden: Brill, 2013), 481.

Calvin operating with a Luther-like distinction between Law and Gospel in his commentaries on Galatians and Romans, and yet this does not prove in any way that he subscribed to the overarching function of the distinction for doing theology. Similarly, it should not surprise us that Calvin subscribes to the elenctic function of the Law and confirms that it is the grace of God alone that makes us fulfil the Law. Of course Calvin is not a theologian who advocates works righteousness, but this does not mean that he subscribes to the role of the Law-Gospel distinction as it had been proposed by Melanchthon. Quite the contrary, both the *Institutes* (in its various editions) and Calvin's many commentaries (as amply illustrated in the footnotes in Hesselink) reveal the powerful emphasis he placed on the unity of the Old and the New Testament, as well as the unity of the Old and the New Covenant, calling the Gospel a 'Law' and the Law a 'Gospel'. Hesselink is very realistic in his assessment of the problem when he writes:

> The real problem, however, is not that of showing that Calvin takes the accusing, condemning function of the law seriously. Rather, the difficulty is to integrate this concept of the law with his understanding of the law as a whole. For it could be maintained that Calvin has not thoroughly integrated this aspect of the law into his system as a whole; and that he operates with two concepts of the law, with the more Pauline one playing a subordinate role. This is a very complex problem, for despite his numerous definitions, warnings, and qualifying phrases (the key one being 'in so far as – quatenus'), no simple solution is readily apparent.[46]

The fact that Calvin explicitly criticizes the Law-Gospel distinction in the sense of a distinction between what God demands and what God promises is significant, but it should not be taken as representative for the whole of the Reformed tradition. Rather, on this point, as in other areas of theology like the doctrine of providence, Calvin is not representative for the Reformed tradition. As we will see below, the later Reformed scholastic tradition generally accepted the Melanchthonian distinction. Nevertheless, Calvin is not unique in his rejection of it, as can be demonstrated by references to the sixteenth-century confessions. In the First Helvetic Confession of 1536, the distinction between Law and Gospel is neither a theme nor does it play a role in the Gallican and Belgic Confessions. This suggests that at least a part of the Reformed tradition does not see the distinction between Law and Gospel as a fundamental issue in theology. A considerable part of that tradition, however, does accept it as such.

---

46. Hesselink, *Calvin's Concept of the Law*, 194. Hesselink quotes a number of very strong passages where Calvin emphasizes the unity between the Old and New Testaments, and then writes: 'Granted, Calvin is overstating his case here, but this "doctrine" which comprises the unity of revelation is not some abstract teaching but Christ himself' (162).

2.3.5 The rule: Reformed scholasticism

If we look at Reformed scholasticism[47] after, or actually already during, the Reformation, a simple pattern emerges. Many Reformed theologians pattern themselves after Melanchthon's *Loci* in the 1535 and later editions. They accept all four elements mentioned above as characteristic of the Melanchthonian distinction between Law and Gospel beginning in 1521, but they also confirm the so-called third use of the Law and affirm the natural law tradition in line with the later Melanchthon. This is, of course, illustrative of Melanchthon's importance for the Reformed tradition. Notable examples of Reformed theologians who follow the Melanchthonian consensus are Girolamo Zanchius (1516–1590),[48] Zacharius Ursinus (1534–1583),[49] Caspar Olevianus (1536–1587)[50] and Gisbertus Voetius.

Voetius is an interesting case in point. In three disputations in the *Disputationes Selectae*, he discusses the relationship between Law and Gospel.[51] What makes Voetius so interesting is the fact that he represents a strand of Reformed scholasticism that had not yet embedded the Law-Gospel distinction within an overarching covenant theology, even though covenant theology is certainly not absent from his work, either. One might say that covenant language in Voetius is embedded in the distinction between Law and Gospel, while for his contemporaries and for later Reformed scholastics it was the other way around.

For Luther and Melanchthon, and also for Calvin, the front they faced was constituted by contemporary Roman Catholic theologians, and later on by various types of radical Reformers, including the Anabaptists and Servetus. Voetius' disputations on Law and Gospel reveal, however, that the primary fronts he is facing are Socinianism, Arminianism and, to a lesser extent, Roman Catholic theology.[52] Large parts of the first and second disputations are devoted to polemics against various Socinian and Arminian views. In this polemic, Voetius powerfully emphasizes that the Gospel in its essence includes no legal element at all. In this context, he makes the remark that I have used as a motto for this book:

---

47. For an introduction to Reformed scholasticism, see Willem J. van Asselt et al., *Introduction to Reformed Scholasticism* (Grand Rapids, MI: Reformation Heritage, 2011).

48. Girolamo Zanchi, *De Religione Christiana Fides = Confession of Christian Religion*, ed. Luca Baschera and Christian Moser (Leiden: Brill, 2007), I, 182–99, 252–63.

49. Willem J. van Asselt, *The Federal Theology of Johannes Cocceius (1603-1669)* (Leiden: Brill, 2001), 255.

50. Clark, 'Hermeneutical Conservatism'.

51. Gisbertus Voetius, *Selectae disputationes theologicae* (Ultrajecti: Johannes à Waesberge, 1648–69), IV, 17–61; these disputations are more easily accessible in the text edited by Abraham Kuyper in Voetius, *D. Gysberti Voetii Selectarum Disputationum Fasciculus*, 341–77.

52. Interestingly, the third disputation is in its entirety devoted to the preaching of Law and Gospel, and especially to the question whether it is easier to preach Law than Gospel, adding a pastoral dimension to the discussion. Unfortunately, Voetius does not explain in detail what issue prompted him to do this.

Objection: The Gospel promises under a condition; this condition is faith, which it demands; therefore, it commands faith. I respond: Properly, directly, and formally a command of the law does not express a mere proposition, or explication, or addition of a condition, but a prescription of duty. However, the Gospel, strictly speaking, insofar as it is distinguished from the law, does not directly and in itself prescribe any duty to us, nor something that we have to do, saying: 'Do this, or believe this, or have faith', or 'Hope for the Lord, expect the Lord, rejoice in the Lord, love the Lord, know the Lord, hold on to eternal life, call upon the Lord, be consoled, persevere until the end, fight the good fight', etc. Rather, it relates, announces, signifies to us what Christ has done for us, and what God promises in Christ, what he wants to do, and what he will do.[53]

Whereas Calvin was forced to emphasize the unity of the Old and the New Testaments, Voetius holds on to the more widespread Melanchthonian tradition and distinguishes clearly between Law and Gospel. The Law signifies all those aspects of revelation that point to what God demands, and the Gospel points to all that God promises. As such, Voetius maintains the unity of the two testaments, while still retaining a distinction between the two elements that are found in both testaments, namely demands and promises. The subtle nature of Voetius' view of Law and Gospel emerges right from the beginning of his first disputation on the topic, when he defines the terms 'Law' and 'Gospel'. In the definitions of both terms, he distinguishes between a broader meaning, which includes 'legal' and 'evangelical' elements in both Law and Gospel, and a stricter meaning, in which 'Law' denotes only the legal aspects (demands) of the Old Testament and the New Testament, while 'Gospel' pertains only to God's promises in both testaments, excluding all legal elements.[54]

An important step towards a more differentiated understanding of the Law-Gospel distinction was taken in the course of the seventeenth century when it came to be included in a refined covenant doctrine, also known as 'federal theology'. On

---

53. Voetius, *D. Gysberti Voetii Selectarum Disputationum Fasciculus*, 348:

> Object. Euangelium promittit sub conditione: conditio autem illa est fides, quam postulat: ergo eandem praecipit. Resp. Proprie, directe, & formaliter praeceptum legis dicit non nuclam propositionem, aut explicationem, aut additionem conditionis; sed officii praescriptionem. Jam vero Euangelium stricte dictum, ut a lege distinguitur, directe & per se non praescribit nobis officium nostrum, aut quid nos facere debeamus, dicendo, hoc fac, aut crede, aut confide; non magis quam, spera in Dominum, exspecta Dominum, gaude in Domino, dilige Dominum, cognosce dominum, apprehende vitam aeternam, invoca dominum, consolare, persevera usque ad finem, certa praeclarum certamen, &c. Sed refert, nuntiat, significat nobis, quid Christus pro nobis fecerit, quidque Deus in Christo promittat, quid facere velit, & facturus sit.

54. Ibid., 341–2.

the continent, Johannes Cocceius was an important figure in this development, with roots further back in time. Cocceius incorporated all the core insights of Melanchthon's vision into his teaching on the covenants.[55] Following an initial controversy about the notion of the relationship between the forgiveness of sins under the Old and the New Covenant, Cocceius' scheme of different stages in the covenant of grace came to be incorporated into the broader Reformed tradition (including that of Voetius and his followers), for example, in Herman Witsius and Francis Turrettin.[56]

Even when the distinction as introduced by Melanchthon was widely adopted by Reformed scholastic theologians, it is still fair to say that it was applied less explicitly and widely in the Reformed tradition than it was in the Lutheran tradition. So too one does not readily encounter it among the Reformed in the discussion of a particular locus or the interpretation of a biblical verse.

On the whole, the Reformed tradition still attempts chiefly to substantiate theological choices by arguing for their biblical basis in an unqualified way, comparing Scripture with Scripture, without explicit indication of the theological framework being used (see Chapter 5). That is to say: theologians from the Reformed tradition typically do not recognize the possibility that a different hermeneutical approach to Scripture may yield a different reading of the available biblical evidence. The texts supposedly speak for themselves. One text is often interpreted in the light of another, but no explicit criterion is given for determining the priority of a particular text. Part of my aim in this book, especially in the chapters on the reception of John, is to show that, in spite of the absence of such an explicit criterion in the Reformed tradition, the criterion operative in classical Reformed theology is the distinction between Law and Gospel.

Given the use of Scripture without a material hermeneutical criterion, it will come as no surprise that the Law-Gospel distinction was not applied to the doctrine of Scripture in the Reformed tradition. This is a step that I will take in this book so as to move beyond the Reformed tradition. In Chapter 5, I apply the distinction to the doctrine of Scripture and examine the consequences for Scripture's role in theology and for Reformed theology as a whole.

2.3.6 The twentieth century: Barth

The subsequent moment in the history of the development of the Law-Gospel distinction that must be addressed here is Karl Barth's reversal of it in the 1930s. At first sight, Barth seems to be continuing an ongoing discussion from the time

---

55. Van Asselt, *Federal Theology*, 254ff.

56. It is interesting to see how the term that Cocceius used to describe the relationship between the covenants, '*abrogatio*', to which Voetius objected, was already used by Melanchthon in 1521 for describing the relationship between the Old and the New Covenant: Melanchthon, 'Loci Theologici [1521]', 192ff; Melanchthon, *Commonplaces*, 151ff. Calvin too accepts the use of the term: Calvin, *Institutes (1559)*, II.7.14ff.

of the Reformation. Upon closer examination, however, it becomes clear that the conditions under which he comes to introduce his view have changed. Barth was writing in a post-Enlightenment context, and, as we will see, this is of considerable influence for the frame of reference in which he uses the Law-Gospel distinction. He opposes the classical form of the distinction for presupposing the existence of two sources of theological knowledge, namely the Law and the Gospel. In this, Barth sees a justification of the idea that religion and knowledge of God are available apart from God's revelation in Christ, on the basis of human reason. Given his cultural context, he understands this notion to offer support to the Kulturchristentum he sees all around him. This is why he poses the challenging thesis that the order of the terms in the distinction must be reversed. He does so in the well-known essay 'Evangelium und Gesetz', published in 1935:

> The traditional order, 'Law and Gospel', has a perfect right in its place, which we shall later describe. It must not, however, define the structure of the whole teaching to be outlined here. The nature of the case is such that anyone who really and earnestly would first say Law and only then, presupposing this, say Gospel would not, no matter how good his intention, be speaking of the Law of God and therefore then certainly not of *his* Gospel.[57]

For Barth, the Gospel has to take precedence over the Law. The source of proper action is not to be found in ourselves, nor can the criterion for proper action be found in reality as we find it around us. The Law follows from the Gospel itself or, more precisely from the life and work of Jesus Christ:

> 'The Law is the manifest will of God.' The definition is correct. But where is the will of God manifest? Certainly God is the Creator of all things and thus Lord of all that occurs. He and his will, and thus the Law, are, however, not manifest to us in all things, in every occurrence, that is, so very manifest that our apprehensions of it could claim to be more and something different than our own theories and interpretations. If the Law is also *God's Word*, if it is further *grace* that God's Word is spoken aloud and becomes audible, and if grace means nothing else than *Jesus Christ*, then it is not only uncertain and dangerous but perverse to want to understand the Law of God on the basis of any other thing, of any other event which is different from the event in which the will of God, tearing in two the veil of our theories and interpretations, is visible as grace in both form and content.[58]

A few lines further on, it becomes clear how the grace of the Gospel turns into a command for us:

---

57. Karl Barth, 'Gospel and Law', in *Community, State, and Church: Three Essays*, trans. A. M. Hall (Garden City, NY: Doubleday, 1960), 71; original emphasis.
58. Ibid., 77; original emphases.

> Because this occurrence of the will of God, therefore the occurrence of his grace, becomes *manifest* to us, the *Law* becomes manifest to us. From what God does *for* us, we infer what he wants *with* us and *from* us. His grace does apply to *us*, it does concern us ... His action does not revolve in itself; instead, it has its goal in our action, in the conformity of our action with his own. 'You must' (*Ihr sollt*) – more exactly and correctly, '*You shall*' (*Ihr werdet*) – 'Be perfect, as your heavenly father is perfect' (Matthew 5:48). Grace can by no means become manifest to men unless it means this offense, unless it moves in this future tense: 'You shall be!' (*Ihr werdet sein*).[59]

Although Barth changes the 'ihr sollt' (you must) from the German Bible into an 'ihr werdet' (you will), he does retain a careful balance between the two. A few sentences later, Barth moves from the 'will' to the 'must', but the commandment always remains embedded in the actuality of God's acts in history. To use Berkouwer's well-known terms, the 'triumph of grace' always precedes the tasks set before us:

> How could the Lordship of Jesus Christ be proclaimed, unless the proclamation as such be a demand for *obedience*? How the incarnation except as the command of self-denial? How the cross of Christ, except as the command to *follow after* him and take up one's own cross? How then his resurrection except as under the admonition of the Easter pericope of the ancient Church (1 Corinthians 5:7f.): 'Cleanse out the old leaven that you may be new dough!'?[60]

In line with Barth's decision to reverse the order between Law and Gospel, there is no mention of the Decalogue in the second part of volume II/2 of the *Church Dogmatics*, which appeared in 1942. Barth's reversal of Law and Gospel (to Gospel and Law) occasioned an intense debate on the third use of the Law in German-speaking Protestant theology.[61] By rejecting the classical order of the terms in the distinction, Barth suggested that there was no room for the first and second use of the Law, the *usus politicus* and the *usus elencticus*. The result would then be a powerful emphasis on the third use, the *usus in renatis*.

We do not need to delve all too deeply into Barth's view on Gospel and Law. Our purpose here is to offer a brief sketch of the way the Law-Gospel distinction has developed throughout the history of Christianity. Barth's polemics may have contributed to the prevalent understanding that the pair of terms is a feature typical of Lutheran theology. But, as we have seen, this understanding has been criticized, and I too am critical of it. Similarly, ecumenical dialogue between Lutherans and Reformed in the 1990s revealed that there is a wide-reaching

---

59. Ibid., 78; original emphases.
60. Ibid., 79; original emphases.
61. Cf. Gerhard O. Forde, *The Law-Gospel Debate: An Interpretation of Its Historical Development* (Minneapolis, MN: Fortress, 1969).

ecumenical agreement on the theological use of the Law-Gospel distinction.[62] So too Lutherans have come to admit that Luther accepted the idea behind what is now known as the third use of the Law, and that the twentieth-century debate on this question was motivated by very specific conditions.[63]

For our purposes, it is relevant to note that the way in which Barth uses the distinction, with an appeal to the Reformed tradition, is in fact neither typically Reformed nor typically Lutheran. In spite of his emphasis on the third use of the Law, Barth's interpretation of this third use is in fact borrowed in a modified sense from an early Lutheran tendency, reflecting Melanchthon's understanding of the role of the Law in the life of Christians in the first edition of his *Loci*. There Melanchthon holds that the Spirit transforms Christians and brings them to obey God's commandments, but that these commandments are therefore no longer needed in the Christian's life. Barth's notion of the 'Ihr werdet' (you will) reminds us of that line of thought, although he is well aware of the risk of cheap grace implicit in it. This is why he adds the 'Ihr sollt', although this is ultimately no real help since these two lines of argument are in constant tension throughout his entire theology. Barth also differs markedly from the Reformed tradition in his interpretation of the Law. His decision to incorporate ethics into dogmatics is reflective of the Reformed tradition, and yet one of the shapes ethics assumes in the Reformed (and traditionally Lutheran) tradition is precisely that of an exposition of the Decalogue.

On the other hand, Barth's tendency to link up the Gospel with the 'Ihr sollt' of the Law, where the Gospel implies the Law, is very problematic from a traditional Lutheran perspective. Lutherans would object to the idea that the Gospel implies obedience, turning Gospel into Law, grace into works. Barth is definitely aware of this risk, which is why he moves back and forth between the 'Ihr werdet' and the 'Ihr sollt' of the Gospel, but still he keeps both onboard. This, however, is problematic not only for Lutherans, but may also be so for Reformed theologians. Barth does not, after all, offer a clear account of the relationship between the 'will' and 'must' in his ethics, which in turn reflects a deep ambiguity in his theology. In Chapter 4, I will argue that it is the ambiguity of his soteriology which makes Barth move back and forth between hard and conditional universalism or, phrased differently, between cheap grace and works righteousness. Barth's doctrine of grace runs the permanent risk of becoming moralistic. If God did everything for us and in us, then either what we do does not matter or we have to live up to what God has done for us. We have to make salvation come true. This also explains how Barth's triumph of grace from the 1940s shifted so easily into the activism of the 1970s. They were two sides of the same coin.

Barth's reversal of the distinction between Law and Gospel introduces two shifts into the meaning and significance of this distinction. So far, we have

---

62. Cf. Bünker and Friedrich, *Gesetz und Evangelium*.

63. Cf. Eilert Herms, *Phänomene des Glaubens: Beiträge zur Fundamentaltheologie* (Tübingen: Mohr Siebeck, 2006), chapter 16.

concentrated on the soteriological shift. The second shift that occurs through Barth's rethinking of the distinction is perhaps even more paradigmatic, although it does not seem to be one he consciously allows. It is a consequence of the modern context in which he finds himself. In this modern context, an epistemological paradigm determines cultural and scientific discourse, constantly posing the question: What is the source of this belief? And is this source reliable? Along these lines, the dominant theological question becomes the one that asks: Does a claim come from God, or is it a human projection? As such, the main question concerns the source of knowledge by which we have access to God, if such access is even possible at all.

As such, the Law-Gospel distinction has entered the epistemological framework of the Enlightenment, where it had never found itself before. Barth's argument is decisively motivated by the question posed by the theology of revelation, which asks how we gain access to the will of God.[64] Does such access come from our side, with natural theology as a consequence, or is it bound to God's revelation in Jesus Christ? If it comes from our side, it can be known and perhaps even be done independently from the obedience of faith. Barth vehemently rejects this, arguing that it is inextricably bound to God's revelation in Jesus Christ. This is because for Barth, influenced as he is by the Enlightenment, the world of creation is no longer an obvious source of revelation.[65]

My intention in this book is to challenge this epistemological paradigm which theology has inherited from modernity and postmodernity, and to develop an alternative that takes the twofold nature of divine revelation seriously – not in the sense of two points of access to God, as if there was one that is human and independent from God and another that depends solely on God, but in the sense of two ways in which God relates to us, both depending on God's revelation. We will continue the conversation with Barth in Chapter 4, where we investigate the development of Barth's Christocentrism.

2.4 Towards a new understanding of Law and Gospel

We have traced the history of the use of the Law-Gospel distinction and seen that it receives new meanings every time it is reintroduced in a new context. This is also true of my own use of the distinction. Perhaps the only difference is that, in contrast with most theologians who reintroduced the distinction, I am trying to be conscious of the innovations I am making. Taking up a range of aspects

---

64. This applies equally to Brunner, notwithstanding his defence of 'natural theology'. Cf. David Andrew Gilland, *Law and Gospel in Emil Brunner's Earlier Dialectical Theology*, T&T Clark Studies in Systematic Theology 22 (London: Bloomsbury, 2015), especially chapter 2.

65. Cf. his admission in the first quotation from *Evangelium und Gesetz* that all creation is indeed from God, although he still denies it as a source of revelation.

from the historical use of the distinction, I rearrange them in my own context in a new way.⁶⁶

As far as Augustine is concerned, we saw him use the distinction between the letter and the Spirit when facing the question of the possibility of a morally perfect life. In this context, he emphasizes that moral perfection is not possible in this life and that concrete directions in Scripture for the moral life must therefore be read as a reminder of our inability to follow them with our own power and of the need for the power of the Holy Spirit. Nevertheless, for Augustine, the keeping of God's commandments with a pure heart remains the primary purpose of the Christian's life. This purpose of Christian life should teach us humility, because the necessity of grace reminds us that every good act we perform must be ascribed to the grace of God alone.

In Melanchthon and those who follow him in adopting the Law-Gospel distinction, we saw that the justification of the godless as we already find it in Paul becomes the anchoring point for the whole of Christian life and therefore the very criterion of theology. As a result, the Law-Gospel distinction begins to function as a hermeneutical key for the reading of all the Scriptures. At the same time, the doctrine of grace, understood in terms of this same distinction, begins to exert a decisive influence on other loci of theology, such as the doctrine of God and Christology. As a consequence, in Reformation times, Christian life no longer revolved primarily around obedience to the commandments and the attainment of moral perfection (or at least moral improvement). Although these two elements still do play a major role in chief Reformation strands, Christian life begins to revolve around personal trust in God's grace revealed in Jesus Christ and living life as a gift of grace.

In Barth, as we have seen, the shifts of meaning in the use of the distinction do not only have to do with the theological concepts that form the immediate context of the distinction between Law and Gospel. Sometimes, this context may seem to remain the same, as it is initially the case in Barth's retrieval of the distinction. Barth does not have his own contextual reinterpretation in view when he modifies the distinction. This was also the case in Melanchthon's reception of Augustine's distinction between the letter and the Spirit. Sometimes, the shift in meaning is not

---

66. There is another significant twentieth-century development after Barth that I do not discuss here. Along the lines of Rudolf Bultmann and Gerhard Ebeling, certain later Lutheran theologians such as Oswald Bayer (cf. especially Oswald Bayer, *Leibliches Wort: Reformation und Neuzeit im Konflikt* [Tübingen: Mohr Siebeck, 1992]) and Gerhard Forde develop a strong opposition between Law and Gospel. Among these theologians, there is hardly any positive role for the Law, which is reason for others (e.g. Robert Jenson) to accuse these scholars of antinomism. For an extensive discussion of this controversy and a defence of the Ebeling tradition, see John D. Koch, *The Distinction between Law and Gospel as the Basis and Boundary of Theological Reflection* (Tübingen: Mohr Siebeck, 2016), especially chapter 2. As one might conclude from the current chapter, my interpretation of the distinction is quite different from those following Ebeling.

so much a deliberate change in theological viewpoints as a change in the cultural and philosophical context in which the distinction between Law and Gospel is used. One might therefore suggest that the distinction receives new meaning as soon as it starts to function as part of a new paradigm.

In Barth, we saw that the Enlightenment context caused a paradigm shift in the sense that he interprets the distinction from the perspective of the question of the sources of theological knowledge implied in this distinction. From this perspective, another question that plays a role is whether salvation is within our own power, not merely as a question of the doctrine of grace but also as a matter of post-Marxist power analysis. Barth denies that salvation can be within our own power, and for that reason reverses the order of the distinction, making the Law fundamentally dependent on the Gospel as free divine revelation. The Gospel as divine and revealed promise must precede the question of how we can live up to that promise. The doctrine of grace is still of major importance in this view, but it is a doctrine of grace that is permeated by an epistemological interest.

In my own use of the distinction, I take up elements from all stages of its development. I assign it a very central role in all of systematic theology, following in this regard the trajectory introduced by Melanchthon's systematization of the distinction. I follow this trajectory even more rigorously than Melanchthon had done, following in this respect the line of Barth when he attempted to reconceive the whole of dogmatics from the perspective of a single locus. Barth too did so in what one might call a post-biblicist context, a frame of reference in which the Bible can no longer be used as a source for dogmatics without qualification. At the same time, I distance myself from Barth in abandoning his single Christological point of access to divine revelation in favour of a double Law-and-Gospel point of access, deliberately retaining this order.

The way in which I use the distinction appropriates another insight from Barth. Like Barth, my theological work is undertaken in awareness of the question of power introduced in modernity by Marx and such critics of religion as Feuerbach and Nietzsche. Barth tries to answer this question by a strict limitation to God's revelation in Jesus Christ. In Chapter 4, I will argue that this Christocentrism causes him to run into the problems that he is at pains to avoid. This is why I myself will argue that the duality of Law and Gospel represents a better instrument for refuting the modern critiques of religion than Barth's Christocentrism does.

Although I take my point of departure in Melanchthon's systematization of the Law-Gospel distinction, I nevertheless take up elements from Augustine's thought in order to effect a partial reversal in the paradigm shift that had occurred in the Reformation. Precisely because of the question of power, I am very sensitive to the danger of cheap grace that seems inherent to the paradigm shift introduced in the Reformation. I already touched on this in the previous chapter (while Chapters 4 and 6 will show that the criticism of cheap grace will also be targeting Barth). Even if Christian life can indeed be lived only on the basis of a fundamental gratitude towards the grace of God, what I have learned from Augustine is that Christian life nevertheless circles around concrete justice and moral perfection. This concrete justice and moral perfection is based not only on the work of the

Spirit in me (cf. the early Luther and Melanchthon) or the structure of God's act in Jesus Christ (cf. Barth) but also on our 'natural' sensitivity towards the Good of which God's Law reminds us.

The biggest innovation in my understanding of the Law-Gospel distinction may well be its reinterpretation in terms of speech act theory, however. As introduced in the previous chapter, following Melanchthon, whose basic insight I combine with Vincent Brümmer's version[67] of Austin's speech act theory,[68] I translate Melanchthon's distinction between what God demands and promises into a distinction between the prescriptive nature of the Law and the commissive nature of the Gospel. The consequences of this step are particularly significant for our understanding of the Gospel, because I borrow from Brümmer the insight that constatives are at work in commissives, but still commissives have a distinct nature.[69] This then leads to my critique of modern dogmatics (as I have already accounted for it in the previous chapter), since it tends to see the whole of dogmatics in constative – or, to use the more common phrase, 'propositional' – terms. This, I argue on the basis of speech act theory, turns Gospel into Law, since each proposition implies a prescriptive to believe it.[70] This argument is not only a philosophical trick but intrinsically connected with my attempt to overcome the power dynamics of theological claims. If the primary character of theological language is propositional, its first aim is to describe the truth about God, and as such, to convince others of what God and God's revelation is. By emphasizing the primarily commissive nature of the Gospel, I am trying to find a way between a merely propositional and a merely expressive account of dogmatics. Dogmatics is not only a reflection on the expressions and experiences of the believing community.[71] It is also a reflection on the community's faithful response to the promises of God. This response to God's promises includes propositional elements, since all commissives presuppose and imply constative (propositional) elements, by virtue of which these propositional aspects are part of Christian faith and theology.

If we allow ourselves to reflect on this step at some greater length, we could say that by combining Melanchthon's understanding of the Law-Gospel distinction with twentieth-century speech act theory, I apply the distinction not just to every *locus* in theology but also to the meta-level of the status of theological language as such. Whereas Karl Barth introduced a shift in the understanding of the distinction

---

67. Vincent Brümmer, *Theology and Philosophical Inquiry* (London: Macmillan, 1981), 9–33.

68. J. L. Austin, *How to Do Things with Words* (Cambridge, MA: Harvard University Press, 1962).

69. Brümmer, *Theology and Philosophical Inquiry*, 29.

70. Ibid., 28–9.

71. Pace e.g. George A Lindbeck, *The Nature of Doctrine: Religion and Theology in a Postliberal Age* (Philadelphia, PA: Westminster, 1984).

in terms of modernity's epistemological turn, I initiate a further shift in terms of postmodernity's linguistic turn.

Finally, I use the distinction between Law and Gospel also as an instrument for elucidating the use of the Bible, taking up the hermeneutical role of the distinction in Melanchthon. In departure from the Reformation tradition, my purpose is not to determine whether a given Bible verse presents us with a piece of Law or a piece of Gospel. To my mind, that is suggestive of an all too direct access to the true meaning of the text. Rather, what interests me is a 'prior' question, namely why the author in question appeals to some verses rather than others. My hypothesis is that some verses are privileged over others because they fit better into what one might rightly call an overarching 'Law and Gospel' framework, even though the authors themselves do not use these terms. In Chapter 3 in particular, I illustrate this at the hand of the reception of the Gospel of John in Augustine and the Reformation.

Chapter 3

SCRIPTURE USE IN AUGUSTINE AND THE REFORMATION

3.1 Introduction

In the previous chapter, we saw that the distinction between Law and Gospel can be used not only in the practice of dogmatic reflection but also to analyse the use of Scripture in the theological tradition. In the present chapter and the next, I will exemplify this by way of an analysis of the reception of the Gospel of John in Augustine, the Reformation and the theology of Karl Barth. It is not without reason that I am using the Gospel of John to illustrate the dynamics between Law and Gospel. As the following will make clear, the Gospel of John triggers the polar opposite of the duality I am defending in this book. In this Gospel we find what we might call a 'Christocentric' reflex, the idea that everything that can be known and has to be done from a Christian perspective must be found in the person of Jesus Christ.

One of the verses triggering this Christocentrism is Jn 14.6, where Jesus says: 'I am the way, the truth and the life, and no one comes to the Father except through me.' We will encounter this verse twice in these two chapters, in Augustine and Barth, and see that they deal with the passage in opposing ways. Theologians who try to resist this Christocentric reflex will have to relate to the Gospel of John in a special way. As I will show, this is what these theologians indeed do, even when they do not explicitly acknowledge that the Gospel of John is problematic for them. Furthermore, the thought of Karl Barth, the modern Christocentric theologian par excellence, will provide an excellent example of a theology fully permeated by the reception of John. Throughout our analysis of Augustine and the Reformation in this chapter, as well as Karl Barth, we will also shed more light on 'Christocentrism' as the concept that forms the background for my defence of systematic theology as operating through the Law-Gospel distinction.

In terms of subject matter, the choice for Christology as the central locus in these chapters should not be surprising. This book does not include specific chapters applying the Law-Gospel distinction to the doctrine of God or to Christology. The main reason for this absence is that I have already done so in my previous book, albeit only implicitly.[1] At the same time, this chapter and the next can be read as an application of the Law-Gospel distinction to Christology, and in that context to the doctrine of the Trinity. First, however, we have to say a little more about Christocentrism as the prominent concept in these chapters.

3.2 Christocentrism

Even when we say that 'Christocentrism' means every dogmatic locus is determined by the Christological dogma, we need to dig deeper and offer a more substantial account of what this term could actually mean. Scholarship has seen a recent emergence of a debate on the use of the label 'Christocentrism' given its varied use as well as its application to both modern and pre-modern theologians.[2] In a departure from McCormack,[3] Cortez[4] and Gibson[5] whose contributions to this question are certainly worthwhile, I am less interested in a definition of Christocentrism that manages to capture all aspects of a specific theology, whether it be that of Barth or others. My interest rather goes out to a systematic account of Christocentrism that provides a taxonomy of systematic-theological options, implying certain ramifications for other theological loci. I will describe this taxonomy by bringing the notion of Christocentrism to bear on three distinctions which may serve further demarcations of what we mean by Christocentrism.

The first pair of terms that I would like to discuss on was one that was introduced roughly a decade ago by Richard Muller.[6] Muller protested against the use – or, at least, the unreflective use – of the term for pre-modern theologians. As a proposal for refinement, he suggested a distinction between soteriological and principial Christocentrism, where the first generally applies to pre-modern theology and the second to modern theology.[7] This distinction between soteriological and principial Christocentrism has been adopted since by David Gibson.[8] With soteriological

---

1. Cf. Maarten Wisse, *Trinitarian Theology beyond Participation: Augustine's de Trinitate and Contemporary Theology*, T&T Clark Studies in Systematic Theology 11 (London: T&T Clark International, 2011).

2. For a helpful survey of the discussion, see Marc Cortez, 'What Does It Mean to Call Karl Barth a Christocentric Theologian?' *Scottish Journal of Theology* 60, no. 2 (2007): 127–43.

3. Bruce L McCormack, *Karl Barth's Critically Realistic Dialectical Theology: Its Genesis and Development, 1909–1936* (Oxford: Clarendon, 1997), chapter 11.

4. Cortez, 'Christocentric Theologian'.

5. David Gibson, *Reading the Decree: Exegesis, Election and Christology in Calvin and Barth*, T&T Clark Studies in Systematic Theology 4 (London: T&T Clark International, 2009), 5–10.

6. Richard A. Muller, 'A Note on "Christocentrism" and the Imprudent Use of Such Terminology', *Westminster Theological Journal* 68 (2006): 253–60.

7. Richard A. Muller, *After Calvin: Studies in the Development of a Theological Tradition* (Oxford: Oxford University Press, 2003), 97–8.

8. Gibson, *Reading the Decree*, 5–10.

Christocentrism, Muller means 'the theological affirmation of the absolute and necessary centrality of Christ to the work of salvation'.[9] What he means is that a theology applying this soteriological Christocentrism draws a distinction between a level on which Christ is indeed central, namely soteriology, and a level in which Christ is not central (albeit also not entirely absent), namely the doctrine of creation. With principial Christocentrism he means, 'still more speculatively, that the Christ-idea must be used as the interpretive key to understanding and elucidating all doctrinal topics'.[10] In a principially Christocentric theology, Christ is central to all speech about creation and salvation.

I myself am happy to admit the distinction between soteriological and principial types of Christocentrism insofar as it delimits the meaning of the term in a certain direction. But as I will argue below, we need more pairs of terms to elucidate the concept of Christocentrism. Basically, Muller's distinction is intended to point out that pre-modern theologians cannot easily be read as 'Christocentric' as scholars often do in the post-Barthian modern history of theology. Moreover, from a theological perspective, Muller would like to get rid of principial Christocentrism for its theological inaccuracy. In line with the subtext of Muller's article, my argument in this book is primarily directed against principial Christocentrism and favours soteriological Christocentrism. Often I will simply speak about a 'Christocentric theology', which must mostly be understood in principial Christocentrism rather than soteriological terms.

However, I am less convinced than Muller that the distinction nicely aligns itself with the distinction between pre-modern and modern theology, as if soteriological Christocentrism applies to pre-modern theology and principial Christocentrism to theology from the eighteenth century onwards. Principial Christocentrism may in a certain sense be as old as Christianity itself. In some form, it can be found in the Gospel of John, as well as in Origen and other church fathers. In early modernity, one finds it in Erasmus and various radical Reformers (see below). As Arnold Huijgen has shown in his book on divine accommodation, Calvin on closer examination proves to be much closer to principial Christocentrism than one might initially expect.[11] In fact, in Calvin all knowledge of God is Christologically mediated. Notwithstanding the dangers flowing from historical complexity, one might suggest that soteriological Christocentrism is a feature of a specific reception of the Augustinian tradition. A milder way of formulating this criticism of Muller's claim is to say that his distinction is probably most helpful as a present-day attempt to identify a difference between distinct, albeit mostly implicit, emphases in the Christian tradition that increasingly came to be played out against one another from early modernity onwards.

9. Muller, 'Note on Christocentrism', 255.
10. Ibid., 256.
11. Arnold Huijgen, *Divine Accommodation in John Calvin's Theology: Analysis and Assessment* (Göttingen: Vandenhoeck & Ruprecht, 2011), 236–44.

Part of what leads Muller astray is the absence of another dimension in his account of Christocentrism that also plays a role when we speak of it and has different connotations and implications. It is for this reason that I would like to propose a second pair of terms for defining Christocentrism: 'epistemological' and 'ontological' Christocentrism.[12] Epistemological Christocentrism entails the thesis that all knowledge of God is mediated by Christ. Ontological Christocentrism means not only that our knowledge of God is mediated by Christ but also that the being of God itself is determined by the Christ event. As such, epistemological Christocentrism need not necessarily imply ontological Christocentrism. The fact that we can only truly know God in Christ does not mean that the incarnation as such is also a defining characteristic of the essence of God. The point can be illustrated as a concrete example. Calvin seems to adhere to an epistemological Christocentrism but not to an ontological Christocentrism.[13] A key decision which every theology must make relates to its view on the question whether or not the history of God's revelation in Jesus Christ is determinative of the essence of God. If so, ontological Christocentrism applies. Here again, one might construe a distinction between pre-modern and modern theology, although care is required even at this point.[14] Generally speaking, a pre-modern concept of God which holds God to be outside of time and beyond all change implies a denial of ontological Christocentrism. At best, these pre-modern theologies may consistently accompany an epistemological form of Christocentrism, whether soteriological or principial.

Ontological Christocentrism implies principial Christocentrism, and principial Christocentrism is often accompanied by ontological Christocentrism. A principial Christocentrism and an ontological Christocentrism will operate on different levels in theological discourse. Principial Christocentrism is a statement about theology and the level to which its discourse is determined by Christology whereas ontological Christocentrism is about the object of theological discourse, that is, God. It states that the Christ event is determinative of the very nature of God.

Epistemological Christocentrism, on the other hand, is not identical with soteriological Christocentrism, nor is the latter implied by the former. Quite the contrary, one might say that epistemological Christocentrism implies some form of principial Christocentrism, since it seems strange to affirm theologically that our knowledge of God is possible only in Christ, while denying that theological discourse must be permeated by Christology. Furthermore, ontological Christocentrism implies epistemological Christocentrism, but not vice versa. This is why I have chosen to use the two pairs of terms alongside each other. In this

---

12. Cortez makes a similar distinction, drawing on TeSelle, but he does not make clear what he means by it: Cortez, 'Christocentric Theologian', 130, 132, 141.

13. Cf. Huijgen, *Divine Accommodation*, 236–44, cited above.

14. Servetus, and possibly other radical Reformers such as the Anabaptists, seem to represent interesting forerunners to modern theology in this respect; see Section 3.5 below.

book, the Christocentrism that I will criticize is both principial and ontological in nature, but it is also epistemological, since I am defending the thesis that God can in various respects be known from creation, such that Christ is not the only path to knowledge of God. The strict version of Christocentrism that is the key target of my critique can be described as follows:

> The incarnation of God in Jesus Christ is essential to the nature of the one God (ontological). Therefore, God can only be truly known in Christ (epistemological). Therefore, Christian theology, as critical reflection on God's revelation in Christ, must necessarily always be Christological in all of its parts (principial).

Now that we have presented two pairs of terms to demarcate the meaning of the term 'Christocentrism', we can finally introduce a third dimension of Christocentrism, which is the distinction between its universalist and particularist forms.

Ontological Christocentrism implies universalism, both from a principial and a soteriological perspective. This is why universalism must follow: if God's character is ontologically determined by the Christ event, our theological discourse is Christocentric through and through, and also our discourse about salvation must be determined by this very nature of God. If, however, God is known in Christ, but the Christ event is not defining for the nature of God, then even if all that we say about God must be found in Christ, one can still be particularist, as the case of Calvin shows. Epistemological Christocentrism does not seem to imply particularism. When one thinks of Origen or other proponents of a subordinationist Trinitarian theology, one might classify them as principial epistemological Christocentrists; and yet, insofar as they hold on to something like *apokatastasis*, they are universalists. The same goes for soteriological Christocentrism. It may well lead to particularism, and in many cases it indeed does, but particularism does not seem to be necessarily implied. One could, after all, hold that Christocentrism applies to the scope of salvation but not creation, while still maintaining that God will save all.

3.3 Augustine on Law and Gospel, 'nature' and 'grace'

In the Introduction, I described how I came upon the idea of doing dogmatics in terms of the Law-Gospel distinction through my reading of Augustine. In Augustine, I constantly saw a dynamic in which the reality of the incarnation of the Son was qualified by an appeal to something else. This 'something else', which I have labelled 'Law' in this book, takes various forms but is very clearly related to the Old Testament and, on an even more fundamental level, to human beings as created by God. As an introduction to my discussion of two sermons from Augustine on the Gospel of John demonstrating this element, I will sketch the two ways in which the Gospel is qualified in terms of the 'Law'.

A leading idea in Augustine's theology is the question: 'Who will see God and live?' Although it is an Old Testament notion (Genesis 32; Exodus 24, 33), Augustine nevertheless associated it with a New Testament text: 'Blessed are the pure of heart, for they will see God' (Mt. 5.8). It is no coincidence that the New Testament text comes from the Gospel of Matthew. In this Gospel, the bond with the Old Testament is very powerful and is framed in terms of living according to God's commandments in concrete ways, in some respects even more radically so than in the Old Testament laws. The Gospel of John likewise contains many references to the Old Testament,[15] but the appeal to the Old Testament is framed differently there, and the Johannine corpus is not as powerfully determined as Matthew by the doing of the actual commandments. On the contrary, in John the life according to the concrete commandments has been replaced by the relationship with the new 'Way': Jesus Christ and the emulation of Jesus as an example.[16] For Augustine's theology, the insight that concrete righteousness in terms of obedience to God's commandments is a condition for entrance into the kingdom is actually so constitutive that it overrules other doctrines. In his Christology, for example, Augustine denies believers direct knowledge of Jesus' divine nature while still on earth (see below, Section 3.3).

Another example, which will be treated at greater length in the following section, is the problematic nature of Christocentrism for Augustine, since it evokes the idea that knowledge of God is impossible apart from Christ. This is an idea that Augustine rejects, regardless of the fact that the Gospel of John does suggest it, and he does so partly because of his context, as he wants to convince pagans that the Christian God relates to the happiness they are already longing for and know to some extent. But to make that point rhetorically, Augustine follows a long apologetic path, whose essence is that human beings as created beings have the ability to know God.

Here, a warning is in place. I want to stress from the start that I am not suggesting Augustine figures here as an example of the entire pre-modern theological tradition, of 'classical Christianity', so to speak. In fact, I would like to suggest that the soteriological Christocentrism identified by Richard Muller is a feature specific to Augustine's theology, possibly more so than it is to the theology of the early Church as a whole. Therefore, when we bring Augustine into the conversation, this does not mean that everyone was with him. Quite the contrary, he seems to have been the exception rather than the rule, although much more extensive research would be required to further substantiate this claim.

---

15. Cf. e.g. Anthony T. Hanson, *The Prophetic Gospel: Study of John and the Old Testament* (London: T&T Clark, 2006); Maarten J. J. Menken, *Old Testament Quotations in the Fourth Gospel: Studies in Textual Form* (Kampen: Kok Pharos, 1996).

16. Cf. Andreas J. Köstenberger, *A Theology of John's Gospel and Letters*, Biblical Theology of the New Testament (Grand Rapids, MI: Zondervan, 2009), 509–24.

3.3.1 Sermon 141

When we turn to sermon 141, we gain an impression of the way Augustine moderated or even implicitly criticized a Christocentric reading of John. Sermon 141, which is on Jn 14.6, begins like this:

> You heard, among other things, when the gospel was read, what the Lord Jesus said: 'I am the way and the truth and the life' (Jn 14:6). Everybody yearns for truth and life; but not everybody finds the way. That God is a kind of eternal life, unchangeable, intelligible, intelligent, wise, bestowing wisdom, this quite a number of philosophers even of this world have been able to see. The truth as something fixed, stable, unalterable, in which are to be found all the formulae of all created things, this they were certainly able to see, but from a long way off; they could see it, but from a position of error; and therefore they did not find the way by which they could reach so great, so inexpressible, so completely satisfying a possession.
>
> That even they did see (as far as any human being can see) the creator through the creature, the producer through the product, the architect of the world through the world, we are assured by the evidence of the apostle Paul, whom Christians, of course, are bound to believe. He said, you see, when he was talking about such matters, the wrath of God is being revealed from heaven upon all ungodliness. These, as you will recognize, are the words of the apostle Paul. 'The wrath of God is being revealed from heaven upon the ungodliness and injustice of men, who hold down the truth in iniquity' (Rom 1:18). Did he say they don't hold the truth? But they hold it down in iniquity. That they hold it is good; what's bad is where they hold it. They hold the truth down in iniquity.[17]

Here we see that Augustine is prompted by the lectionary to preach on 14.6 but seems hesitant to embrace it wholeheartedly. He almost immediately adapts the text to his own interest, saying that everyone longs for truth and life, but not everyone will find the way. Of course, Augustine cannot just bypass the text, nor does he give any explicit indication that this is what he wants to do (and it would also be unthinkable from his theological frame of reference), but he does give several hints in that direction. Having adapted the verse by the statement that the philosophers knew the truth and the life, but lacked the way, he draws on Paul's Letter to the Romans to substantiate this point. In introducing Paul, Augustine explicitly appeals to his authority as an apostle, 'whom Christians ... are bound to believe'. From that point on, Augustine dedicates by far the greatest majority of his sermon to Paul rather than John! As the remainder of the sermon reveals, Augustine plays with the possible resistance among his audience against the Pauline rereading of Jn 14.6.

---

17. Augustine, *Sermons (94A–147A) on the Old Testament*, trans. Edmund Hill, Works of Saint Augustine, III/4 (Brooklyn, NY: New City, 1992), 409.

The identity of those resisting him here is difficult to determine given the scarcity of evidence available for the context of specific sermons. The question is rendered all the more complex by another close reading of 14.6 that has survived in Augustine's corpus. For in tractate 69 from the major homily collection *In Ioannem Evangelium tractatus*, Augustine does not refer to Romans at all.[18] There, he gives no indication whatsoever that Jn 14.6 presents him with a theological conundrum. This supports the suggestion that the problem in sermon 141 is one evoked by his audience rather than his own theology notwithstanding the fact that his position in that sermon aligns very well with the overall shape of his theology. For Augustine was always insistent on defending some form of 'natural theology' (see below). All human beings have within themselves cognitive access to God and a longing for happiness, even after the fall. This natural knowledge of God is insufficient for salvation, however, since human beings can no longer rely on this knowledge of God due to the fall.

One way to read this sermon is as a response to two audiences sitting or standing before the preacher.[19] One audience is composed of confessing Christians, and they are the people to whom Augustine defends his natural theological reading of Jn 14.6 acknowledging that pagans do know something about God, even though they fail to find God along this way. The other part of his audience consists of those who are not yet confessing and baptized Christians but are willing to consider the truth of Christianity and to contemplate becoming Christians. As is evident from Augustine's entire corpus, he is always very concerned about this latter group, if only because he was one of them himself, as that famous seventh book of the *Confessions* makes clear. These people were for the most part intellectually sensitive, probably upper class, and sympathetic to Christianity, albeit not yet so fully convinced as to adopt it full scale as their ultimate source of salvation. Augustine does not want to disappoint these people as if to suggest that you are either a Christian, meaning that you have to abandon all your intellectual skills and convictions, or else no Christian at all. He therefore argues for the intellectual openness of Christianity to all on the one hand, while on the other hand still emphasizing that one must fully commit to it since it is only when you become a member of the church and a humble follower of Christ that you receive all the good things that are part of the Christian faith.

This general pattern is also reflected in sermon 141 on Jn 14.6, which consists of a subtle interplay between flattery and intellectual confrontation. Having introduced Paul with the phrase that the pagans have suppressed righteousness in unrighteousness, Augustine first explains and affirms that pagans indeed have known righteousness in terms of their knowledge of God's existence and the

---

18. The modern translation by Edmund Hill is not yet available. Therefore, we refer to the old translation in the Nicene and Post-Nicene Fathers edition: Augustine, *Homilies on the Gospel of John*, ed. Philip Schaff, Nicene and Post-Nicene Fathers Series I 7 (Grand Rapids, MI: Christian Classics Ethereal Library, n.d.), tractate 69.

19. Cf. more elaborately, Wisse, *Trinitarian Theology*, 17–21.

inscription of God's law written on their hearts, even if they lack all knowledge of revelation.[20] Thus, Augustine appeals to the pagan part of his audience, showing them his respect for their intellectual skills. But in what follows, he explains why they have failed in putting these skills to real success. They have venerated pieces of wood, gold and silver rather than the one true God. Here, Augustine draws on Romans 1 again, but also implicitly on Acts 17, the other classic prooftext of natural theology.

At the end of the sermon, Augustine returns to Jn 14.6.[21] If pagans only have an idea of what God could be, but no capacity to reach the reality behind this idea, there is only one choice: to believe in Christ. The one who was with the Father from the very beginning, God from God and light from light, has become a human being. Rhetorically, there is only one possible way of solving that unbridgeable gap between the one unknowable God and human fallible and creaturely knowledge: the God made man, Jesus Christ. We do indeed know God, but we cannot put that knowledge into practice unless we believe in Christ as the way to God:

> Now because Christ is himself truth and life with the Father, the Word of God, of which it says 'The life was the light of men' (Jn 1:4); so because he is with the Father life and truth, and because we didn't have any way of getting to the truth, the Son of God, who is always in the Father truth and life, became the way by taking to himself a man. Walk along the man, and you arrive at God. You go by him, you come to him: Don't look for a way to come to him by, apart from him. After all, if he had refused to be the way, we would always be going astray.[22]

By its introduction of the theme of morality, the very end of the sermon once again shows a deep concern for respecting non-Christians:

> So he became the way by which you could come to him. I'm not telling you, 'Look for the way'; the way itself has come to you; get up and walk. Walk on your behavior, not your feet. I mean, many people walk very well on their feet, and walk very badly in their behavior. Again, sometimes people who are walking well are running off the way. You will certainly find people who live good lives, and are not Christians. They are running well; but they are not running on the way. The more they run, the further they go astray, because they are moving away from the way. But if such people only reach the way, and keep to it, oh, what relief and security is theirs, because they are walking well, and not going astray! But if they don't keep to the way, however well they walk, oh dear, oh dear, how pitiable it is! I mean, it's better to limp and stagger on the way, than to walk strongly and vigorously off the way. That must be enough for your graces.[23]

---

20. Augustine, *Sermons (94A–147A) on the Old Testament*, 410.
21. Ibid.
22. Ibid., 411; original emphasis.
23. Ibid.

What we have seen here is an example of the way the direct Christocentrism of John is qualified in Augustine's work by an appeal to other voices from the Bible. In this case it is Paul. Someone might say that Paul is in the New Testament. Certainly, but through Paul a line is nevertheless introduced that I would like to call 'Law', a source of knowledge about God and the world that relates to Christ and the Gospel in a similar way as creation relates to salvation. Augustine is shown to adhere here to a soteriological Christocentrism, as Muller would call it. In the Christian tradition, it has also been maintained, long and often, that the insights that come to us through the Decalogue have actually already been placed in us at creation, and this is the view that Augustine is applying here.[24] This notion makes it possible for him to connect the value of the salvation that has appeared in Christ with general human ideals of happiness which can be known or at least desired outside of Christ. One could call that one side of the coin: by resisting Johannine Christocentrism, Augustine creates space for an apologetics that appeals to the ability of non-Christians to know and desire the good. Righteousness is the criterion for the life of faith but also for non-Christian life. However, Christ is the (only) way by which that righteousness can be achieved. On the one hand, this provides Christians with a plus over non-Christians; on the other hand, the claim of righteousness to universality also forces Christians to determine their actions in such a way that they are transparent to others as righteousness. Thus, internal and external criticism of Christians becomes possible through an appeal to universal access to justice as a universal sensibility.

3.3.2 Sermon 229G

In the previous section, we have seen a few reasons why and how Augustine adapts John to his purposes when it comes to knowledge of God through Christ or creation. However, there is a crucial second aspect to Augustine's problems with the Christocentrism of John that has to do with the soteriological level of Christ's work. This is the requirement of righteousness as a precondition for seeing God. This second aspect emerges when we turn to sermon 229G on Jn 14.9. The verse that is being read on that particular Sunday is seriously problematic for Augustine, since Jesus there says: 'who has seen me, has seen the Father' (Jn 14.9). A determinative presupposition of Augustine's theology is the combination of Mt. 5.8 with the Old Testament maxim: 'Who can see God and live?' (cf. Exod. 33.20). Only the pure of heart will see God, and human beings – even believers – who are still on earth never reach this stage of purity of heart in all perfection.[25] As a consequence, what human beings see when they walk around with the human

---

24. Rémi Brague, *The Law of God: The Philosophical History of an Idea*, trans. Lydia G. Cochrane, 3rd edn (Chicago: University of Chicago Press, 2008), 211–19.

25. Maarten Wisse and Anthony Dupont, '"Nostis qui in schola Christi eruditi estis, Iacob ipsum esse Israel": Sermo 122, In Iohannis euangelium tractatus 7 and the Donatist and Pelagian Controversies', *Zeitschrift für antikes Christentum* 18, no. 2 (2014): 302–25.

Jesus is *not* his divine nature but only his human nature.[26] This also explains why it is possible that they do not believe in him. The eye of faith is needed to *believe*, not to 'know' or 'see' that this human Jesus is the Christ and the eternal Son of God. Therefore, God is not really 'seen' in Jesus Christ, since that would imply that people in Jesus' lifetime could see God, even those who did not believe in him, and those who did believe, but were still sinners. Within Augustine's theological frame of reference, Jn 14.9 implies an excessively direct 'seeing' of God that overlooks the fact that seeing God requires purity of heart.

This is not just a detail. Here, Augustine is highlighting something that is a crucial issue for Christian theology. 'Seeing God' marks what we could call the ultimate pursuit of salvation and happiness for human beings. This ultimate enjoyment of happiness and salvation, the Gospel of John says, is possible through faith in Jesus (cf. Jn 3.16). Who has seen Jesus with an eye of faith has seen the Father. What John suggests here, together with all types of theology that develop this type of Christocentrism, is that an act of faith in Jesus is enough to reach the highest religious status, which is that of *visio Dei*. This represents a danger to theologians like Augustine, because it creates an opening for faith to bypass justice. On such a Christocentrism, the highest religious status can be claimed even in the absence of moral purity.

It is at this point that Augustine issues a protest. Regardless of the salvation that the Good News of faith in Christ may bring, one must follow a basic rule of Old Testament faith, namely that no one will see God with an unclean heart. Yes indeed, salvation in Christ is possible, but it is not possible without moral restoration, without purification of heart. Such a theological security measure is set up in order to avoid a radical form of Christianity in which moral purity is cast aside in favour of a free-floating enjoyment of salvation.

In Augustine's broader theology, these are important issues he maintains over against his main opponents throughout his entire career. The Donatists demanded moral purity among the clergy, but Augustine maintains that no one achieves purity in this life, meaning that the Donatists' requirement cannot be appropriate. The Pelagians similarly held that moral perfection is possible, and Augustine likewise refuted their thesis. Thus, Augustine does two things that become characteristic of later Christianity. On the one hand, he denies access to salvation without moral restoration. In this respect, he is perfectly in line with the mainstream of his contemporaries, including the Donatists and the Pelagians. On the other hand (and this is an innovation, or at least an upcoming polemic that had not been as prominent before), Augustine denies that such moral restoration can be complete in this life, and for that reason insists that it is impossible to have access to salvation in this life in a complete sense.[27] Paradoxically, although the denial of moral perfection in this life seems to make moral perfection in the Christian life less important, it is intended to reinforce it. According to Augustine,

---

26. Wisse, *Trinitarian Theology*, 131–4.
27. For more on this, see Wisse and Dupont, 'Nostis qui in schola Christi eruditi estis'.

allowing human beings the possibility of reaching moral perfection in this life would open up the possibility for hubris, pride. Allowing believers such an ideal would, from Augustine's perspective, not help them to become better people but, on the contrary, would seduce them to sin.

Accordingly, it cannot be true that whoever has seen Christ has seen the Father, and yet this is the very thing Jesus says in Jn 14.9! A closer examination of the first part of sermon 229G allows us to see how Augustine tackles this problem. While the rest of the sermon offers a fairly standard account of the equality and yet distinctness of the divine persons, specifically the beginning is interesting for our purposes. After noting that Jesus spoke these words after the resurrection and also introducing the basic Trinitarian confession (i.e. 'the Father is God, the Son is God and the Holy Spirit is God, still no three Gods but one God'), Augustine launches into Jn 14.9, immediately distinguishing between what can be seen in Jesus (his humanity) and what cannot (his divinity):

> What he [Philip, MW] could see, after all, was what the Jews could crucify; he couldn't see the one who was the hidden stumbling block for the Jews. And he assumed that that was all Christ was, what he could look at with his eyes; and that's why he wasn't enough for him, because he couldn't see all of him. And because he thought there was nothing more in Christ, that's why he was asking for the Father as what would be enough for them.[28]

The question, therefore, is why Philip did not see the divinity of Jesus, even though he was already a believer. In order to solve this problem, Augustine introduces the 'Christ hymn' of Philippians and, in connection with it, his own doctrine of the fall and original sin:

> I mean, if he had been able to see the form of God, he would there have seen the Son as equal to the Father; because while he was in the form of God, 'he did not consider it robbery to be equal to God' *(Phil 2:6)*. It wasn't robbery, because it was his nature. And the one for whom it was robbery, fell; and as well as falling, he also pulled down.[29]

This quotation is an example of the associative reading of Scripture so characteristic of Augustine. The idea is that Philip sees Christ in the form of a servant *(forma servi)*, which in the context of Augustine's Christology means that Philip sees Christ's humanity, not his divinity.[30] It was not robbery for Christ to be equal to God, because he was so by nature, both divine and human. And Adam, the first human being, for whom it would be robbery to suggest that he is equal to God, has fallen, and so he is no longer able to see Christ's divinity due to sin.

---

28. Augustine, *Sermons (94A–147A) on the Old Testament*, 289.
29. Ibid., 290; original emphasis.
30. Cf. Wisse, *Trinitarian Theology*, 131–4.

Augustine continues with a few remarks which are highly relevant to his view of deification[31] but not to the present topic. Thereafter, he qualifies the claim from John that it would be possible to see the Father, once again with an associative chain of Scripture verses. This time too it is the Philippians' 'Christ hymn' that plays a key role, together with Psalms and Hebrews:

> It's the form of a servant speaking; look for the form of God. So this is what he meant by, 'If you loved me, you would be glad that I am going to the Father, because the Father is greater than I': What you see me as now, you are seeing me in what I am less. So since you see me in what I am less, if you love me, let me go to where I am equal.
>
> Are you surprised that the Son is less than the Father in the form of a servant? I'm telling you that he's even less than himself, because 'he emptied himself, taking the form of a servant' (Phil 2:7). But if you can see that it's about him that it said 'He has been lessened to a little less than the angels' (Ps 8:5; Heb 2:7); so now, if you have attached yourself to the form of a servant, don't stop there; go a step higher, confess that Christ is equal to the Father. Why are you pleased to hear, 'The Father is greater than I?' You should be more pleased to hear, 'The Father and I are one' (Jn 10:30).[32]

In fact, John's message that those who have seen Jesus have seen the Father has effectively been dismantled to mean: believe in Jesus, which means – believe in his divinity! The elevated meaning of 'seeing the Father', which in Johannine terms means participating in the communion of Father, Son and Spirit,[33] has been reduced to the state of faith that is still unable to see God. Augustine therefore adapts what John might say or even actually says through an implicit use of his controlling notion from Mt. 5.8. For Augustine, what John seems to be saying – namely that the full reality of God has come within the believer's grasp and possession through faith, even in the absence of moral perfection, of perfect obedience to the Law – cannot be true. Salvation in Christ must be moral restoration and cannot be radical participation in God through faith.

3.4 The Johannine prologue in the Reformation

So far, we have taken a few snapshots from the work of Augustine as an illustration of the way in which he struggles with Johannine Christocentrism and also dealt with his reasons for these struggles. Although, strictly speaking, it lies beyond

---

31. Cf. ibid., chapter 6.
32. Augustine, *Sermons (94A–147A) on the Old Testament*, 291; original emphases.
33. Köstenberger, *A Theology of John's Gospel and Letters*, 376–8; Hans Burger, *Being in Christ: A Biblical and Systematic Investigation in a Reformed Perspective* (Eugene, OR: Wipf and Stock, 2009), 318–54.

the scope of my argument, I would still like to suggest that Augustine's work has been very influential in this regard, even though there are certainly also other trends in the medieval reception of the early Church that run more or less counter to this trajectory. Here, one might think of the work of Dionysius Areopagite, for example, which also witnesses a strong reception in medieval theology, including its powerful participation language. It is probably fair to say that by the time the church's tradition arrives at the Reformation, it bears within itself a variety of different ways for construing the relationship between the reality of the incarnation and various available options for participation in the incarnation through faith. These options are accompanied by different controlling 'lawlike' notions that aim to protect the difference between this reality of the incarnation and our participation in it through faith and practical obedience.

The Reformation, then, returns to Scripture in new ways, and is therefore more or less forced to find a way to effect a new balance between the two sides of the theological tradition. It does so not so much in a theoretical abstract fashion but in the middle of an experiential revolution in which faith rediscovers in a radically new way what it means to be in Christ. It is only in the period that follows that various Reformation strands begin to sort out what this rediscovery means for the way we read the Bible as a whole, and by far not all are reading the Bible as a whole in the same way. As we will see when we turn our attention to the reception of the Johannine prologue in the Reformation (in the awareness that it may also have precursors), some radical trends start reintroducing a more radical reading of the Gospel of John, while others, and in particular the Reformed tradition of Bucer and Calvin, insist on the Augustinian adaptation of this Gospel's radical message.

Up till now, in both the previous and the present chapter, we have paid particular attention to several passages from John 14, especially verses 6 and 9. From now on, we will be turning our attention to the Johannine prologue. The prologue is not just one biblical passage among many others, and this also holds true for both the early modern period and the early Church. In various periods of Christian history, the Johannine prologue has functioned as no less than the very touchstone of Christian orthodoxy – especially in the early Church, but also in later ages.[34]

The following will reveal that the appeal to the Johannine prologue on the part of traditional Nicene orthodoxy is far less obvious than it seems. This becomes particularly evident when we expand our horizon beyond the mainstream Reformation so as to include also various forms of radical Reformation. As we will see, it was not only the mainstream Reformation that claimed the Johannine prologue as a source of support for traditional Nicene theology and Christology. On the contrary, for such proponents of radical Reformation as Michael Servetus and the Anabaptists, the Johannine prologue likewise represented a main source of inspiration for their particular forms of reform.

---

34. Cf. Wijnand Boezelman, *Athanasius' Use of the Gospel of John* (Lewiston, NY: Edwin Mellen, 2019); T. E. Pollard, *Johannine Christology and the Early Church* (Cambridge: Cambridge University Press, 1970).

I will propose that the reason for this two-sided appeal must be located in the ample opportunity presented by the prologue for developing various forms of Christocentrism. The most fascinating aspect of the Johannine prologue is not the fact that it forms the basis for traditional Christian orthodoxy but that it includes so great a tension between orthodoxy and heterodoxy that almost everyone will find something in it to support their position. The different forms of Christianity that emerge from different receptions depend on the way in which various aspects of the prologue are brought into conversation with one another and with other notions from Scripture, and on the aspects that take centre stage and therefore suppress others because they do not fit into the reader's overall theology.

3.5 The problem in a nutshell

Before we take a closer look at early Reformation receptions of the prologue, we will briefly show how the big tensions within the Johannine prologue itself enabled later traditions to appeal to it in strikingly different ways. One might say that all the varieties of principial and soteriological Christocentrism are present in the prologue in some way. What they need to be brought to the fore are readers who have an interest in pursuing them. In departure from the writers of the synoptics, John allows himself to link up the historical figure of Jesus of Nazareth with cosmological and metaphysical language. Here a central role is played by the Logos language and the relationship between this Logos and God. At first sight, this grants the historical person of Jesus a high status. At the same time, it enables the developing Christian tradition to also pursue the universal and metaphysical implications of the Christ event. Something happens to Christ, but by that very same account something is happening also to metaphysics.[35]

It is here that we find the first opportunity to develop a Christocentric theology in terms of the Johannine prologue, that is, in terms of the introduction of a mediator of creation at the beginning of the prologue: 'Through him all things were made; without him nothing was made that has been made. In him was life, and that life was the light of all mankind' (Jn 1.3-4; NIV). Whenever this element was pushed hard, it offered an opening towards a very positive view of creation and of human beings. Christ is already present, not only among believers but also among all human beings! Accordingly, theology must be Christocentric theology because an independent doctrine of creation, separated from soteriology, is from the very start an impossibility: creation is already in Christ and cannot be understood apart from Christ.[36]

---

35. Cf. Markus Enders and Rolf Kühn, eds, *Im Anfang war der Logos: Studien zur Rezeptionsgeschichte des Johannesprologs von Antike bis Gegenwart*, Forschungen zur europäischen Geistesgeschichte 11 (Freiburg im Breisgau: Herder, 2011).

36. Cf. Frances M. Young, 'Christology and Creation', in *The Myriad Christ: Plurality and the Quest for Unity in Contemporary Christology*, ed. Terrence Merrigan and Jacques Haers, BETL 152 (Leuven: Peeters, 2000), 191–205.

If pushed hard, a theology on the basis of Jn 1.3-4 ends up making the incarnation presented in Jn 1.14 almost superfluous. If Christ is already so powerfully present in all of creation, why does God need to become even more present in a single human being? As John Milbank would call it, the incarnation becomes something like an affirmation in excess, an affirmation of what has been the case from the beginning, namely that everything has always been in Christ, so that all creation is a form of incarnation, but we need to know it.[37] This getting to know what is the case from the beginning is the purpose of the incarnation. In Erasmus, we see a similar pattern, when he in his reading of the prologue develops what one could call a 'pedagogical theology'.[38] God has been calling people to the kingdom. From the very start, God has been educating his people, speaking to them as the *Sermo Dei*, the Word of God:

> The word of God has always been in the world – not that he who is immeasurable can be contained by any boundary of space, but he was in the world as the intelligence of the craftsman is in his handicraft, as the pilot is in that which he steers. The light was even then shining in the world, somehow making plain through what had been marvellously created the divine might, wisdom, and goodness, and in this way even then he was speaking in some fashion to the human race.[39]

The incarnation is not so much an interruption of this divine education programme as its culmination. Having spoken to us through the fathers and the prophets, God finally speaks through his Son:

> Now we will trace how he first became known to the world, though earlier he was not thought to be other than a man even by his own brothers. For he chose to become known gradually, lest a thing so novel not find credence among makind if it sprang up suddenly. And indeed much had taken place already that could in some measure prepare the hearts of mortals for belief: the authority of the prophets; the foreshadowings of the law.[40]

Other readers are disappointed by this reading of the prologue, claiming that it is too general to be really adequate to our current fallen human condition. If Christ and his saving work are so powerfully present in the whole of reality, how can we take the presence of evil seriously? We need something more than what we already have by virtue of the good of creation. As we will see, Anabaptists were

---

37. John Milbank, *Being Reconciled: Ontology and Pardon*, Radical Orthodoxy Series (London: Routledge, 2003), 67, 70; cf., Wisse, *Trinitarian Theology*, 109–14.

38. Desiderius Erasmus, *Paraphrase on John*, trans. Jane E. Phillips, New Testament Scholarship 46 (Toronto: University of Toronto Press, 1991), http://www.deslibris.ca/ID/417447. This is an English translation of Desiderius Erasmus, *Paraphrasis in Euangelium Secundum Ioannem* (Basel: Froben, 1523).

39. Erasmus, *Paraphrase on John*, 20.

40. Ibid., 24.

among them. The prologue contains something radical: God not only assumed human flesh, as if to remain the same in spite of this, but God *became* a human being. Hence, Jesus is not only divine, as traditional orthodoxy argues primarily on the basis of Jn 1.1, but the divine has also become human, enabling – following Athanasius' dictum – the human to become divine.[41]

According to the Anabaptist readers, this has tremendous implications for believers in the here and now. Deification is possible, and it is possible in the here and now. You only have to believe. It is radical: it is not just Jesus who is at once divine and human, but once you believe in Him, you will become divine as well! Believing in Jesus gives us 'the right to become children of God and' (Jn 1.12), quite radically, to see the Glory of the Lord in Jesus (1.14), not just in some distant future, but in the here and now. This reading of the Johannine prologue is more radical and particularistic, but still optimistic: you can do it, if you only believe! It is also Christocentric, but in a particularist sense: Knowing God is not just about accepting the existence of a being. Knowing God is always and immediately saving knowledge of God, and therefore, it is knowing God in Christ. To quote another passage from John: 'this is eternal life, that they know you and me whom you have sent' (Jn 17.3). It is Christocentric in the sense that the life of God is defined by the incarnation. If God just *assumes* human flesh, both God and human flesh remain the same, and there is no possibility for human beings to cross the border between God and creation because God does not cross that border in the incarnation either. But when God crosses the border in Christ, then God freely enters our history, our story, and so the incarnation is not just external but something intrinsic to the life of God.

To yet other readers, finally, the above still stops short of taking serious account of the full message of the Johannine prologue. It is true that, for this last category of readers to be able to take these extra elements of the Johannine prologue seriously, they have to downplay others. Immediately after Jn 1.4 ('the light was the light of human beings'), we find 1.5, which says: 'and the light was shining in the darkness, and the darkness comprehended it not'. Several verses later, in 1.10-11, the prologue repeats its dark side: 'He came into the world, and the world has been made by him, but the world did not acknowledge him. He came to his own, but his own did not accept him.' This forms a strict contrast with the optimism that we have encountered so far. Erasmus downplays the radically negative anthropology present here by urging some ongoing education. Of course, people have often not fully understood that Christ was educating them, he acknowledges, but let us hope for the best. This sounds pleasant, radical pessimists argue, but it misses the clear point of the prologue, which is that those who believe in Christ do not do so from their power but have been born from God. A doctrine of predestination can be found not only in Paul but also in John.[42]

---

41. Cf. Athanasius, *De incarnatione verbi*, 54.3.

42. Roland Bergmeier, *Glaube als Gabe nach Johannes: Religions- und theologiegeschichtliche Studien zum prädestinatianischen Dualismus im vierten Evangelium* (Stuttgart: Kohlhammer, 1980).

It should not go unnoticed that the rejection of an optimistic anthropology also implies the rejection of a universalist theology or a radical Christology. Erasmus' educational programme is bound to fail because human beings are so bound to sin that they are unwilling to say yes to God's friendly invitation. And so, the creator Christ who is the light of all cannot bring with him the whole of salvation. Ultimate salvation needs to be yet another act of God in which God becomes God incarnate in order to bring sinful human beings back to a state of being in which they are able to say yes again. The same goes for radical Christology. The radical Christology of the Anabaptists, in which becoming human is part of God's nature, must be rejected because the salvation that is offered is not something for us to realize through faith. If saving humans is part of God's essence, while it is up to us to appropriate this universal love of God through faith and participation in Christ, then an optimistic anthropology is still in place. We will see that the Reformed tradition of Bucer and Calvin in particular shows itself immediately sensitive to this when it says that Christ does not come for the salvation of all, but only for those predestined to faith (see below). In addition, because Christ comes to save some rather than all, saving humans does not belong to the nature of God, but to his sovereignty. Therefore, the radical Christology offered by the Anabaptists on the basis of Jn 1.14 has to be rejected in favour of the traditional reading of 'became' as 'assumed'. Christ did not really condescend into the human condition, 'becoming' human, but only 'assumed' a human nature in unity with an otherwise immutable divine nature.

Therefore, it is not only optimistic universalist readers who find in the Johannine prologue their favourite texts but also pessimistic and particularist readers, as if John is *totus noster*. In what follows, we will explore this variety of readings of the Johannine prologue during the Reformation period. We will show how the different readings of John reflect different ways of seeing the relationship between the Christ event and everything else. If Christ is present already and sufficiently in creation, so that the incarnation is only a matter of reminding us of what is already the case, then the Christ event is no longer a radically new event in world history. Put in terms of Law and Gospel, it means that the Gospel in such views is part of the Law: it is about hearing God's message and doing it.

However, if the incarnation offers a radically new possibility of becoming divine in the here and now, the radical potential of the Gospel over against the Law is granted full force and the old structures of creational life can be overruled by the new structures of the community of faith. The Anabaptist experiment in the city of Munster was a deterrent example of what could happen then, at least to sixteenth-century believers, regardless of whether or not they were adherents of the mainstream Reformation. The significance of the Christ event must be balanced out against other aspects of divine revelation, and the divine commandments in particular. Finally, the balance between the Christ event and the commandments had to be sorted out by the mainstream Reformers because they wanted to uphold the all-encompassing significance of Christ's work on the cross for the believer's justification, without the involvement of human works at all involved. On the other hand, they struggled with the role of the divine commandments, because the Christian life could not be so free that good works end up no longer having any significance at all.

3.6 Radical receptions of the Johannine prologue

3.6.1 Michael Servetus

We will start our exploration of the ways in which various Reformation strands interpret the Johannine prologue with the Radical side. We will first have a look at a universalizing interpretation, and then consider particularizing readings. An excellent example of a theology from the radical Reformation in which an Erasmian universalizing tendency takes centre stage is Michael Servetus' magnum opus *Christianismi Restitutio*, published in 1553.[43] Born in Spain, Servetus was already subjected to vehement criticism for his anti-Trinitarianism by Bucer in Strasbourg in the 1530s, before his infamous burning with his books in Calvin's Geneva.

In *Christianismi Restitutio*, Servetus confronts his readers with a radicalized version of a Johannine Christianity. Although he uses much more than just the Gospel of John, this gospel – and more precisely its prologue – can still be said to provide the hermeneutical key to his understanding of the Christ event.[44] Servetus consistently refuses to read the prologue in terms of a traditional two-nature Christology and doctrine of the Trinity.[45] Although Servetus is best known for his anti-Trinitarianism, what follows will reveal that his attack is actually directed against a two-nature Christology rather than some version of the Trinity. Servetus would have been quite content with a modern version of the doctrine of the Trinity, for example. What he attacks is the idea of a Son who is not the Son here on earth, the human person who was born from Mary, walked around in Galilee and died on the cross. To use the terms of Joseph Ratzinger, for example, one might say that Servetus argued vehemently against the idea of 'Christ as an ontological exception' to all other human beings, which is something that Ratzinger himself opposes.[46] In the time of the Reformation, however, this was still a revolutionary viewpoint, especially if it came with the radical implications that Servetus drew from it.

---

43. Even today, Servetus' works are not all that readily available. For this reason, we will be referring to two different editions: (1) Michael Servetus, *Christianismi restitutio*, 1790, which contains the Latin text and is easily accessed e.g. in: Alexander Street Press, ed., *The Digital Library of Classic Protestant Texts*, http://alexanderstreet.com/products/digital-library-classic-protestant-texts; and (2) Michael Servetus, *The Restoration of Christianity: An English Translation of Christianismi Restitutio, 1553*, trans. Marian Hillar and Christopher A. Hoffman (Lewiston, NY: Edwin Mellen, 2007).

44. Michael Servetus, *Christianismi restitutio*, 1790, 47–52; Servetus, *The Restoration of Christianity*, 69–77.

45. E.g. Servetus, *The Restoration of Christianity*, 5–11, 20–3.

46. Joseph Ratzinger, 'Retrieving the Tradition: Concerning the Notion of Person in Theology', *Communio* 17 (1990): 449ff.

Servetus' Christology could be summarized as follows: the Word, the Son, was not as a separate *Res* ('entity' in the new English translation) or Person with the Father, as Servetus suggested Christianity had always claimed.[47] Departing from the tradition and choosing rather to follow Erasmus, Servetus sees the Word not as a separate substance alongside the Father but as the dynamic creating Speech of God.[48] Hence, rather than construing Jn 1.1 as an eternal prelude to the act of creation in 1.2, Servetus construes them as a single moment. Everything has been created through God's dynamic speaking, and this speech gives light to everyone who comes into the world (1.9). This Word is divine, because it is none other than God who is speaking in his creative discourse.[49]

Of course, for a Christian message of salvation to make sense, Servetus needs a notion of a fall or sin. The light of the divine creative Word shines in the darkness from the very beginning of creation, but 'the darkness does not comprehend it'. Through sin, human beings have lost their eye for the true and divine nature of the world.[50] Therefore, God has to speak the Word anew in a specific way, and this is what God does in Christ. In the incarnation, God as the Father speaks creatively again. Through the Spirit of God, the Father breathes on Mary, and thus God creates Jesus, the Son, in whom the Word, the divine speaking of the Father, becomes flesh.[51] God does not speak differently in Christ, but God speaks anew, as one might put it with reference to the theologies of Karl Barth or John Milbank. In contrast to the Anabaptist radicals, Servetus does see a decisive role for Mary in the incarnation, because the Son, Jesus, is really this human being born of the Virgin Mary. Time and again, Servetus draws attention to the fact that the New Testament does not speak about a pre-incarnate Son in heaven but always points to the human earthly Jesus when it speaks about Jesus as the Son of God the Father. In the language Servetus uses in the context of the incarnation, Jesus is very much like the child of God the Father and Mary, and his language for this divine-human couple borders on the erotic. Jesus has a truly human and divine nature according to Servetus, although he will avoid these terms. These are not two natures, but they are two perspectives on the one person of Christ. We too have this divine nature, although we at first do not know it.[52] Christ shows us again what we have always

---

47. Servetus, *Christianismi restitutio*, 15–16; Servetus, *The Restoration of Christianity*, 21–2.

48. Servetus, *Christianismi restitutio*, 48: 'Verbum in Deo proferente est ab aeterno ipsemet Deus loquens, et in nubis caligine apparens'; Servetus, *The Restoration of Christianity*, 71.

49. At this point, Servetus follows Erasmus but draws consequences that the latter does not draw: Erasmus, *Paraphrase on John*, 15–16; Erasmus, *Paraphrasis in Euangelium Secundum Ioannem*, ad Joh. 1: 1.

50. Servetus, *Christianismi restitutio*, 186; Servetus, *The Restoration of Christianity*, 150–1.

51. Servetus, *Christianismi restitutio*, 49; Servetus, *The Restoration of Christianity*, 72–3.

52. Servetus, *Christianismi restitutio*, 129; Servetus, *The Restoration of Christianity*, 180.

been, and what we acknowledge through faith and baptism, namely that we are daughters and sons of God.

Servetus does not seem to be fully consistent in pursuing this incarnational metaphysics.[53] The soteriology flowing from his Christology is still postlapsarian in books 1-3 of *Christianismi Restitutio*. It is also strongly rooted in biblical language. Servetus calls his readers to the acknowledgement of Jesus as the Son of the Father, to believe in him,[54] and to be baptized in order to be one body with the Son.[55] Therefore, in the first three books, there is no de facto radical, universalistic interpretation of the Johannine prologue in the sense that Christ, faith and baptism are presented in such a way as to become superfluous because we have always already been in Christ. In books 4 and 5, however, this changes. As we have shown above, God's act of creation in the Word of creation and in the Word of salvation is one and the same creative act. It has to be so, because Servetus otherwise cannot uphold the true divine and human nature of Jesus Christ. If the world was not divine, the divine breath on Mary would result in a new human being at best, but not a Christ who is at once divine and human. Part of the genius of Servetus' theology was its introduction of a clever path between pantheism and Arianism (although it, in a sense, was both). Jesus does not merely have a divine origin, but he is divine, and we are likewise.

All of a sudden, in book 4, where Servetus discusses the names of God, he introduces Platonic forms of speech and places such emphasis on the idea of the eternal light, in which we all live and have our being, that the other aspects of the prologue lose their significance.[56] The incarnational understanding of reality has put aside the particularity of the incarnation in Jesus Christ; otherwise stated, Jn 1.4 has overruled 1.14.

3.6.2 Sebastian Franck

Servetus shares these universalistic tendencies with other so-called Spiritualists of his time, among whom Sebastian Franck (1499-1543) is a good example.[57] In both Servetus and Franck, these universalistic tendencies lead to a new evaluation of non-Christian religions.[58] As early as the 1530s, we find similar

---

53. Arie Baars, *Om Gods verhevenheid en Zijn nabijheid: De Drie-eenheid bij Calvijn* (Kampen: J. H. Kok, 2004), 153-5, 162-3, 165-6.

54. Servetus, *Christianismi restitutio*, 3-4, 13; Servetus, *The Restoration of Christianity*, 2, 18.

55. Servetus, *Christianismi restitutio*, 196; Servetus, *The Restoration of Christianity*, 280.

56. Servetus, *Christianismi restitutio*, 133ff; Servetus, *The Restoration of Christianity*, 189ff.

57. For biographical information, see Patrick Marshall Hayden-Roy, *The Inner Word and the Outer World: A Biography of Sebastian Franck*, Renaissance and Baroque Studies and Texts 7 (New York: Peter Lang, 1994).

58. Servetus, *Christianismi restitutio*, 34-6; Servetus, *The Restoration of Christianity*, 48-51.

and strongly Johannine ideas in Sebastian Franck's, *Das Gott das ainig ain*.[59]

The main thesis of this work already emerges clearly from the long version of its title. It reveals a strongly 'Johannine' line of thought, especially the universalist reading of the prologue that we have already encountered in Erasmus and Servetus. The full title of the work, in my English translation, begins as follows:

> That God, who is the only one, and highest good or being, almighty, true and living Word, will, art, law, 'Sun', meaning, character, light, life, image, realm, arm, spirit, power, hand, Christ, the new human being, and the seed of a woman, next to the seed of the Serpent, is in the heart of every human being.

This is actually only the first half of the very long title, and the content of the work is mainly concerned with demonstrating the truth of this first half. However, there is also a second part to the title which offers a crucial qualification of Franck's view:

> However, this is not enough for salvation, because we also need to be in God, in Christ and in his reign as he is in us. Likewise it could be said that the Word, Christ, the new human being, is found and received in us, so it is then born, known, read, used, and put to service. The witness of Holy Scripture, pagans and old doctors and fathers.[60]

Following the title, one finds a reference to Deut. 30.14 and Rom. 10.8: 'The Word is near to you, in your mouth and in your heart.' What we see here is that Franck is not simply satisfied to affirm that God is in all of us and that God enlightens us, but he also acknowledges that a human response is required to turn the salvation given to all into a reality.

The first sentence of the work then more or less repeats the title, albeit with a different wording:

> That God is the essence/being of all beings, that he lives in every creature, fills it, and creates it through his Word, so bears it, feeds it and keeps it. That he lives in human beings, whom he created after his image and temple, with a special

---

59. Sebastian Franck, *Das Gott das ainig ain, und höchstes gut, sein almechtigs, wars, lebendigs wort, will, kunst, gesatz, Sun, sinn, Caracter, liecht, leben ... in aller menschen hertz sey: Zeügnuss der hailigen schrifft, der Hayden, alten lerern und vättern*, 1534.

60. In the actual body of the work, the witness of Scripture, pagans, doctors, and fathers does not follow this order. The pagans come at the end and are only few in number. The bulk of the discussion is devoted to Scripture and the fathers. Among the fathers, Franck gives a special place to the mystic Johannes Tauler. Unlike Servetus, Franck does not restrict himself to earlier church fathers such as Irenaeus and Tertullian; he also brings Augustine, Jerome, Gregory the Great and Bernard of Clairvaux into the service of his argument.

privilege, as in his own realm and property, so that every creature is filled with him, and God is and works all in all. The witness of Scripture.

Later on in the work, Franck refers to Bible chapters rather than specific verses. For him, references to Scripture aim to show a broad level of support for his view. The key to the overall shape of Franck's theology is the lack of discrimination between various ways in which the Spirit/Word/Hand of God is present in human beings. For example, when Paul says in 1 Cor. 6.19, 'Do you not know that your body is a temple of the holy Spirit', Franck reads this as a reference to something that applies to all human beings rather than just those who believe in Christ.[61] We have seen this already in the title of the work, where it is not without reason that Franck calls human beings in particular not just 'images' but also 'temples' of the Holy Spirit. Similarly, when Paul says that in the eschaton God will be all in all, Franck applies it to the current condition of humankind, as is evident from the first sentence of the body of the text.

Of course, as the second part of the title indicates, Franck is aware that he is universalizing the presence of God, Christ and the Spirit. It was not without reason that Schimansky gave his book on Franck the title *Christ ohne Kirche* (Christ without Church).[62] In fact, the idea of Christ without a church is the core of Franck's theology and the root of his concern. His spiritualist concern is rooted in the observation that both Rome and Reformation ascribe more value to external things, to belonging to a certain community, to bearing a certain name, to participation in certain rituals and sacraments than to a person's actual inward renewal and participation in Christ. In order to overcome this problem, Franck universalizes the saving presence of Christ to such an extent that no particular representation is necessary to mediate this salvation. Salvation is a purely spiritual and inward phenomenon.

There is much more at stake here than just an interesting historical phenomenon foreshadowing a development that would not come to full force until the theology of the nineteenth and twentieth centuries. What we see here is the introduction of a type of Christocentrism and a view on the consequences of such a type. A universalizing type of Christocentrism puts an end to a problem that is deeply intrinsic to the Christian tradition: the problem of mediation. What Christ did for human beings – or, to use a more particularistic formulation, to believers – needs to be appropriated somehow. Such an appropriation requires some place, some institution or some representing body which mediates our participation in what Christ has done for us; or, at least, this is what Christians have predominantly presupposed. They call this the church.

However, any such representing body runs the risk of deterioration. Such a church may run into all sorts of problems, such as a fall in the moral status of its

---

61. Ibid., b ii.
62. Gerd Schimansky, *Christ ohne Kirche: Rückfrage beim ersten Radikalen der Reformation: Sebastian Franck* (Stuttgart: Radius-Verlag, 1980).

members, the purely external performance of rites or legalism. Appropriation of salvation as it happened in Christ is supposed to require external acts of affirmation, such as baptism, which as such do not tell us anything about the inner intention or state of mind of those who perform them. These problems were acute long before the Reformation, as can be seen in the disputes surrounding Montanism, Donatism and Pelagianism. At bottom, all of them revolve around an interest in presenting faith in Christ as a participation in ultimate salvation, while at the same time maintaining correct moral behaviour.

Here we again encounter the problem of balancing out Law and Gospel. The Law prescribes that an appropriate state before God depends on proper behaviour. Proper behaviour is at least objectively observable, and so it seems to be able to withstand the dangers of deterioration. The Reformation, however, saw what happens when people abuse a faith that has been entirely transformed into an elaborate system of rites; externalism goes to such lengths that it extensively justifies false behaviour. It leads to legalism and therefore to grave forms of injustice. This is why the Reformation insists on salvation being independent from human acts. However, it quickly proved that such speech about salvation is equally if not more open to abuse, because believers say they believe in Christ and will go to heaven, but they still do not act as is proper!

Universalist Christocentrism must be seen as another attempt to cope with these problems. Its solution was certainly not entirely new to the Reformation era; precursors included at least Eckhart and other medieval mystics may be mentioned as a precursor. If Christ is everywhere and salvation is a matter of fact, then the problem of externalism has passed. The only thing that matters is your personal intention, your attention to something that is already the case. The problem is that this opens up two possibilities, already clearly seen in the Reformation itself: trivialization and works righteousness. These two are polar opposites but still two sides of the same coin. With trivialization, I mean a line of reasoning that claims that if salvation is a fact, one can do whatever one wants and enjoy the darker sides of human life because in the end all will be good.

The second problem, which is that of works righteousness, is a direct strategy to avoid trivialization by emphasizing the need for an appropriate human response to salvation, as it is beautifully illustrated in the second part of the title of Franck's work. With works righteousness, I mean a line of reasoning that says that because Christ is everywhere and salvation is a fact of our existence, it is now up to us to live a life of gratitude worthy of our fate. In the sixteenth century, views like these as propagated by Servetus and Franck were still perceived by most of their contemporaries as horrible heresies deserving severe forms of punishment. In Franck's case, he probably escaped because he avoided creating a movement.[63] In the case of Servetus, the story ends with the famous death penalty inflicted on him in Geneva. Servetus and Franck's ideas would have to wait at least until the nineteenth century before they began to be embraced by the masses.

---

63. Hayden-Roy, *The Inner Word and the Outer World*, 1.

3.6.3 Melchior Hoffman and Menno Simons

Now that we have taken our starting point for understanding the radical reception of the Johannine prologue in the theology of Servetus and Franck, it will be relatively easy to understand the Anabaptist reception in the work of Melchior Hoffman and Menno Simons. In making this transition, we need to recall that what we now describe as distinct categories of radical Reformers was at that time not necessarily perceived as such, although there were indeed marked differences between spiritualists and Anabaptists. The view of the incarnation and soteriology typical of Hoffman and Simons was likewise decisively determined by a specific reading of the prologue, although in their case the central role was played by Jn 1.14 rather than Jn 1.4.[64] In contrast with Servetus and Franck, the Anabaptist reading was permeated by a particularist spirit rather than a universalist one.

Hoffman and Simons, one might say, read the whole of Scripture from the perspective of Jn 1.14, rather than reading this text from the perspective of the whole of Scripture, as mainstream theology before and after them does. As we have seen above, Servetus can only uphold the true divinity and humanity of Jesus if he draws a universalizing parallel between God's speaking in creation and God's speaking in the new creation in Christ. Precisely this move is an impossible one to the Anabaptist spirit, because everything would be lost to it.[65] While sin was for Servetus primarily a matter of perception (i.e. we are divine, but we are not aware of it properly), for Anabaptists the fall has much more serious consequences and the distinction between God and the world is much stronger. We are human beings, and fallen human beings are lost as long as it is not a radically new human being that is born. The conception of this new human being must take place without any human intervention at all. Since according to these radical strands of the Reformation, Mary was seen an ordinary human being, the new human nature had to come from elsewhere, since Mary too was considered a fallen, sinful human being. It is precisely at this point that Jn 1.14 speaks: '*The Word became flesh*' – not in the sense of the assumption of a human nature, but in the sense of God's creation of a new sinless human being in Jesus Christ.[66]

Ordinary humans become partakers of this new being through faith and baptism. Through this union with Christ, they become a new community, purified and kept holy through suffering and brotherhood, until the return of the Lord.[67]

---

64. Sjouke Voolstra, *Het Woord is vlees geworden: De melchioritisch-mennniste incarnatieleer* (Kampen: J. H. Kok, 1982), chapter 4.

65. George Huntston Williams, *The Radical Reformation*, Sixteenth Century Essays & Studies 15, 3rd edn (Kirksville, MO: Sixteenth Century Journal, 1992), 492–5.

66. Melchior Hoffman, 'Van der ware hochprachtlichen eynigen Magestadt Gottes und vann der worhaftigen Menschwerdung des ewigen Worttzs und des aller Hochsten, eyn kurtze Zeucknus und Anweissung allen Liebhabern der Ewigen Worheit', in *Het Woord is vlees geworden: De melchioritisch-mennniste incarnatieleer*, ed. Sjouke Voolstra (Kampen: J. H. Kok, 1982), 233.

67. Voolstra, *Het woord is vlees geworden*, 28.

While for Servetus the presence of God in God's creative speaking activity was already so strong that the eschaton received its locus already in the present life, the Anabaptists tend to understand the eschaton as a redemption *from* this world. This world is a world full of evil and sin. Accordingly, the persecution of Anabaptists is not something unexpected, since it belongs to what true believers will experience in the last days of the world. In the last days, Anabaptists take up the apocalyptic traditions of the synoptics, as only a few will understand the call of our Lord Jesus Christ. These few will have to suffer much, but after a short time, the Lord will come to save them.

We therefore find two extremes in the radical Reformation: one extreme of incarnational universalist affirmation of the world, and another extreme of exclusivist world denial. What drives people to develop these theologies is not a mere exegetical conviction, or a rationalistic mindset, but a real-life worldview that flows from and resonates with fresh understandings of specific biblical passages or reconfigurations of biblical material. The adherents of the radical Reformation's various strands discovered something that brought them so much existential joy and assurance that they were found willing to die for their faith with many, because their way of seeing things makes up the very core of their faith. In some instances, it took ages for their views to become more or less mainstream, and by far not all early, Reformation adherents and later, nineteenth- and twentieth-century adherents to these views have clear historical connections between them. Servetus' theology was almost eradicated in his own time, but anyone who studies Servetus and modern theology in parallel will discover many similarities between them. Many modern Christian churchgoers may not know who Sebastian Franck was but still hold views that resemble ideas he introduced.

3.6.4 Martin Bucer and John Calvin

While radical Reformers such as Servetus, Franck, Hoffman and Simons appealed to the Gospel of John for justifying their claims, it is not as if those whom we would now call 'mainstream' Reformers put this Gospel aside. Quite the contrary, the Gospel of John is the church's primary doctrinal authority for Luther, Bucer and Calvin as well.[68] It is this variety of powerful appeals to the Johannine prologue that makes an exploration of the variety of Reformations in terms of their receptions of John so interesting. The question was not *whether* one had to make a primary appeal to the Gospel of John for developing one's particular Reformation variety, but rather *how* this appeal had to be made. We will approach the mainstream reception in reverse chronological order, starting with the Reformed tradition and closing with Luther.

---

68. Martin Luther, *Das new Testament yetzund recht grüntlich teutscht* (Basel: Adam Petri, 1522), http://www.e-rara.ch/zuz/content/titleinfo/198933; for Calvin, see Erik de Boer, *The Genevan School of the Prophets: The Congregations of the Company of Pastors and Its Influence in the 16th Century* (Geneva: Librairie Droz, 2012), chapter 6.

The reason for starting with the Reformed tradition is that it uses the simplest hermeneutical key for resolving the tensions in the prologue. Its adherents simply 'delete' all the radicals' key passages. Of course, pre-modern theologians will never admit that they are 'deleting' anything from Holy Scripture but only insist that they are giving a proper explanation of the meaning of a passage within the context of Scripture's overall message. Depending on how one looks at it, however, they at least in practice do remove the radical potential implicit in the text. According to Calvin as well as Bucer before him, the eternal light that enlightens every human being who enters the world (cf. Jn 1.4 and 1.9) is not Jesus Christ, God incarnate, but God in general. The basic interpretive steps at this point were not first taken by Calvin, but by Bucer. Bucer already contributed to the rising flow of commentaries on John in 1528,[69] when he published his *Enarratio*, in which his primary attacks are directed against Luther's view of the Eucharist as well as various radicals who had found a rather safe refuge in Bucer's city of Strasbourg.[70] A key passage that plays a role time and again, as early as Erasmus' Paraphrases, in this deradicalization of Jn 1.4 and 1.9 is Romans 1, the passage concerning the so-called natural theology.[71] Christ is present in the world not in any truly salvific way, but as God in general, who can be known by all.

In Bucer and Calvin, it is the doctrine of grace that determines the interpretation of Jn 1.4 and 1.9.[72] Hence, Jn 1.5 ('The darkness comprehended it not') and 1.13 ('who are not from blood, from the will of the flesh, nor of the will of a man, but who have been born from God') are read more radically by Bucer and Calvin than they are by Servetus, the Anabaptists and Erasmus. The line of reasoning is a simple one: In Jn 1.4 and 1.9, Jesus Christ cannot be intended as the subject of this enlightenment because it would imply one of two options: either everyone would be saved or else salvation would be a possibility for everyone while its reality would depend on the free choice of believers. Both options must be rejected.[73] Scripture speaks against the former option, and the doctrine of grace speaks against the latter. With the latter option, it would be up to us to decide whether we want to be saved or not. Reformed anthropology, however, is rather pessimistic at this point. If salvation in the end boils down just to a beautiful offer, it is no salvation at all. Salvation can only be real if it is radically given, so that our salvation no longer depends on our faith.[74]

---

69. Cf. Timothy J. Wengert, *Philip Melanchthon's Annotationes in Johannem in Relation to Its Predecessors and Contemporaries* (Geneva: Librairie Droz, 1987), 235–53.

70. Martin Bucer, *Enarratio in Evangelion Johannis* (Strasbourg, 1528), 1, verso.

71. Erasmus, *Paraphrasis in Euangelium Secundum Ioannem*, on Jn 1.4.

72. Cf. Calvin, *Institutes (1559)*, ed. John T. McNeill, trans. Ford Lewis Battles (Kentucky: Westminster, 1960), books II.2.12, 14, 19.

73. Bucer, *Enarratio in Evangelion Johannis*, on Jn 1.3-4; John Calvin, *Commentarius in Evangelium Ioannis*, Calvini Opera 47, 1892, on Jn 1.3–4.

74. Bucer, *Enarratio in Evangelion Johannis*, 11, verso: 'Hic ergo status et scopus in hac sacra historia est, Dominum nostrum Iesum, non hominem tantum, quanquam & hominem

The next verse that is bereft of its radical potential is Jn 1.14. Already in the *Enarratio*, Bucer points out that the words of this verse can never be understood in the sense of a radical becoming.[75] The Word has assumed flesh but was never changed into flesh. Of course, this point is ultimately linked to the controversy surrounding the Reformation understanding of the Eucharist, as Bucer defends this understanding of the verse also against Luther. In fact, however, the whole project of the Reformation is at stake; this world is world, we are human beings and the incarnation does not change this. The new world is not this world, so no revolution of worldly authority, no radical understanding of the Christian community, no universalistic optimism or proto-prosperity Gospel is an option, as the Anabaptists proclaimed them. The world should be governed as if it were business as usual. To the Reformed tradition, therefore, the prologue can only be the foundation of right doctrine if its potential to radicalization is eradicated from the beginning.

3.6.5 Martin Luther

And then we finally come to Luther. In the context of this chapter, I will have to restrict myself to him, although there would be ample opportunity to discuss other Lutherans, since the 'John-hype' was particularly strong in their camp.[76] A first question we have to address is our choice to end this discussion with Luther, rather than following the historical sequence where things start with him.

I am well aware of the peculiarity of my approach to the various strands of the Reformation. The simplest way to answer the question is to say that when we discuss Luther at the end, one can characterize his reading of the prologue by suggesting that we find in him everything that the others say, but then united in the theology of a single thinker. This is the characteristic aspect of Luther's interpretation of the prologue. Luther seems to be the only one in that era to leave the extreme tension between universal and particular salvation intact. Whoever isolates specific passages in Luther from others easily turns Luther into Servetus or Franck, but also Simons, Bucer or Calvin – but this happens only if one loses the whole and the true Luther from sight.

If one were to read Luther's early interpretation of Jn 1.4 in the so-called Church Postill of 1522 in isolation, for example, one could readily conclude that Luther thought along the same lines as Servetus. In the Church Postill, Luther applies the message of Jn 1.4 in such a powerful way to the incarnate Christ's presence in the whole world that it would inevitably lead to a universalist incarnational view of

causa tollendi nostra peccata, sed et Deum esse ac salvatorem omium in se credentium, hoc est, eorum quos illi pater ab aeterno in hanc fortem destinatos donavit.'

75. Bucer, *Enarratio in Evangelion Johannis*, on Jn 1.14; Calvin, *Commentarius in Evangelium Ioannis*, on Jn 1.14.

76. See Wengert, *Philip Melanchthon's Annotationes in Johannem in Relation to Its Predecessors and Contemporaries*, 235–53, for a list of early commentaries on John.

salvation.⁷⁷ Luther's reading of Jn 1.9, however, offers a healthy corrective to this. Against the reading of the majority of scholars, who relate the enlightenment of all human beings to Christ's presence to all, Luther restricts this enlightenment to believers.⁷⁸ This is even more true of the much later '*Reihenpredigt*' (1537), in which the interpretation of Jn 1.4 is no longer applied to the universal presence of the incarnate Christ but to the creative and sustaining presence of the divine Word, which is pointedly distinguished from the saving work of the incarnate Jesus Christ.⁷⁹ In general, one can see how Luther is in the later '*Reihenpredigt*' much more on guard against ideas that could be used to support a universalization of salvation, probably under the influence of his disputes with various radical Reformers.

Even if Luther becomes more careful in avoiding a universalization of salvation in his later work, he in his 1537 sermons on the prologue does not turn into a Calvinist. This becomes evident from his beautiful rendering of Jn 1.14, which receives much more colour and greater depth in his later work than it does in the early Church Postill. Although Luther clearly confirms and emphasizes a two-nature Christology, he goes almost as far as his radical contemporaries in emphasizing the paradigmatic character of this verse. Bucer and Calvin do not have much more than a formal affirmation of a two-nature Christology at their disposal when they discuss this verse. For Luther, however, it is the full heart of the Gospel that we hear beating in this verse. It is beautiful to see how Luther in that late sermon from 1537 returns in a thoroughly positive way to his Roman Catholic

---

77. See WA 10 I, 197, as e.g.: 'Nu ists yhe offinbar, wie der teuffer Johannes habe gepredigt von Christo nit nach der hohen speculation, da sie von reden, ßondern eynfelltiglich und schlecht, wie Christus eyn liecht unnd leben sey allen menschen tzur selickeyt.' Here, Luther's aim is to draw as tight a connection as possible between the presence of Christ in creation and faith.

78. Ibid., 221, e.g.:

> Widerumb das es nit von dem gnadenliecht sey gesagt, dringet, das er sagt, es erleuchte alle menschen, die da kommen yn diße wellt; das ist yhe fast klar gesagt von allen menschen, die geporn werden. S. Augustinus sagt, es sey alßo tzuuorstehen, das keyn mensch erleuchtet werde denn von dißem liecht, auff die weyße alß man pflegt zu sagen von eynem lerer in eyner stat, so keyn lerer mehr drynnen ist: dißer lerer leret sie alle ynn der stadt, das ist: es ist keyn lere ynn dißer stadt, denn der alleyn. Er hat alleyn alle iunger; damit wirt nit gesagt, das er alle menschen ynn der statt lere, ßondernn das nur eyn lerer drynnen sey, und niemant von eynem andern geleret werde.

79. WA 46, 562: 'Aber ohne das Liecht, das allen Menschen, beide, fromen und boesen, gemein ist, ist noch ein sonderlich Liecht, das Gott den seinen gibt, auff welchem da bleibet alles, was herhernacher Joannes vom Wort schreibet, nemlich, das sich das Wort seinen Ausserwelten durch den heiligen Geist und durchs muendliche Wort offenbaret, und wil seines Volcks Liecht sein.'

youth when he discusses the verse from the Johannine prologue. He reminds his audience of the fact that even under the papacy, this wonderful word sounded in every church service, even when its profound message was not always clearly seen.[80] One gets a sense of how close this verse really is to Luther's heart when he says: 'Es were auch nicht wunder, das wir noch fuer freude weineten, ja, wenn ich auch nimer selig solt werden (da der liebe Gott fuer sey), sol michs doch froelich machen, das Christus, meines fleisches, gebeins und Seelen, im himel zur rechten Gottes sitzet, zu den ehren ist mein gebein, fleisch und blut komen.'[81]

A similar difference separates Luther from Bucer and Calvin with respect to the doctrine of grace and predestination. In Bucer and Calvin, predestination is already determinative for their exegesis of Jn 1.4 and in fact for their entire interpretation of the prologue. With Luther, the doctrine of grace is indeed in play, but this is not so for predestination. In both his early and late interpretation of 1.13 ('those who are born from God'), Luther draws a strict connection from new birth from God to faith. To be born anew means to believe in Jesus Christ.[82] As the radicals of his time did, so too Luther held Jesus Christ to be present to all human beings,[83] and for him, at first sight, it seems as if faith in this universal offer of salvation is left up to the human being's own decision.

Summarizing our findings, it seems not to have been without reason that Luther in 1539, at the end of his career, held a disputation on the philosophical consistency and comprehensibility of the opening words of Jn 1.14,[84] and that he in 1540 in the *Disputatio de divinitate et humanitate Christi*, extensively problematized the philosophical status of Christological expressions.[85] For theology not to lose sight of the heart of the Gospel, so Luther argued, it can only speak about the mystery of salvation in Christ with many words. If these words are taken out of their context and absolutized, they all lead to heresy. This was already the case among the church fathers,[86] and Luther's own Christology witnesses to this as well. Perhaps

---

80. Ibid., 624–5.

81. Ibid., 626–7.

82. WA 10 I, 231: 'Die gotliche gepurt ist nu nichts anderß, denn der glaub.' WA 46, 614, e.g.: 'es gilt hie nichts mehr denn aus Gott geboren sein durch den glauben an den Son Gottes, der Mensch ist worden.'

83. WA 46, 623: 'Das also alle, niemand ausgeschlossen, er sei Man oder Weib, die Christus wort hoeren, an in gleuben, die gewalt und das recht haben, das sie mit warheit sagen koennen: Ich bin durch Christum Gottes kind und ein Erbe aller seiner himlischen gueter, und Gott ist mein Vater.' See also ibid., 610–13. My point here is not to deny that Luther ascribes the act of faith to the work of the Holy Spirit, because he does. Rather, my point is that he draws so close a connection between the work of the Spirit and faith that there is no room for questions of predestination or an operation of the Spirit apart from faith; if there is faith in Christ, the Spirit must be working there. At this point, Bucer and Calvin would bring the doctrine of predestination into play.

84. WA 39 II, 1–33.

85. Ibid., 92–121.

86. Ibid., especially the theses 10–16 and 49–50.

the difference between Luther and the later Lutherans is best located here as well, since the latter all take up some aspect of Luther's theology, but for the most part attempt to resolve the tension that is so characteristic of Luther himself.

3.7 Conclusion

In this chapter, we explored the role played by the Law-Gospel dynamics in the interpretation of the Gospel of John, and its consequences for the adoption or non-adoption of a form of Christocentrism by Augustine and Reformation theologians. In Augustine, we saw that he has two motives for keeping the dynamics between Law and Gospel going, even when the Gospel of John leaves little room for him to do so. On the one hand, this was apologetically motivated. He wanted to show non-Christians that the things which Christians pursue are the same good that non-Christians long for and to some extent also know. In this way, Augustine sought to motivate non-Christians to become Christians, so that they might achieve justice through faith in Christ and be able to see God. The second motive for maintaining the Law-Gospel dynamics is Augustine's conviction that faith in Christ can never be a way to circumvent the need to perform concrete acts of justice in the life of believers. Only the pure of heart will see God, and there is no one in this life who is pure of heart. By following this path, Augustine qualifies the rights to salvation which believers receive through faith in Christ. Those rights remain limited because one's relationship to Christ through faith can never trump the requirements of concrete justice. As such, Augustine end up teaching believers a specific form of humility that appears not to be present in the Gospel of John.

Something similar emerged from our exploration of the interpretation of the Johannine prologue in the Reformation. To some interpreters, the entire Gospel is already present in creation. For this party, which included Michael Servetus and Sebastian Franck, there is no fundamental difference between the levels of creation and salvation. In this respect, they are in a certain sense Christocentrists, but their form of Christocentrism leads to a universalist and cosmopolitan perspective on Christianity. To Anabaptists such as Melchior Hoffman and Menno Simons, there is a fundamental difference: In Christ, a radical form of salvation is possible that was impossible through creation. In Christ, something radically new appears, and therefore the present order of creation is of secondary importance. The Anabaptists are Christocentrists as well, but their Christocentrism evokes in them a dynamics opposed to that the universalist thinkers Servetus and Franck. The Anabaptists draw a 'sectarian' conclusion from their Christocentrism. Salvation happens to a small group that participates radically in Christ, rather than in the whole of creation.

The mainstream Reformation finds itself in between these two radical streams. The mainstream Reformers recognize the old order of the Law, of creation, but they at the same time speak of a restoration of the current order. Luther is in doubt. He is so preoccupied with the radical newness of the Gospel that he almost goes so far as to put the old order of the Law aside, and sometimes he even actually does. On the other hand, especially when he sees the consequences of the rejection of the creation order in radical forms of Reformation, he sticks to the old order of the Law in the life of believers.

In the next chapter, we will continue our exploration of the dynamics between Law and Gospel and its role in reading the Gospel of John. We do so by means of an elaborate discussion of the theology of Karl Barth. Barth in particular was one to defend a radical form of Christocentrism in the twentieth century. However, as we will see when we explore his theological development, he did not arrive at his mature Christocentrism without hesitation. We will see how he came to his Christocentrism through an exploration of the various side paths offering ways of doing theology that differ markedly from the one he finally opted for. Following Barth's line of thinking can help us to see the different ways in which the Law-Gospel distinction may be used for theological reflection, and how they relate to the mature 'Christological concentration' that has exercised such a profound influence on theology in the twentieth and twenty-first centuries.

Chapter 4

CHRISTOCENTRISM IN KARL BARTH, THE GOSPEL OF JOHN AND THE POSSIBILITY OF NATURAL THEOLOGY

4.1 Introduction

In the previous chapter, we explored the way in which the distinction between Law and Gospel could be used as a key to the use of Scripture in Augustine and the Reformation. On the one hand, Augustine and in particular the mainstream Reformation embraced the Gospel of John and specifically the prologue, but on the other hand, they constantly needed ways to moderate the at-times far-reaching claims in this gospel – and they did so, as I attempted to show, through an appeal to the Old Testament tradition. This Old Testament tradition, which I labelled 'Law', received greater emphasis in New Testament books other than John. Time and again, the disputes occasioned by the Gospel of John in the later tradition concern the extent to which believers can 'grasp' the revelation and salvation which we encounter in Jesus Christ. Are believers taken up into the condescending movement of Christ, and, through it, also into the ascending movement? In the answers given by theologians and believers, they construe a balance between Law and Gospel.

In this chapter, we take the next step in exploring this balance between Law and Gospel through an engagement with the work of Karl Barth. In his time, Barth struck a new balance between revelation and reason, grace and nature, church and culture. He did so through by a powerful resistance against what he called 'natural theology'. Prompted by the disastrous consequences of a theology that focuses one-sidedly on culture, on the human and the civic, Barth opted for a radically opposite standpoint and claimed to depart exclusively from revelation. Christocentrism or, as others call it, a 'Christological concentration', became the hallmark of Barth's theology.

Resistance against Christocentrism forms one of the reasons for this book developing an alternative in terms of the Law-Gospel distinction. This in itself already makes engagement with Barth a near inevitability. The presence of Christocentrism in present-day systematic theology is inconceivable without the theology of Barth, making engagement with his thought a matter of primary importance for appreciating the theological reasons for this Christocentrism. It is only when we take these reasons most seriously that we can develop a credible alternative. At the same time, the reasons extend further back than Barth. Barth did not arrive at his Christocentrism without a struggle. As an experimental theologian, he experimented with all sorts of contextually determined trajectories for doing theology in a new way. There are certain sensibilities in all these attempts, but they do not form a perfectly consistent whole.

My aim in this chapter is to explore the reasons for the rise of Christocentrism in contemporary systematic theology by thinking along with Barth. I will develop my own approach in conversation with the various attempts he made towards his mature Christocentric theology. By exploring several of the decisive moves in Barth's emerging Christocentrism in the 1920s and 1930s, I will reassess the choices he made. The purpose is to learn from the steps Barth took, to evaluate the alternative trajectories that he explored but put aside and to see how an alternative trajectory in terms of Law and Gospel could offer a solution to the problems he tried to solve Christocentrically. In a certain sense, my aim is an ambitious one: I aim to '*überbiet*' Barth, to do better than he did. I attempt to show that Barth would have reached his own goals better with a duality between Law and Gospel than he did with the Christocentrism he settled on.

The reader will notice soon enough that not only the development of Barth's Christocentrism but also the specific reception of the Gospel of John continues to play a role in this chapter. I hope to show how tracing the development of Barth's reception of John sheds light on the development of his Christocentrism. I would like to suggest that the reception of John in Barth can be used to monitor the development of his Christocentrism.[1] I will follow a circular trajectory, starting with Barth's appropriation of Barmen in *Church Dogmatics* (CD) II/1. Subsequently, I will go back to 1922 and trace a path through several essays from the 1920s and 1930s, before finishing with CD volume I/2.

4.2 Barth as an experimental theologian

Barth's Christocentrism has received extensive attention over the years. The responses vary, ranging from strikingly pejorative evaluations, such as the

---

1. That the role of the Gospel of John in the development of Barth's Christocentrism did not receive its proper due may well be related to McCormack's thesis concerning Christocentrism and the doctrine of election, since McCormack's thesis leads Gibson to put the reception of Romans at the centre of his otherwise excellent treatment of exegesis and Christocentrism in Barth. Cf. Bruce L. McCormack, 'Grace and Being: The Role of God's Gracious Election in Karl Barth's Theological Ontology', in *The Cambridge Companion to Karl Barth*, ed. J. B. Webster (Cambridge: Cambridge University Press, 2000), 92–110; David Gibson, *Reading the Decree: Exegesis, Election and Christology in Calvin and Barth*, T&T Clark Studies in Systematic Theology 4 (London: T&T Clark International, 2009), 18–20.

oft-heard charge of 'Christomonism',[2] to many favourable accounts and historical investigations. One might say that Barth's Christocentrism became the de facto starting point for many systematic theologies from the second half of the twentieth century. The revival of interest in the Christian doctrine of the Trinity in recent decades is directly related to Barth's Christocentrism. His rethinking of the doctrine of God, in the sense that God is truly God in Christ from all eternity through God's decision to be God with us, follows directly from his Christocentrism. Not only has this Christocentrism become the common starting point of contemporary dogmatics but it also easily aligns itself with a broad Christocentric spirituality as it is found especially in the evangelical world.

On the level of historical research, Bruce McCormack's groundbreaking study of the development of Barth's theology produced a new consensus among Barth scholars.[3] Barth's mature Christocentrism is now commonly connected to his doctrine of election as presented in volume II/2 of the CD, although McCormack traces the roots of this development as far back as 1936, when Barth was introduced to Pierre Maury and heard his paper on election and faith. From that point on, so the current consensus suggests, Barth's mature Christocentrism was in place. Recent scholars most commonly follow McCormack's reconstruction on this point.[4]

2. Marc Cortez, 'What Does It Mean to Call Karl Barth a Christocentric Theologian?' *Scottish Journal of Theology* 60, no. 2 (2007): 130.

3. Bruce McCormack, 'Christonomie', in *Barth Handbuch*, ed. Michael Beintker, Theologen-Handbücher (Tübingen: Mohr Siebeck, 2016), 226–32; Bruce L. McCormack, *Karl Barth's Critically Realistic Dialectical Theology: Its Genesis and Development, 1909–1936* (Oxford: Clarendon, 1997), 453–63; McCormack, 'Grace and Being'.

4. For example, although Cortez provides an elucidating analysis of the meaning of the term 'Christocentrism', he makes no attempt to reconstruct its historical development: Cortez, 'Christocentric Theologian', 127. While Cortez may mention Barth's own 'How I changed my mind', Barth does not actually mention the doctrine of election in that particular text at all. Gibson, who is interested in the relationship between exegesis and the doctrine of election, does not question McCormack's theory either: Gibson, *Reading the Decree*, 5–10. So too on the continent, van 't Slot, who is very sensitive to the historical developments in the exchange of ideas between Barth and Bonhoeffer, follows the view of McCormack as well: Edward van 't Slot, *Negativism of Revelation? Bonhoeffer and Barth on Faith and Actualism*, Dogmatik in der Moderne 12 (Tübingen: Mohr Siebeck, 2015), 171–7; Edward van 't Slot, 'Die christologische Konzentration: Anfang und Durchführung', *Zeitschrift für Dialektische Theologie* 61, no. 1 (2015): 12–31. In the Barth handbook from 2016, various scholars provide an introduction to the genesis of Barth's theological thought in line with McCormack's analysis. McCormack himself summarizes his view in the separate chapter on Barth's mature Christocentrism: McCormack, 'Christonomie'; Michael Beintker, 'Dialektische Theologie', in *Barth Handbuch*, ed. Michael Beintker, Theologen-Handbücher (Tübingen: Mohr Siebeck, 2016), 200–5; Michael Beintker, 'Der Dialektiker als Dogmatiker', in *Barth Handbuch*, ed. Michael Beintker, Theologen-Handbücher (Tübingen: Mohr Siebeck, 2016), 206–10; Wolf Krötke, 'Erwählungslehre', in *Barth*

In this chapter, I make no attempt to challenge this consensus. My contribution will be of a different nature, albeit still broadly compatible with the profound historical work done by McCormack and many others. While van 't Slot follows one series of Barth's early essays, a recent article on the development of Barth's Christocentrism,[5] I follow a different series of essays and thus a different line of development in his early Christocentrism. My primary interest is not to reconstruct Barth's development, but to see how several moments in this development can be used to reassess its Christocentric outcome. While this indeed requires a partial account of the historical development, my analysis is by no means intended to offer a new genetic analysis.

I also see an additional reason why genetic analysis is not of primary interest for my present purpose. It is tempting to read Barth's writings as pieces of abstract systematic theology, as moments in the development of an intellectual who had no care but the consistency and brilliance of his ideas. And if this is already the case for a single article, it is even more tempting to read the hefty volumes of the CD in this way. Every volume looks the same and is big, deep and wide; therefore, the idea that this is simply one of those famous systematic theologies from the history of Christianity is but a reflex of the interpreter's brain.

This reflex, however, is wrong.[6] Not even Barth saw those volumes in that way, even though the more human part of him may have had the tendency to do so every now and then. The prefaces to the various volumes testify to a sober self-awareness. At the beginning of the first volume, he explains how he approached his own development when, following the appearance of the *Christliche Dogmatik im Entwurf*, he started all over again with volume I/1 of the CD:

> My experience of twelve years ago in re-editing the Römerbrief was repeated. I could still say what I had said. I wished to do so. But I could not do it in the same way. What option had I but to begin again at the beginning, saying the same thing, but in a very different way?[7]

Handbuch, ed. Michael Beintker, Theologen-Handbücher (Tübingen: Mohr Siebeck, 2016), 221–6; by way of overall summary, see: Michael Beintker, 'Resümee', in *Barth Handbuch*, ed. Michael Beintker, Theologen-Handbücher (Tübingen: Mohr Siebeck, 2016), 232–7.

5. Van 't Slot, 'Christologische Konzentration'.

6. Beintker, 'Resümee', 232–3.

7. Karl Barth, *Church Dogmatics*, trans. Geoffrey William Bromiley and Thomas F. Torrance (Edinburgh: T&T Clark, 1975), I/1, xii; hereafter CD. Karl Barth, *Die Kirchliche Dogmatik* (Zollikon-Zürich: Evangelischer Verlag, 1932–70), I/1, vi: 'Was ich vor zwölf Jahren bei der Neubearbeitung des Römerbriefs erlebt hatte, wiederholte sich: ich konnte und wollte dasselbe sagen wie einst; aber so wie ich es einst gesagt, konnte ich es jetzt nicht mehr sagen. Was blieb mir übrig, als von vorn anzufangen, und zwar noch einmal dasselbe, aber dasselbe noch einmal ganz anders zu sagen?'

Many years later, at the beginning of volume IV/2, he explained at greater length how he viewed the coherence of his dogmatic work:

> I can certainly confirm his [one of his critics, MW] view to this extent. When I take up the theme of each part-volume, or even embark upon each new section, although I keep to a general direction, only the angels in heaven do actually know in detail what form the material will take. But to me it is very comforting that the angels in heaven do know, and as far as I am concerned it is enough if I am clear that at each point I listen as unreservedly as possible to the witness of Scripture and as impartially as possible to that of the Church, and then consider and formulate whatever may be the result. I am, therefore, a continual learner, and in consequence the aspect of this Church Dogmatics is always that of quiet but persistent movement. But is the same not true of the Church itself if it is not a dead Church but a Church which is engaged in a living consideration of its Lord? Would it not be abnormal if I were in a position to show the eternal mysteries, and the truths of the Christian faith as they are revealed in time, like a film which has been taken and fixed, as though I were myself the master of them? Of course it would. Am I then groping in the dark? Is anything and everything possible? Not at all.[8]

In fact, if one studies the themes running through the CD, one can indeed see what Barth is saying here: there are key insights that return, but often they appear in a different form with virtually no notice, prompted by different questions and different conditions of the surrounding culture. As we will see below, for example, Barth's discussion of Barmen in II/1 differs markedly from

---

8. Barth, *CD*, IV/2, xi–xii; Barth, *KD*, IV/2, viii:

> Darin kann ich aber seine Ansicht bestätigen, daß mir, wenn ich jeweils an das besondere Thema eines neuen Teilbandes herantrete, ja sogar bei der Inangriffnahme jedes neuen Paragraphen, wohl die Richtung des Ganzen vor Augen steht, daß dann aber im Einzelnen zunächst in der Tat nur die Engel im Himmel wissen, wie sich die Sache gestalten wird. Eben daß die Engel im Himmel es schon wissen, ist mir dabei sehr tröstlich, und was mich betrifft, so genügt es mir, mir darüber klar zu sein, daß ich jetzt wieder und wieder, je auf einen bestimmten Punkt ausgerichtet, möglichst vorbehaltlos auf das Zeugnis der Schrift und möglichst unparteilich überlegend auch auf das der Kirche zu hören und dann eben aufzupassen und zu formulieren habe, was herauskommt. Da habe ich dann fortwährend hinzuzulernen, und daraus folgt, daß das Gesicht «dieser kirchlichen Dogmatik» fortwährend in einer stillen, aber bestimmten Wandlung begriffen ist. Muß das nicht auch von der Kirche selbst gelten, sofern sie nämlich nicht tot, sondern im Aufmerken auf ihren Herrn lebendig ist? Wäre es nicht abnorm, wenn ich etwa in der Lage wäre, die Darstellung der ewigen Geheimnisse und der in der Zeit offenbarten Wahrheiten des christlichen Glaubens, als ob ich ihrer Meister wäre, wie einen zuvor aufgenommenen und fixierten Film ablaufen zu lassen? Das sei ferne!

his discussion of it in later volumes. The critique of natural theology and the Christological exclusivism that were not yet present in 1933 took centre stage in 1937/38–40, disappeared again in IV/2 and was then accompanied by a turn towards culture that was typical of the post-war years of Protestant Germany. Notwithstanding all the volumes of that 'dogmatic system', it is more helpful to look at the CD and at Barth's theology as a whole as a contextual theology centred around the insight that the church lives from Jesus Christ alone and that it must remain true to his message, which nevertheless needs to be expressed in new language every time.

This meandering and dynamic approach to the central concerns in Barth's theology will become clear in what follows. Barth has reasons to resist over-systematizing his own ideas. To his mind, theology is not allowed to become a 'system', since that would suggest that the truth about God can be caught in a stable structure, while for Barth the truth about God is an event that has to happen anew every time.[9] This is also why I think that it makes sense to enter into a conversation with Barth along the various stages in his own development, because Barth is at every point in this development deeply aware of the present contextual issues at stake at that particular moment, and he allows himself to frame those issues in ways that fit the particular context, drawing on theological notions which are already given in the context. By analysing how Barth theologizes in those particular contexts, scrutinizing the concerns urgent to him then and there, we get a view on how we can address those concerns in ways that go beyond his approach, but still take them seriously.

4.3 The Barmen Declaration

After this brief methodological detour, we are now ready to embark on our journey through the development of Barth's Christocentrism. We take our starting point in volume II/1, since it is there, in Barth's discussion of the Barmen Declaration, that we find a clear example where his mature Christocentrism, the rejection of natural theology and the Gospel of John all come together. Barth's reception of Jn 14.6 will provide a helpful lens through which the development of Christocentrism and his critique of natural theology can be brought into focus. What we also find here is a reflection from Barth's side on the Barmen event, a reflection that occurs a few years after the event itself, which, as we will see below, proves to be important for his interpretation of it.

But before we examine Barth's discussion of Barmen in CD II/1, we will first take a look at the Barmen Declaration itself. The Barmen Declaration's opening thesis contains a clear statement of what one might call 'Christocentrism', based on two key quotations from the Gospel of John:

---

9. Beintker, 'Resümee', 233; Rinse Reeling Brouwer, *Grondvormen van theologische systematiek* (Vught: Skandalon, 2009), 18.

'[Jesus says:]¹⁰ I am the way, the truth, and the life: no man cometh unto the Father, but by me' (Jn. 14:6).

'Verily, verily, I say unto you, He that entereth not by the door into the sheepfold, but climbeth up some other way, the same is a thief and a robber ... I am the door: by me if any man enter in, he shall be saved' (Jn 10:1,9).

Jesus Christ, as He is attested to us in Holy Scripture, is the one Word of God, whom we have to hear and whom we have to trust and obey in life and in death.

We condemn the false doctrine that the Church can and must recognise as God's revelation other events and powers, forms and truths, apart from and alongside this one Word of God.¹¹

It is a well-known fact that Barth was the Barmen Declaration's main author.¹² Each thesis contains three components: first, the Bible verses; second, the positive statement; and, finally, the 'anathema'. While we will elaborate on the Bible verses below, a noteworthy aspect about the positive statement is an allusion to the Reformed tradition when it says that we have to trust and obey Jesus Christ 'in life and death'. This may be read as a reference to the well-known first question of the Heidelberg Catechism: 'What is your only comfort in life and in death?'¹³ Barth therefore links up the Catechism's reference to only one

---

10. These two introductory words in square brackets are absent from the final edition of the first thesis, but do appear in Barth and Asmussen's so-called 'Bonner Entwurf'. As we will see, this phrase also plays a role in Barth's discussion in the *CD*. Cf. Karl Barth, *Vorträge und kleinere Arbeiten, 1934–1935*, ed. Michael Beintker, Michael Hüttenhoff and Peter Zocher, Karl Barth-Gesamtausgabe 52 (Zürich: Theologischer Verlag, 2017), 270–2, 296. The *Gesamtausgabe* offers no details as to why the words 'Jesus speaks' in the Bonner Entwurf were left out in the version of the Declaration accepted by the synod.

11. Barth, *CD*, II/1, 173; Barth, *KD*, II/1, 194:

«[Jesus spricht:] Ich bin der Weg und die Wahrheit und das Leben, niemand kommt zum Vater denn durch mich» (Joh. 14, 6). «Wahrlich, wahrlich, ich sage euch, wer nicht zur Tür hineingeht in den Schafstall, sondern steiget anderswo hinein, der ist ein Dieb und ein Mörder ... Ich bin die Tür; so jemand durch mich eingeht, der wird selig werden» (Joh. 10, 1. 9). Jesus Christus, wie er uns in der Heiligen Schrift bezeugt wird, ist das eine Wort Gottes, das wir zu hören, dem wir im Leben und im Sterben zu vertrauen und zu gehorchen haben. Wir verwerfen die falsche Lehre, als könne und müsse die Kirche als Quelle ihrer Verkündigung außer und neben diesem einen Worte Gottes auch noch andere Ereignisse und Mächte, Gestalten und Wahrheiten, als Gottes Offenbarung anerkennen.

See also: Barth, *Vorträge und kleinere Arbeiten, 1934–1935*, 296.

12. Eberhard Busch, *Karl Barths Lebenslauf nach seinen Briefen und autobiographischen Texten*, 4th edn (München: Kaiser, 1986), 258.

13. Philip Schaff, *The Creeds of Christendom*, Bibliotheca Symbolica Ecclesiæ Universalis (New York: Harper & Brothers, 1882), III, 307.

comfort to the idea of following only one Lord in life and death. At the same time, the idea to trust Jesus Christ alone as the true God is a small but entirely meaningful modification of a key notion from the Lutheran tradition. For Luther, in his Large Catechism, putting one's trust and faith in Jesus Christ alone is the fulfilment of the first commandment.[14] Barth modifies this by saying that you trust God *and obey* God by following Jesus Christ. The notion of obedience is absent from Luther's discussion of the first commandment, and, given the addition of a legal dimension to faith in Christ, it will certainly have rung a bell among a Lutheran readership.[15]

For the present topic of Christocentrism, the anathema at the end is also relevant, because it rejects any resources for faith and theology apart from Christ. Of course, this must be read primarily and historically against the background of the danger of the subsummation of the church into the totalitarian state under Adolf Hitler's Third Reich.[16] Every power that claims absolute authority, so the Barmen Declaration states, is to be rejected as an idol. However, it is Barth himself who extends the scope of the first thesis in the interpretations of the declaration he was to give in subsequent years. One such interpretation is his famous discussion in CD II/1 in the context of his critique of natural theology.[17]

In this volume, Barth looks back at the events taking place in the years 1933/34. Volume II/1 was published in 1940 and have their origin in Barth's lectures in dogmatics from the years 1937/38. The discussion of the Barmen Declaration has its place in Barth's critique of natural theology. In an extensive discussion on the possibility of knowledge of God, Barth deals with what he understands to be the historical circumstances which led to the writing of the Barmen Declaration. At the end of the essay, he discusses the role of the Bible verses quoted at the top:

---

14. Martin Luther, 'Large Catechism', in *Triglot Concordia: The Symbolical Books of the Ev. Lutheran Church*, trans. F. Bente and W. H. T. Dau (St. Louis: Concordia, 1921), http://www2.hn.psu.edu/faculty/jmanis/m~luther/mllc.pdf, on the first commandment.

15. For Barth's view of faith and obedience in his earlier work, in conversation with the Lutheran view, see Karl Barth, «Unterricht in der christlichen Religion»: *Zweiter Band*, ed. Hinrich Stoevesandt, Karl Barth-Gesamtausgabe 20 (Zürich: Theologischer Verlag, 1985), sec. 17, pp. 207ff; Karl Barth, *Die christliche Dogmatik im Entwurf*, ed. Gerhard Sauter, Karl Barth-Gesamtausgabe 14 (Zürich: Theologischer Verlag, 1982), sec. 19, pp. 417–34. For these references I am indebted to my colleague Rinse Reeling Brouwer.

16. Barth did not, however, directly attack Adolf Hitler and National Socialism at the time of writing the Declaration; see Paul Silas Peterson, *The Early Karl Barth: Historical Contexts and Intellectual Formation, 1905–1935*, Beiträge Zur Historischen Theologie 184 (Tübingen: Mohr Siebeck, 2018), 312–28.

17. Barth, *KD*, II/1, 194–200. For another interpretation, see Busch, *Karl Barths Lebenslauf*, 259–60. The latter, however, is a very late reflection (1964), probably prompted by Barth's ecumenical interests of the time, which is the topic he highlights there.

For the understanding of what the first article of Barmen has to say in detail, it is perhaps advisable not to pass over the preceding verses from Jn. 14 and Jn. 10, but to understand everything from them as a starting-point. The emphasis of everything said previously lies in the fact that Jesus Christ has said something, and, what is more, has said it about Himself: I myself am the way, the truth, and the life. I myself am the door. The Church lives by the fact that it hears the voice of this 'I' and lays hold of the promise which, according to this voice, is contained in this 'I' alone; that therefore it chooses the way, knows the truth, lives the life, goes through the door, which is Jesus Christ Himself alone. Moreover, it is not on its own authority, or in the execution of its own security programme, but on the basis of the necessity in which Jesus Christ Himself has said that no man comes to the Father but by Him, and that any by-passing of Him means theft and robbery, that the Church makes its exclusive claim, negating every other way or truth or life or door apart from Him.[18]

Barth thus presents the Bible verses quoted at the beginning of the Barmen Declaration not just as illustrations of what is written in the thesis, but as the very foundation and centre of the thesis itself. Barth does two things in this interpretation. First, he argues for Christological exclusivism: All true knowledge of God is knowledge of Christ. God is available to us because God has freely made himself available in Christ. This is justified in terms of the text from John. But there is more at stake, since Barth also makes a second, more drastic, statement, and he seems fully aware that he needs it for substantiating the first, more modest claim. For in the event this Christological exclusivism were an invention of the Confessing Church or, even worse, of the theologian Karl Barth, then it would still be Barth who had decided that no longer Nature or Scripture but Christ alone

---

18. Barth, *CD*, II/1, 178; Barth, *KD*, II/1, 199:

> Zum Verständnis dessen, was der erste Satz von Barmen inhaltlich im Einzelnen zu besagen hat, ist es ratsam, die vorangeschickten Stellen aus Joh. 14 und 10 ja nicht etwa zu überschlagen, sondern vielmehr alles Andere gerade von ihnen aus zu verstehen. Der Nachdruck alles nachher Gesagten liegt darauf, daß Jesus Christus etwas gesagt und zwar dies von sich selbst gesagt hat: Ich bin der Weg und die Wahrheit und das Leben. Ich bin die Türe. Die Kirche lebt davon, daß sie die Stimme dieses Ich hört und die Verheißung ergreift, die laut dieser Stimme ganz allein in diesem Ich beschlossen ist: daß sie also den Weg wählt, die Wahrheit erkennt, das Leben lebt, durch die Türe geht, die ganz allein Jesus Christus selber ist. Wiederum nicht in eigener Vollmacht, nicht in Ausführung eines eigenen Sicherungsprogramms, sondern auf Grund der Notwendigkeit, in der Jesus Christus selbst gesagt hat, daß niemand zum Vater komme denn durch ihn, daß jedes Vorbeigehen an ihm Diebstahl und Mord bedeute, vollzieht dann die Kirche auch die Exklusive, spricht sie ihr Nein zu Allem, was außer ihm Weg, Wahrheit, Leben, Türe sein möchte.

is the criterion of theology. As such a human being would still be the ground for choosing Christ as the only criterion.[19]

This is what Barth refutes with his interpretation of the statement. His claim is that, through Jn 14.6 and 10.1,9, it is Jesus himself who is speaking to the Confessing Church and installing a Christological exclusivism. This is then also the reason why the Bible verse is more important than the thesis that follows. In the verse, Jesus himself is speaking, whereas in the thesis, it is the church that responds to the words of Jesus. Therefore, the true subject of the Barmen Declaration was not the Confessing Church or the theologian Karl Barth but Jesus Christ himself. Barth had made this explicit a little earlier on when he wrote:

> If we want really to understand the genesis of Barmen, we shall be obliged to look finally neither to the Confessional Church as such nor to its opponents. For there is not much to be seen here. The Confessional Church was, so to speak, only the witness of a situation in which simultaneously there took place a remarkable revelation, as there had not been for a long time, of the beast out of the abyss, and a fresh confirmation of the one old revelation of God in Jesus Christ. It was only a witness of this event. Indeed, it was often a most inconspicuous and inconvenient witness.[20]

There was only one natural possibility. As the church had done so over all the previous centuries, it had to go for a view in which next to Jesus Christ, even nature and culture were accepted as sources of theological truth. However, thanks to divine providence, Jesus Christ ruling the church from heaven above, Christological exclusivism was now defended as the only viable foundation for the church's life.

In Barth's interpretation of the Barmen Declaration, the Bible verse thus comes first. Even more, Barth identifies the statement of the Barmen Declaration with the very Word of God. This point likewise emerges from the fact that the Bible verse quoted (Jn 14.6) was adapted somewhat to give better expression to Barth's claim. Jn 14.6 opens with Jesus' answer to a question posed to him by Thomas: ('Lord, we do not know where you go. How can we know the way?'), and then continues: 'Jesus speaks to him (*autoi*)'. In its official version, the Barmen Declaration omits

---

19. Cf. Klaus Wengst, 'Der Beitrag der neutestamentlichen Zitate zum Verständnis der Barmer Theologischen Erklärung', *Theologische Zeitschrift* 41, no. 3 (1985): 297.

20. Barth, *CD*, II/1, 178; Barth, *KD*, II/1, 198–9:

> Man wird, wenn man die Genesis von Barmen wirklich verstehen will, letztlich weder auf die bekennende Kirche als solche, noch auf ihre Gegner sehen dürfen. Es ist hier nicht viel zu sehen. Die bekennende Kirche war sozusagen nur Zeuge einer Situation, in der es gleichzeitig zu einer merkwürdigen, so schon lange nicht mehr dagewesenen Offenbarung des Tieres aus dem Abgrund und zu einer neuen Bewährung der einen alten Offenbarung Gottes in Jesus Christus kam. Sie war nur Zeuge dieses Geschehens, ein oft sehr unaufmerksamer und störender Zeuge sogar.

the phrase 'Jesus speaks to him', and Barth and Asmussen's proposal drops the words 'to him', even though these words end up playing a decisive role in Barth's interpretation of the thesis.[21] Jesus' contextual reply thus ends up being changed to sound like a universal, timeless statement.

Barth himself saw his rejection of all forms of natural theology as an innovation, even a 'purification':

> The same had already been the case in the developments of the preceding centuries. There can be no doubt that not merely a part but the whole had been intended and claimed when it had been demanded that side by side with its attestation in Jesus Christ and therefore in Holy Scripture the Church should also recognise and proclaim God's revelation in reason, in conscience, in the emotions, in history, in nature, and in culture and its achievements and developments. The history of the proclamation and theology of these centuries is simply a history of the wearisome conflict of the Church with the fact that the 'also' demanded and to some extent acknowledged by it really meant an 'only'. The conflict was bound to be wearisome and even hopeless because, on the inclined plane on which this 'also' gravitated into 'only', it could not supply any inner check apart from the apprehension, inconsistency and inertia of all interested parties.[22]

4.4 A historical deconstruction of Barth's reading of Barmen in Church Dogmatics II/1

Thus far we have therefore found a very close connection between Barth's Christocentrism and his use of the Gospel of John, in particular Jn 14.6. This

---

21. Barth, *Vorträge und kleinere Arbeiten, 1934–1935*, 270-2, 296.
22. Barth, *CD*, II/1, 178; Barth, *KD*, II/1, 194:

> Wie denn schon in den Entwicklungen der vorangehenden Jahrhunderte zweifellos nicht nur ein Teil, sondern das Ganze gemeint und gefordert war, wenn man der Kirche zumutete, Gottes Offenbarung neben ihrer Bezeugung in Jesus Christus und also in der heiligen Schrift auch in der Vernunft, auch im Gewissen, auch im Gefühl, auch in der Geschichte, auch in der Natur, auch in der Kultur, in ihren Errungenschaften und in ihren Fortschritten zu erkennen und zu proklamieren. Die Geschichte der Verkündigung und der Theologie dieser Jahrhunderte ist eine einzige Geschichte der mühsamen Auseinandersetzung der Kirche mit der Tatsache, daß das ihr zugemutete und von ihr weithin anerkannte «auch» in Wirklichkeit ein «allein» bedeutete. Diese Auseinandersetzung mußte mühsam, sie mußte geradezu hoffnungslos sein, weil es auf der schiefen Ebene, auf der dieses «auch» zum «allein» strebte, ein inneres Aufhalten außer der Angst, der Inkonsequenz, der Trägheit aller Beteiligten nicht geben konnte.

Christocentrism is put to the service of a strong repudiation of any kind of a second source, something that determines theological discourse 'next to' Jesus Christ.

Interestingly, however, in terms of Barth's historical development, the interpretation of Barmen and especially the link between Barth's Christocentrism and his use of the Gospel of John are more complex than this. The passages from CD II/1 that have been quoted above were published in 1940, but were based on the seminar on natural theology which Barth gave in Basel during the winter semester of 1937/8. In 1985, Klaus Wengst published an article in the *Theologische Zeitschrift* (in celebration of fifty years of *Barmen Theologischer Erklärung*) detailing the story of the Bible verses in the Barmen Declaration. Wengst consulted the Barth archive in Basel and discovered that at first – that is, during the January free synod of the Reformed churches in Germany, which was likewise held in Barmen but took place a few months prior to the more well-known synod of the Reformed, Lutheran and united churches – there were no Bible verses accompanying the theses.[23] The Bible verses must therefore have been added during the period between the Reformed synod in January 1934 and the 'Evangelical' synod at the end of May 1934. In this process, Jn 14.6 was in fact one of the last verses to be added, since thesis one was initially preceded only by the quotation from John 10. Moreover, the addition of Jn 14.6 is to be credited to the Bavarian bishop Hans Meiser, who protested somewhat to the inclusion of John 10 and proposed Jn 14.6 instead. Hans Asmussen and Barth, most probably prompted by this proposal, then added the reference to Jn 14.6 to the top of the first thesis only days before the final Barmen synod was held from 29 to 31 May 1934.[24]

Against this background, it is clear that Barth significantly rewrote the role of the biblical passages in the events leading to the composition of the Barmen Declaration. In contrast with what Barth suggests in CD II/1, the historical context indeed contributed decisively to the way in which the Barmen Declaration was formulated. This is not to suggest that the biblical passages were not relevant at all. Quite to the contrary, it means that Barth's reconstruction of Barmen needs to be treated with greater suspicion than we find in some secondary literature, including such authoritative works as Busch's *Karl Barths Lebenslauf*.[25] That Barth's reconstruction of the events leading up to Barmen developed over time, to put it mildly, also seems to follow a pattern. Every time he reconstructs Barmen, he presents the significance of the event in terms of the pressing issues of the day, whether that be natural theology (1937/8), just war (1954),[26] theology of culture (1959)[27] or ecumenism (1964).[28]

---

23. Wengst, 'Der Beitrag der neutestamentlichen Zitate zum Verständnis der Barmer Theologischen Erklärung', 295–6.

24. Ibid., 299. See also: Barth, *Vorträge und kleinere Arbeiten, 1934–1935*, 287.

25. Busch, *Karl Barths Lebenslauf*, 259; the two sources of Barth's perception in this work are CD II/1 and a conversation in 1964.

26. Dietrich Braun, 'Karl Barths Texte zur Barmer Theologischen Erklärung', *Evangelische Theologie* 45, no. 1 (1985): 83–4.

27. Barth, *KD*, IV/3, 95–6.

28. Busch, *Karl Barths Lebenslauf*, 259–60.

4.5 'The Word of God as the task of theology' (1922)

Having examined the way Barth uses the Gospel of John to attack natural theology in volume II/1 of the CD, we now take a step back to explore the trajectory that led him to this mature form of Christocentrism in the various volumes of the CD. We will see that his mature Christocentrism was not always there, and an exploration of the steps leading towards it will allow us to consider the theological options that Barth explored earlier on, only to leave them behind in his later work. We start our trajectory with Barth's famous text from 1922, 'The Word of God as the task of theology'[29] ('Das Wort Gottes als Aufgabe der Theologie'). The first edition of the text appeared in 1922 in the journal *Zwischen den Zeiten*. That same year also saw the publication of the famous second edition of the *Römerbrief*. While the appearance of the first edition already was an event, this second edition was to bring Barth even greater fame.

Our choice to start with this article is motivated by its significance for what is called Karl Barth's 'dialectical theological method', a phrase that appears towards the end of the text. While that can indeed be found in the article, students who start reading Barth should be aware that the article was never intended to do what it in hindsight did. The article was not written as an exercise in devising a new theological method. On the contrary, it was written as a heroic attempt at doing theology by an angry young man, fearful and trembling, who had been invited to set out his controversial ideas before his critics' main society, the 'Christian World'.[30] More than the exposition of a method, therefore, it is a piece of rhetoric, a masterpiece, as we will shortly see.

It is to this flexibility and rhetorical skill that the article 'Das Wort Gottes als Aufgabe der Theologie' testifies in a marvellous way. Although the name of Jesus Christ as the centre of Christian theology appears only at the very end, his name and person are present from the very beginning. As Barth remarks at the end: 'Although I have touched upon the *actual* theme of my presentation a few times, I have not expressly named it. All of my thoughts circle around the one point which is called "Jesus Christ" in the New Testament.'[31]

Particularly relevant to the theme of this chapter is the nature of Barth's 'dialectical theological method'. It is about not being able to speak theologically

---

29. Karl Barth, 'The Word of God as the Task of Theology', in *The Word of God and Theology*, trans. Amy Marga (London: T&T Clark International, 2011), 171–98. This is a translation of the edition from the Gesamtausgabe, including the introduction and annotations to that edition: Karl Barth, 'Das Wort Gottes als Aufgabe der Theologie', in *Vorträge und kleinere Arbeiten 1922–1925*, ed. Holger Finze-Michaelsen, Karl Barth-Gesamtausgabe 19 (Zürich: Theologischer Verlag, 1990).

30. Barth, 'Word of God', 171–3.

31. Ibid., 197; original emphasis. Barth, 'Wort Gottes', 176: 'Ich habe das eigentliche Thema meiner Darlegungen einigemal berührt, aber nie ausdrücklich genannt. Alle meine Gedanken kreisten um den einen Punkt, der im Neuen Testament Jesus Christus heißt.'

but nevertheless being obliged to do so, about a 'yes' and a 'no'. What readers often seem to forget is that it is for the most part about what Barth calls *die Mitte* or 'the centre':

> From the outset, this [dialectical, MW] way takes seriously the positive unfolding of the thought of God on the one side and the critique of the human and all things human on the other. Neither one, however, happens on its own accord but with constant reference to their common presupposition, to the living truth itself, which itself is naturally not a reference. Rather, it stands in the center and gives each one its position and its negation, its sense and meaning. Here we consistently see the living truth, the decisive content of a genuine speaking of and by[32] God – that God (really God!) becomes human (really human!). But how should we establish the necessary relationship of each side to the center? The true dialectician knows that this center is incomprehensible and invisible. He will let himself get carried away into direct communication as seldom as possible, for he knows that every direct communication about *it*, whether it is positive or negative, is *not* communication *about it*. Instead, it will always be *either* dogmatism *or* self-critique.[33]

When, later on, Barth asks whether this dialectical method, taking inspiration from Luther's distinction between Law and Gospel, will be more successful than the other methods mentioned, he responds in the negative.[34] If the dialectical method solved the riddle of speaking about God by just saying 'yes' and 'no' all the time (in other words, by looking at every issue from two opposing sides), it would

---

32. I added the word 'by' to the English translation, since the German has a double meaning that the existing translation failed to capture sufficiently.

33. Barth, 'Word of God', 190–1; original emphases. Barth, 'Wort Gottes', 167:

> Hier ist mit dem positiven Entfalten des Gottesgedankens einerseits und mit der Kritik des Menschen und alles Menschlichen andrerseits von vornherein Ernst gemacht; aber beides darf nun nicht beziehungslos geschehen, sondern unter beständigem Hinblick auf ihre gemeinsame Voraussetzung, auf die lebendige, selber freilich nicht zu benennende Wahrheit, die in der Mitte steht und beiden, der Position und der Negation, erst Sinn und Bedeutung gibt. Daß Gott (aber wirklich Gott!) Mensch (aber wirklich Mensch!) wird, das ist da gleichmäßig gesehen als jenes Lebednige, als der entscheidende Inhalt eines wirklichen Von-Gott-Redens. Wie aber soll nun die notwendige Beziehung von beiden Seiten auf diese lebendige Mitte hergestellt werden? Der echte Dialektiker weiß, daß diese Mitte unfaßlich und unanschaulich ist, er wird sich also möglichst selten zu direkten Mitteilungen darüber hinreißen lassen, wissend, daß alle direkten Mitteilungen *darüber*, ob sie nun positiv odder negative seien, *nicht* Mitteilungen *darüber* sondern eben immer *entweder* Dogmatik *oder* Kritik sind.

34. Ibid., 171.

mean that theology is in the end a human construct and that the God-talk of such a theology is an awful idol or a form of pagan magic. Theology speaks, and it does so with a 'yes' and a 'no', but in doing so, it can only hope for God to speak through and to it. In speaking, it can only wait for the '*Mitte*' of all true theology, a centre that no human being can master or control, the living person of Jesus Christ in the here and now.

Another important aspect to this early article is the level of 'natural theology' present in it. An introductory account would suggest that Barth, especially in this early period, was very critical of 'natural theology' and that he held a highly transcendent view of God, denying every point of contact between God and the world.[35] 'God is in heaven and you are on earth', as the preface to the second edition of the Letter to the Romans has it.[36] The dialectical method presented in this 1922 article would be ample evidence of this. We have to speak about God, but we cannot.

This, however, is a rather one-sided picture of what Barth says and does in this article. Throughout the text, one can notice how thoroughly Barth was acquainted and reckoned with the theology of his audience and how carefully he plays with their theology of culture throughout his argument. In spite of all the rhetorical pestering of his audience, Barth also makes a profound appeal to their anthropocentric concerns by stressing time and again that the Gospel is not something completely foreign to human longing, to human experience and to human culture. Quite to the contrary, what human beings long for, what a minister of the Word is asked for, what the basis of human culture is is something from the outside but at the same time fully human:

> We have misunderstood our office if we fail to see it as an index and sign of the truth. We must see it as a distress signal of the dilemma that extends over the *entire* range of actual and possible human circumstances in which the human finds himself as one among many: the moral *with* the immoral, the spiritual *with* the unspiritual, the pious *with* the impious, the human in his humanity, which means limitedness, temporality, creatureliness, and separation from God, whether he knows it or not. His situation only gets worse the less aware he is, the less he can tell us what he is missing. It then becomes easier for his fellow human, who is eager to help, to misunderstand him. The human in his humanity cries out for God, not for *a* truth, but for *the* Truth, not for *something* good, but for *the* Good, not for answers but for *the* Answer that is directly connected to his questions. For he himself, the human, is the question. Therefore the answer must be the *question*. It must be *himself*, but himself as answer, as answered question. The human does not cry for solutions, but for

---

35. See e.g. Stanley J. Grenz and Roger E. Olson, *20th Century Theology: God & the World in a Transitional Age* (Downers Grove, IL: InterVarsity, 1992), 68–9.

36. Karl Barth, *Der Römerbrief: zweite Fassung, 1922*, ed. Cornelis van der Kooi and Katja Tolstaja, Karl Barth-Gesamtausgabe 47 (Zürich: Theologischer Verlag, 2010), 17.

salvation, not for something human again, but for God as the Saviour of his *humanity*.[37]

Barth's Christocentrism is in fact already in play here, but it is interwoven with a theology of culture with which his audience was well acquainted. What human beings are longing for is the very person of Christ! Theology, in the way in which it responds to human longing, experience and culture, must be a Christocentric theology. This Christocentric figure is present as early as 1922, but, as van 't Slot and others have shown, it is not the Christocentrism we find in the later Barth.[38]

So far so good for our analysis of Barth himself. In the remainder of this section, I will attempt to bring this article to bear on my exploration of the role of Law and Gospel as instruments for doing systematic theology. The article also offers an interesting insight for our interest in Christocentrism and the role of Law and Gospel. This insight has to do with how precisely we interpret the Christocentrism running through this dialectical-theological method. There are two ways of interpreting it.

The first could be formulated as follows: Since we must be able to speak of God from a theological perspective, a dialectical method of theologizing implies that we have to look at each theological question from two, in principle, contradicting sides. We do that because we know that our human language and human understanding are fundamentally unable to grasp the reality of God in

---

37. Barth, 'Word of God', 179; original emphases. Barth, 'Wort Gottes', 154–5:

> Wir haben unser Amt als Theologen nicht verstanden, solange wir es nicht verstanden haben als Exponenten und Wahrzeichen, nein Notzeichen einer Verlegenheit, die über die ganze Skala wirklicher und möglicher menschlicher Zuständlichkeiten sich ausbreitet, in der sich also der moralische mit dem unmoralischen, der geistige mit dem ungeistigen, der fromme mit dem unfrommen Menschen, in der sich der Mensch einfach als Mensch befindet. Der Mensch in seiner Menschlichkeit, die als solche Beschränktheit, Endlichkeit, Kreatürlichkeit, Getrenntheit von Gott bedeutet, ob er sich dessen nun mehr oder weniger bewußt sei. Seine Lage ist um so schlimmer, je weniger er sich dessen bewußt ist, je weniger er es uns sagen kann, was ihm fehlt, je leichter ihn die hilfsbereite Mitmenschheit mißversteht. Der Mensch als Mensch schreit nach Gott, nicht nach *einer* Wahrheit, sondern nach *der* Wahrheit, nicht nach *etwas* Gutem, sondern nach *dem* Guten, nicht nach Antworten, sondern nach der Antwort, die unmittelbar eins ist mit seiner Frage. Denn er selbst, der *Mensch*, ist ja die Frage, so muß die Antwort die *Frage* sein, sie muß er *selbst* sein, aber nun als Antwort, als beantwortete Frage. Nicht nach Lösungen schreit er, sondern nach *Erlösung*. Nicht wiederum nach etwas Menschlichem, sondern nach Gott, aber nach Gott als dem Erlöser seiner *Menschlichkeit*.

38. Van 't Slot, 'Christologische Konzentration', 17–22.

our language and from our human perspective.³⁹ From a Christological viewpoint, this is appropriate because we must always speak Christologically with two words, namely from the perspective of Christ's divinity and humanity. These two perspectives can, therefore, never be rationally aligned.

The later Barth seems to interpret and construe his dialectical method in this way. A good example from the CD is the discussion of the knowledge of God in II/1, where Barth in section 25.1 carefully describes all knowledge of God as mediated, but then in 25.2 construes it on the basis of the true mediation of Christ, as direct and real and therefore in a certain sense unmediated. Similarly, in Barth's account of the essence of God in the same volume, he elaborates the concept of God at once from the notion of love and the notion of freedom.⁴⁰

But I also think there is a second way to interpret his dialectical method, particularly on the basis of the discussion of the '*Mitte*' at the end of this 1922 article. In the first interpretation, the Christocentric moment is actually already present in dialectics. The dialectic takes the form of the Christological dogma and speaks theologically in a certain way because Christ is a dialectical reality. In the second reading, Christ is not 'in' the 'yes' and 'no'. Christ is, as Barth himself puts it, the centre, the '*Mitte*'. Christ as such is always beyond what we say, whether that be a 'yes' or a 'no'. Christ is a person and what the Chalcedonian formula aims to do is protect our theological language from forgetting about this irreducible personality of Christ and turning him into a formula.⁴¹

Therefore, indeed through an application of the Chalcedonian formula, the 'yes' and 'no' intend to speak of theology and of Christ in such a way that Christ remains Christ, a living presence who can never be turned into a formula, but is this concrete person present among us in Word and sacraments? Everything else – God, creation, human beings and salvation – can never be conceived without this Light throwing light on it and qualifying it, because it determines their meaning, their destiny.

If we further elaborate this interpretation of the dialectical method in a way that Barth himself chose not to follow, it will have consequences for Christocentrism. Christocentrism does not mean that Christ is always the centre of every dogmatic locus, as Barth was indeed to do in his later work, as we will see below. What it means is that Christ is the centre, around which Christ is often *not* spoken of. After all, if Christ is in the middle, then, in order to do justice to that centre, there are all kinds of other themes in Christian faith and theology that are not primarily and explicitly about Christ. These other loci are connected to Christ, however, and they shed light on and co-determine the meaning of Christ as the centre of theological

---

39. Michael Beintker describes this way as the later form of dialectics in Barth: Beintker, 'Der Dialektiker als Dogmatiker', 209.

40. Barth, *CD*, II/1, section 28.

41. Cf. Maarten Wisse, *Trinitarian Theology Beyond Participation: Augustine's de Trinitate and Contemporary Theology*, T&T Clark Studies in Systematic Theology 11 (London: T&T Clark International, 2011), 147–8.

and religious thinking. To use a famous dictum from the Dutch theologian Arnold van Ruler, who intended something similar but with a different outcome: 'in Christian faith, it's about creation, but revolves around Christ'.[42]

Theology is, on the one hand, a discourse in which we give words to the mystery that has come to us in Christ. In that respect, the Gospel is a testimony to the reality of God's acts in Christ. On the other hand, theology is a qualification of God's acts in Christ in terms of God's acts in creation and God's commandments given in the Law. Accordingly, theology aims to protect the mystery of God's acts in creation and Christ as the '*Mitte*' of theology. As such, Christ is at the very centre, more radically so than we find him in Barth, especially in his later work. Christ is in the middle, and we should not attempt to capture God in Christ in Christological language, but we ought to try to respect God's current and actual presence by balancing out the language of the Gospel with the language of the Law. The Law provides language emphasizing that God is always different from us, while the Gospel bears witness to the fact that the reality of God has truly entered our human reality.

I am well aware that this line of reasoning goes beyond Barth and even reads him against the grain of his own writing, but I would like to suggest that it offers an alternative trajectory from this 1922 lecture that would avoid what I see as pitfalls in Barth's theology, even if Barth himself partly succeeds in circumventing them himself (cf. below). One of the reasons why he succeeds in this is the fact that he very much avoids over-systematizing his own theology.

Of course, part of the price to pay for my alternative reading from the 1922 article is that dogmatics can no longer be reduced to Christology. If we are to do Christology appropriately, then the specificity of Christology over against the other loci must be bolstered and protected rather than undone. If we want to receive an appropriate view of what it means to say that God became a creature, an ordinary human being, then for us to have a proper understanding of the significance of this insight it is crucial to have an independent, non-Christologically defined idea of what creation is, and even who God is, and who human beings are, because it is the distinction between God and creation, the goodness of creation, the moral nature of human beings and truly creaturely destiny that determine what Christ does in restoring this destiny. This is not an awful defence of natural theology but rather a sincere confession of the fact that if we receive creation from God, it must be allowed to have a theological significance, preceding and thereby qualifying God's incarnation in Jesus Christ.

My proposed alternative reading may also imply that a price must be paid with respect to Barth's idea of having to speak about God, but not being able to. It implies a potential critique of the overarching character of negative theology.[43]

---

42. See e.g. A. A. van Ruler, *Verzameld werk*, ed. D. van Keulen, vol. 4A (Zoetermeer: Boekencentrum, 2011), 139–65. The nuance of the original Dutch dictum is difficult to express in another language: 'Het gaat om de schepping en het draait om Christus.'

43. Wisse, *Trinitarian Theology*, 88–93.

If practiced in the way apparently suggested by Barth's two maxims, negative theology becomes all encompassing.

An altogether negative theology is difficult to practice, precisely because it is all encompassing. If you have to take back everything you say, also on the fundamental level, it raises the question of what you actually want to say.[44] For this reason, I have the impression that even Barth's own followers hardly practice this radical dialectical approach. In Barth, this approach works out positively because he, in spite of it, still offers so many ingenious insights that we continue to read his texts anyway and, moreover, can continue to use them in all sorts of different ways, depending on a particular line of thought we want to pursue. In this sense, the strongly dialectical nature of Barth's theology partially explains the broad scope of his reception. Moreover, in the end, Barth himself does not persist in his dialectics, either. It was not without reason that Berkouwer spoke about the triumph of grace in Barth's theology.[45]

But this notion of the triumph of grace as a step beyond the dialectic also immediately signals the accompanying problems. After all, the earlier Barth had good reasons to opt so decidedly for his radical dialectics. Choosing one of the two poles of the dialectic in fact means nothing less than grasping absolute power, since the 'yes' of the Gospel then unqualifiedly outdoes the 'no' of the Law. This leads precisely to the consequence of Barth's teaching regarding the triumph of grace. It leads to universalism, even though Barth usually refused to draw that conclusion.[46] It is not without reason that I plead elsewhere in this book for the doctrine of double predestination. This plea was partly prompted by a resistance to the universalism of twentieth-century theology prompted by the triumph of grace in Barth's theology, even though Barth himself was most often wise enough to reject it.

Methodologically, a strict dialectic represents a difficult starting point. Elsewhere I have argued for designating two specific areas in systematic theology as being particularly bound to forms of negative theology: Christology and the doctrine of the Trinity.[47] The fact that theological discourse is neither Christological nor Trinitarian in an overarching way ensures that such discourse is not dominated by negative theology from beginning to end. Sometimes theology can and must

---

44. Cf. Vincent Brümmer, *Speaking of a Personal God: An Essay in Philosophical Theology* (Cambridge: Cambridge University Press, 1992), chapter 2.

45. Cf. G. C. Berkouwer, *De triomf der genade in de theologie van Karl Barth* (Kampen: J. H. Kok, 1954).

46. For the discussion of Barth's universalism, see Suzanne McDonald, *Re-imaging Election: Divine Election as Representing God to Others and Others to God* (Grand Rapids, MI: Eerdmans, 2010); Tom Greggs, *Barth, Origen, and Universal Salvation: Restoring Particularity* (Oxford: Oxford University Press, 2009); and van 't Slot, *Negativism of Revelation?*, 181–2.

47. Wisse, *Trinitarian Theology*, chapters 2 and 3.

speak. At other times it should not speak contradictorily but keep silent or speak negatively about what God, Christ or this world are not.

Such discourse differs fundamentally from speaking about God in contradictions. In the latter, one says all kinds of things about God, Christ and this world, pretending that these things are true statements that are only qualified by the fact that one at the same time also confirms the opposite. At the end of the day, it means constantly speaking in heresies that one recognizes as such and with consequences that one very clearly sees, as was the case with Barth. Such an approach. however, is not only difficult to take seriously but also ignores the real risks associated with those heresies. We do not reject certain theological ways of speaking simply because we think they do not correspond to the truth of the Gospel on the level of theory. Rather, we reject them because they are associated with practices of belief and morals that are potentially harmful to the integrity of the Christian community and society at large.[48]

4.6 'The first commandment as theological axiom' (1933)

After this extensive discussion of Barth's dialectical method, we proceed to another article that antedates the CD, and, according to the current scholarly consensus, also comes before or stands at the beginning of the decisive turn towards Barth's mature Christocentrism. The article in question dates from 1933, going back to lectures he gave in Copenhagen and Aarhus in Denmark during the month of March in that same year. These were the turbulent years following Hitler's rise to power, when Barth still served as professor at the University of Bonn and the struggle of the Confessing Church was beginning to take shape.[49]

It would be surprising to find this 1933 article absent from the present discussion of Barth. In it, around the time of the Barmen Declaration, Barth can be found defending the thesis – or so at least it seems – that the Decalogue, and more specifically the first commandment, must be the criterion of Christian theology. Implicitly, one might conclude, this would imply that it is not Christology, or at least not Christology alone, which Barth is designating as the criterion of theology. But as we will see, a close reading of the article leaves no doubt that this is not at all the argument Barth is trying to make. Yet it is still worth seeing where he is headed instead. In the introduction to his lecture, Barth announces the programmatic significance of the first commandment as follows:

---

48. Cf. chapter 1, section 5. See also Maarten Wisse, 'De integratie van theologie en religiewetenschap in Stefan Paas' Vreemdelingen en priesters: De Utrechtse theologische faculteit in de jaren '90', *Soteria* 35, no. 1 (2018): 19–31.

49. For the historical context of this essay, see Karl Barth, *Vorträge Und Kleinere Arbeiten, 1930–1933*, ed. Michael Beintker, Michael Hüttenhoff and Peter Zocher, Karl Barth-Gesamtausgabe 49 (Zürich: Theologischer Verlag, 2013), 209–14.

If there is also an axiom of *theology*, as the title of this address implies, then what is meant is this: theology too rests in regard to the proof of its statements on an ultimate and decisive presupposition. As such, it can neither be proven nor is it in need of proof. It contains in itself everything which is necessary for its proof.[50]

At first sight, we might indeed be surprised to find Barth taking his starting point in the Decalogue here, given that we have already seen him in 1922 very much developing his theology from a Christocentric point of view, albeit in a less mature form. Yet such surprise is not altogether justified. For it is also a worthwhile confirmation of what we have argued before, namely that Barth's theology developed in a much more rhetorical manner than one might think. It is significant that Barth delivered the lecture as the basis of this article in Aarhus and Copenhagen, suggesting a predominantly Lutheran audience. Contemporary theologians may assume – partly due to their training in the tradition of Barth's theology! – that there is little separating a Reformed and a Lutheran frame of reference, but this would be an anachronistic misunderstanding. Barth was very aware of his audience, not, as we have seen above, in the sense that he adapted his views to the argument of his audience, but in that he responded to and built on the set of presuppositions expected by his audience, often by playing creatively with them, and even turning them upside down, but still always taking them seriously.

In the 1933 article, Barth does this with Luther's interpretation of the Decalogue, in particular as it appears in the Large Catechism.[51] Luther connects the first commandment and the concept of God by suggesting that the thing in which we trust, to which our heart clings, is our God.[52] The one true God, however, is the God of revelation, the God who became incarnate in Jesus Christ. Believing in God does not simply mean adhering to a principle or a set of propositions, but it is the trust of one's heart. This is why faith in God, entrusting oneself to the true God, revealed in Christ on the cross, is the only way to fulfil the Law and the first commandment.[53] Barth does refer to Calvin as well, but his fundamental line of reasoning has its place within the Lutheran theology of the Decalogue. Barth

---

50. Karl Barth, 'The First Commandment as an Axiom of Theology', in *The Way of Theology in Karl Barth: Essays and Comments*, ed. H. Martin Rumscheidt, Princeton Theological Monographs 8 (Allison Park, PA: Pickwick, 1986), 63; original emphasis. Karl Barth, 'Das erste Gebot als theologisches Axiom', in *Gottes Freiheit für den Menschen. Eine Auswahl der Vorträge, Vorreden und kleinen Schriften* (Berlin, 1970), 132: 'Wenn es, wie der Titel meines Vortrages behauptet, auch ein theologisches Axiom gibt, so ist damit gesagt: auch die Theologie beruht hinsichtlich des Beweises ihrer Sätze auf einer letzten entscheidenden Voraussetzung, die als solche weder bewiesen werden kann noch bewiesen zu werden nötig hat, sondern die Alles zu ihrem Beweise Nötige selber sagt.'
51. Barth, 'First Commandment', 69.
52. Luther, 'Large Catechism', 581.
53. Ibid., 583, 585.

makes an attempt to show that it is not the modern Protestants of the time but his own theology of revelation that has the true reading of Luther.

Barth links up the key notions of his own theology with Luther's reading of the first commandment. All key notions of this theology from the 1930s are covered: a powerful critique of *Neuprotestantismus*, a strong emphasis on the distinction between ordinary human reasoning and science, and Christian theological reasoning, and, finally, a Christocentric theology that is more revelation centric and Word oriented than Christocentric in the proper sense of the term.[54] The latter is evident, for example, in that the first key aspect of the theological axiom which Barth emphasizes is that it is *written*:

> The first commandment '*is written*' in Exodus 20. It is essential to the axiom of theology that it 'is written', that it is part of the document in relation to which the church exists as the church in the world. The church exists in her reading and proclaiming this document as the unique witness of God's unique revelation, in reading, proclaiming and reading again, proclaiming, reading and proclaiming again. In this movement of life of the church, theology also exists. For this reason, the statements of theology basically can be only interpretation.[55]

This language about the Word of God is embedded in a persistent emphasis on what is now known as Barth's actualism. Faith in God is not faith in a principle. The theological axiom of the first commandment is actualistic, it is historical, pointing to a God who reveals himself concretely, who always speaks, in Barth's words, a 'Konkretissimum'.

Along with these notions that we know from this period, however, it is fascinating to find Barth deriving virtually every other aspect of his later theology just from the first commandment here. We see the typical language of his later doctrine of election in the form of the claim that the first commandment involves God's self-determination to be God with us, which is so typical of Barth's doctrine of God in CD II/1.[56] To believe in God along the lines of the first commandment

---

54. McCormack, 'Christonomie', 226; cf. also van 't Slot, 'Christologische Konzentration', 23–5.

55. Barth, 'First Commandment', 64–5; Barth, 'Das erste Gebot', 133–4:

> Das erste Gebot 'steht geschrieben' im 20. Kapitel des Buches Exodus. Es ist dem theologischen Axiom wesentlich, daß es 'geschrieben steht', das heißt, daß es Bestandteil der Urkunde ist, auf die bezogen die Kirche in der Welt als Kirche existiert. Die Kirche existiert, indem sie diese Urkunde als das alleinige Zeugnis von Gottes alleiniger Offenbarung liest und verkündigt und wieder liest, verkündigt und liest und wieder verkündigt. In dieser Lebensbewegung der Kirche existiert auch die Theologie. Darum kann ihre Voraussetzung nur sein, was 'geschrieben steht'; darum können ihre Sätze grundsätzlich nur Auslegung sein.

56. Barth, 'First Commandment', 67–8.

does not just mean to believe in a detached principle but to entrust oneself to the mercy of God in Jesus Christ, a thesis that must have rang a strongly Lutheran bell among his audience.

We also hear, however, that believing in God is about obeying a commandment.[57] One is '*aufgefordert*', to follow, to obey the God who calls us from sin and alienation. Faith is obedience, and for this reason ethics follows dogmatics, as Barth paradigmatically shows in CD II/2, elaborating on it in later volumes. God's choice for us (the doctrine of election) is immediately followed by our obedience (the commandments).

In short, even if he is developing all these notions from the perspective of the first commandment, Barth shows himself to be a good Lutheran by interpreting the commandment as the sum of the Gospel rather than the basis of works righteousness. Instead of emphasizing the distinction between Law and Gospel, Barth draws on the parallel between the Law as promise and God's fulfilment of this promise on the cross. Although, as we have seen, he in CD II/1 criticizes the tradition for the idea of revelation next to natural theology, in 1933 he still defends the Reformers for their approach to natural law and natural knowledge of God, duly recognizing that their theology differed substantially from that of his arch enemy *Neuprotestantismus*:

> If theology is aware of its responsibility but deems it necessary to relate the concept of revelation to some other criterion, which for some reason is important, by means of that little but weighty word 'and', then this responsibility will express itself by speaking of revelation with a notably heightened seriousness and interest, and by speaking of that other criterion only secondarily and for the sake of revelation. In the obviously unequal distribution of its zeal and passion, theology will show plainly where its heart is and where it has its god, namely at the point where God, in the commandment, has placed himself. The reformers, as it is well known, did not refuse all recognition to nature, natural theology and natural religion. Nevertheless, it is quite plain where their heart and their god was in their quest for the foundation and law of the church. In recent Protestant theology however, from Buddeus and Pfaff to Hirsch and Althaus, Gogarten and Brunner, it is not clear whether or not their zeal and passion is meant for that other authority.[58]

57. Ibid., 70–1.
58. Barth, 'First Commandment', 73; Barth, 'Das erste Gebot', 141:

> Wenn die Theologie, wissend um ihre Verantwortlichkeit, es für nötig hält, den Begriff der Offenbarung mittels des auf alle Fälle folgenschweren Wörtleins,und'zu einer andern aus irgendeinem Grund für wichtig gehaltenen Instanz in Beziehung zu setzen, dann wird sich diese Verantwortlichkeit dahin zeigen, daß sie in merklich erhöhtem Ernst und Interesse von der Offenbarung, und nur beiläufig und um der Offenbarung willen von jener andern Instanz reden wird. In der merklich ungleichen Verteilung ihres

The juxtaposition of Barth's Christocentrism and his interest in the first commandment is most beautifully rendered in a statement about the status of the first commandment as a theological axiom:

> When we speak here and now of no other than the first commandment, we identify a quite specific passage of that document. We believe that there we hear very clearly the axiom of theology. Of course, we could hear it in other passages in the document. We could cite as the axiom of theology John 1:14 ('The Word became flesh, he dwelt among us, and we beheld his glory') or Matthew 11:28 ('Come to me, all who labour and are heavy laden') or 2 Corinthians 5:19 ('God was in Christ reconciling the world to himself'). All these verses tell us basically what the first commandment tells us. Nothing is said in the first commandment that is not also said in those versions in their own manner and in their own context.[59]

What was Barth after in this talk, which was held only weeks after Hitler came to power in Germany in 1933? He is aiming to secure the uniqueness of revelation over against humanity and culture. The Gospel does not come from human beings, has no linking pin to which a connection can be made. That is why the first commandment is a theological axiom, a point of departure from the outside. The words come to us, and we have not created them ourselves. All the words we ourselves make are idols in the light of the first commandment. Here Barth is on his way to the insight that he will later express in the first Barmen thesis: we

---

> Eifers und ihres Pathos wird sie zeigen, wo sie ihr Herz, wo sie ihren Gott hat: daß sie ihn da hat, wo er in seinem Gebot sich selber hingestellt hat. Es ist bei den Reformatoren, die bekanntlich der Natur, dem Naturrecht und der natürlichen Religion nicht jede Anerkennung versagt haben, ganz klar, wo sie bei ihrer Frage nach dem Grund und Gesetz der Kirche ihr Herz und also ihren Gott haben. Es ist aber in der neueren protestantischen Theologie von Buddeus und Pfaff bis und mit Hirsch und Althaus, Gogarten und Brunner nicht klar, ob ihr Eifer und ihr Pathos nicht vielmehr jener andern Instanz gilt.

59. Barth, 'First Commandment', 65; Barth, 'Das erste Gebot', 134:

> Wir schlagen, in dem wir hier und heute gerade das erste Gebot namhaft machen, eine ganz bestimmte Stelle dieser Urkunde auf, weil wir in ihr das theologische Axiom besonders deutlich zu hören meinen. Wir könnten es gewiß auch an andern Stellen hören. Wir könnten auch das Wort Joh. 1,14:'Das Wort ward Fleisch und wohnte unter uns und wir sahen seine Herrlichkeit', wir könnten auch das Wort Matth. 11, 28:'Kommet her zu mir alle, die ihr mühselig und beladen seid!', wir könnten auch das Wort 2. Kor. 5, 19:'Gott war in Christus und versöhnte die Welt mit ihm selber'als das theologische Axiom angeben, weil alle diese Worte uns grundsätzlich nichts anderes zu hören geben als das erste Gebot und weil im ersten Gebot nichts anderes gesagt ist, als was alle jene Worte an ihrem Ort und in ihrer Weise auch sagen.

are expected to obey only one person, and that is God who reveals himself in Jesus Christ. Barth perceives, here especially in conversation with the Lutheran tradition, that this contention is somehow related to the first commandment. In this, he is helped by the close relationship which Luther draws between obeying the first commandment and having faith in Christ.

At the same time, quite a few loose ends remain. I see one such loose end emerge in the last passage cited above, where Barth identifies the message of the first commandment without reservation with the message of Jn 1.14, Mt. 11.28 and 2 Cor. 5.19. I would like to raise two concerns in Barth's move to see no difference between the first commandment and Jn 1.14 when it comes to the recognition of both as potential candidates as axiom of theology. The question one might raise is whether that identification does not proceed too fast, and, secondly, whether it does not lead to the very opposite of what Barth actually wants to achieve.

The first question is rather modest: even if faith as obedience to the revelation of God is the fulfilment of the first commandment, this does not mean that the proclamation of the first commandment is identical to the proclamation of the Gospel that Barth sees exposed in the above passages from the New Testament. The content of the first commandment is a commandment, a claim on human beings. That requirement may come from the outside, but that does not necessarily make it identical to the second word that God speaks, the word of the Gospel. Barth does identify the two with each other here, and this is characteristic of his theology. Here in 1933 he does so from the first commandment; he identifies the commandment with the Gospel. In 1934, with the Barmen Declaration, as we have seen, he does it again, but then from the side of the Gospel, by identifying everything that God has ever said and all we have ever obeyed with the person of Jesus Christ. The upshot of this is that an important sensitivity to the duality of Law and Gospel ends up getting lost. Hans-Joachim Iwand, a renowned Lutheran theologian of the time, pointed to the loss of this Law-Gospel duality in his commentary on the first Barmen thesis in a very friendly but resolute manner.[60] In the Lutheran tradition, the dynamics of Law and Gospel continue to exist in a way that disappeared in Barth.

Barth seems to be overlooking something, namely the difference in kind of what God speaks. He pretends that the only thing that matters is the question of whether or not God speaks 'from the other side', determined as he is to this by the Enlightenment frame of reference inherited from his context. Barth's struggle is to find the courage to say that God indeed speaks in a post-Kantian context, and to dare to start his theological undertaking from that other side. But because of that, he has no eye for the question of whether and how that word from that other side relates to and is differentiated from us. In his view, it must by definition be a word either from our side or from the other side. But he goes along with that in a Kantian construct that is hardly compelling in its own right and is moreover

---

60. Hans-Joachim Iwand, 'Die 1. Barmer These und die Theologie Martin Luthers', *Evangelische Theologie* 46, no. 3 (1986): 214–31.

problematic in view of a Christian doctrine of creation. Why should the word that comes to us from creation not also be a word that God speaks to us? Besides, Barth neglected the difference in kind between God's revelation as Law and Gospel.

If the word that God speaks in the Law is not directly a word of mercy but a demand from God to us, appealing to our place as creatures before God, it is a word that, even if in keeping with our nature, does not necessarily come from our nature as the content of our salvation. For this we need a second word that, although it enters our reality as a proclamation of our salvation, does not necessarily coincide with that reality. God does not speak one word but speaks at different moments, and those moments are not necessarily of the same kind, although both qualify as revelation. The Gospel testifies to God's grace in Christ and invites faith, while the Law demands and appeals to our creaturely condition. This differentiated way of speaking is, as I hope to show in the rest of this book, necessary in our context and under the conditions of the twenty-first century.

This leads to a second problem. By not differentiating between Law and Gospel,[61] Barth runs into problems that he is at pains to avoid. Barth's identification of Gospel and Law leads to a generalization of the Gospel and therefore jeopardizes his actualism and its Christocentric nature. A close reading of the entire of this article, even if beyond the scope of this chapter, will show that it makes a choice between entrusting oneself to the gracefulness of creation and to Jesus Christ on the cross an almost arbitrary one. If everything is Christocentric, then faith is not so much a specific relationship to Jesus Christ on the cross for a specific reason (i.e. sin), but it is a general 'attitude' of entrustment towards life. This is because, if God speaks only one word, the nature of faith is defined by accepting, believing and embracing this word. What the content of that single message is is no longer relevant. It comes from the outside, and that is what counts. In this sense, Barth is not as far removed from an existentialist theology as his polemics against anthropocentric theologies would suggest. Barth reception, and perhaps especially the postmodern reception, shows how Barthian lines of reasoning can slip into a generalized incarnational theology.[62] This is no coincidence. The root of this is already present in Barth himself. If God speaks two words of two different kinds, the specific relationship between these two words and kinds determines the nature of one's response to it. Faith in Christ is

---

61. Or more precisely: 'By now not differentiating sufficiently' – this observation is based on Barth's remark here on the first commandment and the New Testament passages. As I have shown in chapter 3, Barth does distinguish between Gospel and Law, but even then he embeds the Law in the Gospel. This leaves my argument in this paragraph intact. It could even be reinforced by a more precise analysis of the meaning of the 'Law' in Barth's theology, where it refers to following the divine actions in Christ rather than the concrete commandments of the Decalogue. This leads to a much more 'inward' and 'intentional' concept of 'Law' in Barth than a more robust distinction between Law and Gospel would allow for, reinforcing the 'existentialist' thrust of his theology.

62. Cf. Wisse, *Trinitarian Theology*, chapter 1.

not primarily one's trust into a word from the outside, it is our response to Christ's specific invitation in the Gospel, fulfilling the demands of the Law, thus turning us away from evil and putting us on the path of justice.

4.7 'Three basic patterns of theology' (1936)

As a penultimate step in our journey through Barth's developing Christocentrism, we make a stop at the lecture Barth gave at the University of Basel in 1936, which goes back to a series of lectures delivered in Paris as early as April 1934, only a year after his Copenhagen lecture.[63] These were turbulent times, both in 1933 and 1934, the time when the Barmen Declaration was written and eventually accepted, and the conflict with Brunner over natural theology came to full force. By 1936, Barth had left Germany and returned to Switzerland.

As we saw in the previous section, Barth did not deal with Jn 14.6 in his Denmark lecture but referred rather to Jn 1.14 as a key verse of the New Testament witness. In the 1936 Basel lecture, it is Jn 14.6 that comes to take centre stage as it provides the basic structure. After introducing the object of theology as the basis for every true theology, which Barth now explicitly identifies as Jesus Christ, he proceeds with a discussion of three moments of true theology – the way, the truth and the life – enveloping all three of them in a discussion of freedom. The reference to Jn 14.6 is not even explicit, and it is linked to Jn 1.14 as if to designate these two words from John as the matrix for all true theology:

> Jesus has called himself the *way* according to the same Gospel in which it is said, that the Word became flesh.[64]

Barth's reading of Jn 14.6 is very associative. The three labels 'Way', 'Truth' and 'Life' are more appropriately associated with Hegel's 'thesis-antithesis-synthesis', or as exegesis, systematic theology and practical theology, than they are a serious interpretation of Jn 14.6 or a reflection on the person of Jesus Christ. In spite of this, the 1936 lecture still contains a number of interesting insights for our aims. First of all, it is of course important to see that Barth, having bound theology to the first commandment in his Denmark lectures, now seems to be suggesting that a Christological foundation alone is sufficient and necessary:

> The subject of theological thinking, from which it receives its basic forms, however ..., is the reality in which the Christian Church is rooted, the reality

---

63. Karl Barth, *God Is God: zes voordrachten uit 1930–1936*, trans. Nico T. Bakker (Kampen: J. H. Kok, 2004), 123.

64. Karl Barth, 'Die Grundformen theologischen Denkens', in *Theologische Fragen und Antworten* (Zollikon: Evangelischer Verlag, 1957), 285: 'Er [Jesus Christus] hat sich selbst (nach demselben Evangelium, in welchem es heißt, daß das Wort Fleisch wurde) den *Weg* genannt.'

that shapes the substance of its life and the subject of its message: the man *Jesus Christ*. He is present in the here and now through the Holy Spirit in the witness of the Old and New Testament and thus, he is God himself in his truth. This is to say: in his revelation – God who reveals and judges human sin, takes it onto himself and forgives – God who gives the hope of eternal life and through this, takes the human being into his service.[65]

The difference is less striking than it might initially seem, however. As we have seen above, Barth sees no sharp distinction between the first commandment as axiom of theology, and New Testament key verses such as Jn 1.14. In the above quotation, we see that the Holy Spirit testifies to the man Jesus Christ in both the Old and the New Testaments.

In this 1936 lecture, we once again find a powerful concern for the basis of theology in revelation. Barth is here, as before, very worried about a theology that starts from below, from human experience or human thinking. The starting point must be revelation, or, more concretely, the 'way', Jesus Christ.

For our attempt to go beyond Barth, it is interesting to see how he, in the two steps that follow 'the way', distinguishes between the truth and the life in a sense that seems to resonate with the way in which I distinguish between Law and Gospel. The second moment that he introduces, the moment of truth, is particularly centred around the critical role of theology. From the perspective of the encyclopaedia of theology, the basic form of truth is associated with systematic theology:

> Secondly, theological thinking must be a differentiating, Greek: *critical* thinking. It must differentiate what it has heard, listening to those documents, from what the past, and in particular the present, has put into or in addition to these. It must distinguish in the service of that object, in the midst of it, what the Church believes it is supposed to say today: that which is its own from that which is alien to it and therefore the divine glory from the well and less well-meant pseudo glories which want to push in their place, and so, the truth from error and lies.[66]

---

65. Ibid., 284; original emphasis:

> Der Gegenstand des theologischen Denkens, von dem es seine Grundformen empfängt, ist aber ... diejenige Wirklichkeit, in der die christliche Kirche begründet ist, die die Substanz ihres Lebens und die den Inhalt ihrer Botschaf bildet: der Mensch *Jesus Christus*, durch den Heiligen Geist im Zeugnis des Alten und Neuen Testamentes heute gegewärtig wie gestern und so God selbst in seiner Wahrheit, will sagen: in seiner Offenbarung – Gott, der des Menschen Sünde aufdeckt und richtet, auf sich selbst nimmt und vergibt – Gott, der dem Menschen die Hoffnung ewigen Lebens gibt und ihn eben damit in seinen Dienst nimmt.

66. Ibid., 286; original emphases:

> Theologisches Denken muß also zweitens ein unterscheidendes, griechisch: ein *kritisches* Denken sein. Unterscheiden muß es nämlich das, was es, auf jene

Although Barth seems to associate the three basic forms of theology with three theological subdisciplines, he still does not want to reserve the critical task of theology for systematic theology. A little later on, he brings this to bear on the role of exegesis in theology and the possibility of an overly exegetical theology:

> The task of biblical interpretation, if one wanted to overlook this second form of theological thinking, could be misunderstood as a mere inventory of distant, past things as such. A biblical and ecclesiastical historicism – perhaps suspiciously poor in its succession of incomprehensible facts, or perhaps also suspiciously rich in the magnificence of any elevation of intellectual history, one way or another producing blind views – could take the place where the testimony of God's revelation is to be interpreted: neutral towards the question of truth, to which revelation does not allow us to be neutral.[67]

What this makes clear is that an allegedly biblical theology can go wrong. This is nothing new insofar as it points to a well-known aspect of Barth's hermeneutics: a critique of historicism, and an emphasis on the 'Sache', the subject matter, of the text, instead. It is still interesting in the sense that Barth shows himself to be well aware that theology is much more than an explanation of the meaning of the biblical texts. Theology has to see sharply. One might say that within the biblical witness, Barth sees two instruments to take on the task of speaking theologically in the present: a critical focus on where theology goes wrong (i.e. a critique of all sorts of idolatries), and the Good News of salvation in Christ. This second instrument is then discussed in the third part of the lecture, on Jesus Christ as 'Life'. Accordingly, theology does indeed need to be scriptural, but in order to be truly scriptural, it needs a critical instrument that separates helpful readings of Scripture for the

> Urkunden hörend, vernommen hat, von dem, was die Vergangenheit und insbesondere die jeweilige Gegenwart einlegend oder sonst aus freiem Gutdünken danebengestellt hat. Unterscheiden muß es im Dienste jenes Gegenstandes inmitten dessen, was die Kirche heute sagen zu sollen glaubt: das diesem Gegenstand Eigene von dem ihm Fremden und also die göttliche Herrlichkeit von den gut und weniger gut gemeinten Pseudoherrlichkeiten, die sich an deren Stelle drängen wollen, und also die Wahrheit vom Irrtum und von der Lüge.

67. Ibid., 286–7:

> Es könnte ja die Aufgabe der biblischen Auslegung, wenn man diese zweite Form des theologischen Denkens übersehen wollte, mißverstanden werden als eine bloße Bestandesaufnahme ferner, vergangener Dinge als solcher. Es könnte ein biblischer und kirchengeschichtlicher Historismus – vielleich verdächtig arm in seiner Aneinanderreihung unverstander Tatsachen, vielleich auch verdächtig reich in der Pracht irgendeines geistesgeschichtlichen Aufzugs, so oder so blinde Anschauungen produzierend – an die Stelle treten, wo das Zeugnis van Gottes Offenbarung auszulegen ist: neutral gegen die Wahrheitsfrage, der gegenüber uns gerade die Offenbarung keine Neutralität erlaubt.

present from unhelpful or erroneous ones. The helpful or unhelpful nature of this instrument cannot simply be argued on the basis of what we find in Scripture. It is fundamentally something that happens in the present, in the exchange between the data from the text and one's critical analysis of the signs of the times, culminating in the positive Good News of the Gospel.

When Barth takes the next step and speaks about Jesus Christ as 'Life', he addresses theology's aim towards the practice of the proclamation of the Gospel:

> The Church, whose thinking it is, becomes visible now as the community of the faithful, who, time and again, have to hear and are allowed to hear that as such they are not lost, but have eternal life.[68]

The lecture closes with a powerful emphasis on the theme of freedom in theology. Both at the beginning and at the end, Barth stresses that theology needs to be a free thinking about its object. In theology, Jesus Christ as the object of theological reflection forbids any attempt to speak final words. Again, Barth shows himself very concerned about the suggestion that theology would try to grasp its object as if it comprehended it from beginning to end, as if true theology were a once-and-for-all truthful copy of its object. Theology must be dynamic, or else, again, it will turn into idolatry. At the end of his lecture, Barth speaks about the mystery that belongs to the object of theology, not just the mystery of Christ, but the mystery of human life. In his eyes, this is also the reason why a certain plurality is worthwhile in theology, caused by the permissible one-sidedness of individual theologians. Sometimes, therefore, peace is possible where there are now too many polemics. On the other hand, when theology loses hold of its object, polemics are necessary where there is now often too much peace.

When we evaluate Barth's proposal for theology in terms of Jn 14.6, we see him struggling to derive both the affirmative and the critical aspects of theology from a single criterion and a single kind of revelation. Again, it is because Barth, now assisted by a Johannine discourse that poses such a single criterion to some extent, sees revelation primarily as a revelation of what is. What is, what God does in Christ, is our salvation, and it is from everything God does that we can and must derive what we want to say theologically. As a result, theology's task is to represent what God has done. Theology thus 'duplicates' reality in a way typical of an Enlightenment concept of knowledge: True is what corresponds to its object; true theology is theology that corresponds to the reality of God's revelation. Barth is very aware that this is not possible and that, moreover, such attempts insofar as they are attempted are forms of idolatry and power abuse. At the same time, he gives himself no other choice because he limits the Christian faith to the Gospel and the person of Jesus Christ. If Jesus Christ is both the critical criterion and

---

68. Ibid., 287: 'Die Kirche, deren Denken es ist, wird jetzt sichtbar als die Gemeinde der Glaubenden, die immer wieder hören müssen und hören dürfen, daß sie als solche nicht verloren sind, sondern das ewige Leben haben.'

the salvific subject matter of theology, then those two aspects of salvation in Christ are constantly competing with each other. This is why Barth puts so much emphasis on the theme of freedom. He is at pains to make sure that the salvation that appeared to us in Christ does not petrify, as if it were a stable representation of God in our human hands. On the contrary, he wants to ascertain that truth must be found every time anew, because it ought never to become a stable resource for our access to God.

But it is precisely from there that the emphasis on freedom in theology is actually very problematic, as if theology would be free to twist the truth of God's revelation in Jesus Christ, misrepresenting it, knowingly, and then do it again! From Barth's emphasis on the human, limited nature of theology by the simple inability of language to represent God, such is understandable, but from the fact that it is ultimately a question of really adequately proclaiming God's acts in Jesus Christ, it is highly problematic.

Now that we live in a post-Enlightenment era, we can try to speak about divine revelation in a different way. As such, we may also attempt to reach Barth's two goals for speaking theologically. On the one hand, to speak critically, and, on the other hand, to speak affirmatively. I propose to do so by locating the critical moment in the Law and the affirmative moment in the Gospel. First, God speaks through the Law, in line with our critical ability to distinguish between good and evil. Revelation ties in with our power to distinguish good from evil because we have become fallible human beings through sin. This is why we constantly need to be reminded of and confronted with the true Good. However, this reminder of and confrontation with the Good resonates with our conscience, and therefore fits in with what has been implanted in us at creation. The point here is not to represent and duplicate revelation in theology but to hear the call of the Law and to have our words and actions subjected to the criticism of the Law, not only practically and morally, but also theologically. It is then a matter of discovering and unmasking all of the moments in which we take what is of God, implicitly or explicitly, and domesticating it as if it were our own.

At the same time, God speaks a second word, a word of salvation and forgiveness. Here, too, the purpose of theology is only in a secondary sense to represent or duplicate that revelation. In its primary sense, theology is about investigating and confirming the depth of revelation and bearing witness to that revelation in new words. We do not have to represent the second word of salvation, because it is already among us as what and who it is, and, although among us, it can and must never coincide with us. It is and remains the Word of God, Jesus Christ, present among us in proclamation and sacrament. Nor does it make a claim towards affirmation as a proposition in the first place, although it certainly includes propositions,[69] but first and foremost theology has the character of a promise inviting us to entrust ourselves to it and embrace it. Theology, as a critical reflection on our faith, moves back and forth between these two poles of

---

69. Cf. also Chapter 9.

110 Reinventing Christian Doctrine

Law and Gospel. It examines our testimony to salvation in Jesus Christ, testing to see whether we appropriate that salvation too easily. It asks whether we serve other gods, other people or ourselves with the confession of our Lord on our lips. At the same time, Christian theology also inspires us to grow in communion with the Lord and in a deeper awareness of what God has done for us in Christ.

4.8 Christocentrism in the Church Dogmatics I/2

As a final step to close the circle, we will now have a look at Barth's Christocentric statements in CD I/2, published in 1938, one year before volume II/1, with which we opened this chapter. This step does not present a truly different track in comparison with the Basel lecture we just examined. In fact, the substance of Barth's argument in CD I/2 was probably written around the same time as the material for the Basel lecture, as both go back to the years 1933–4. After all, volume I/2 has its origins in the lectures Barth delivered during the winter semester of 1933/4, roughly half a year after the publication of the lecture on the first commandment as axiom of theology.[70] Right at the beginning of the Christology section in volume I/2, Barth makes a remarkable statement that could be seen as the formal expression of his mature Christocentrism, even though many would, of course, suggest that it would take until II/2 before Barth finally found the material expression of it in his doctrine of election. Regardless, we now seem to come upon a rather strict criterion for the task of a 'CD':

> A church dogmatics must, of course, be christologically determined as a whole and in all its parts, as surely as the revealed Word of God, attested by Holy Scripture and proclaimed by the Church, is its one and only criterion, and as surely as this revealed Word is identical with Jesus Christ. If dogmatics cannot regard itself and cause itself to be regarded as fundamentally Christology, it has assuredly succumbed to some alien sway and is already on the verge of losing its character as church dogmatics.[71]

Interestingly, Barth now no longer speaks only about the fact that Christian theology should be oriented towards its object, Jesus Christ, but he also speaks of

---

70. Barth, *Vorträge und kleinere Arbeiten, 1934–1935*, 550.
71. Barth, *CD*, I/2, 124; Barth, *KD*, I/2, 135:

> Eine kirchliche Dogmatik muß freilich im ganzen und in allen ihren Teilen christologisch bestimmt sein, so gewiß das von der Heiligen Schrift bezeugte und von der Kirche verkündigte offenbarte Wort Gottes ihr eines und einziges Kriterium ist und so gewiß dieses offenbarte Wort eben mit Jesus Christus identisch ist. Wenn die Dogmatik sich nicht grundsätzlich als Christologie versteht und verständlich zu machen weiß, dann ist sie gewiß irgendeiner Fremdherrschaft verfallen, dann steht sie gewiß schon im Begriff, ihren Charakter als kirchliche Dogmatik zu verlieren.

a dogmatics that ought to be wholly determined by 'Christology', and, if it is not, has been surrendering itself to a foreign lord. Immediately after this polemical statement, in the small print that follows, Barth sets his sights on natural theology and, in a departure from the Denmark lecture, not only points at Neo-Protestantism but also includes the entire theological tradition of the early Church, the Middle Ages and the Reformation. What they did was wrong, for they found a source of theological truth outside the person of Jesus Christ, even outside Christology as the theological language about the person of Christ. Apart from criticizing the pre-modern theological tradition, Barth also admits that the modern theological tradition of Ritschl and Schleiermacher did indeed develop a forerunner to his own Christocentrism, although that tradition was already so severely infected by 'natural theology' that the Christocentric direction could not bear real fruit:

> And so Schleiermacher's romantic conception of history and Ritschl's Kantian metaphysics on the one hand, and their christocentric efforts on the other, could only render each other unworthy of credence.[72]

In what follows, Barth develops the sum of the Gospel from the perspective of what he had already announced in the Denmark lecture as a verse paralleling the first commandment, namely Jn 1.14. Adumbrating his doctrine of God in CD II/1, Barth reads Jn 1.14 primarily through a dialectics of freedom and love, between God's enduring freedom and sovereign lordship on the one hand, and his condescending love and humanity on the other. More than in his later work, he stresses here the freedom of the incarnating God over the humanity of God, and emphasizes the primacy of the divinity over against the assumed humanity emphasized. But also here, Barth's Christocentrism implies that God is essentially God with us, because one cannot speak about God apart from the person of Jesus Christ, God and man, the Word made flesh. Towards the end of his discussion of Jn 1.14, Barth sketches the enduring tension in his theology between the freedom and humanity of God in terms of the two traditions – Lutheran and reformed – that come together in his theology, suggesting that these two traditions bear something of the necessary plurality, alluding to the plurality he had noted in his lecture on the three basic patterns of theology:

> Perhaps there can be no resting from the attempt to understand this ἐγένετο. Perhaps there can be no amicable compromise in Evangelical theology as regards the order of merit between these two views. Perhaps if it is to be Evangelical theology at all – and truly so, it may be, only when this necessity is perceived – there always has to be a static and a dynamic, an ontic and a noetic principle, not

---

72. Barth, *CD*, I/2, 124; Barth, *KD*, I/2, 135: 'Und so haben Schleiermachers romantische Geschichtsauffassung und Ritschls kantische Metaphysik auf der einen, ihre christozentrischen Bemühungen auf der anderen Seite sich nur gegenseitig unglaubwürdig machen können.'

in nice equilibrium, but calling to each other and questioning each other. That is, there must be Lutherans and Reformed: not in the shadow of a unitary theology, but as a twofold theological school – for the sake of the truth about the reality of Jesus Christ, which does not admit of being grasped or conceived by any unitary theology, which will always be the object of all theology, and so perhaps inevitably of a twofold theology – object in the strictest sense of the concept. It may even be that in the unity and variety of the two Evangelical theologies in the one Evangelical Church there is reflected no more and no less than the one mystery itself, with which both were once engrossed and will necessarily be engrossed always, the mystery that ὁ λόγος σάρξ ἐγένετο.[73]

Here we very clearly see again the way in which Barth tries to preserve his critical awareness of the fact that God's acts always come from God's side. But at the same time, it is becoming clear that he still sees theology and Christology as instruments of representation, as discourses aimed at duplicating the divine reality in theological discourse. Precisely his conviction that all our representations of the divine revelation in theological discourse go astray leads him to a plea for theology as an ongoing conversation between two conflicting discourses, as if this were the only way to remain aware of the limitation and sinfulness of our human discourse. As I have already argued above, things can and must be done differently. Barth's plea for two contradictory discourses does not do justice to the genuine contradictions that are present in the two discourses, and therefore does not do justice to the valid arguments each side has against the other. The price that must be paid for this is that readers will often pick those arguments from Barth's discourse that suit them best.

73. Barth, *CD*, I/2, 172; Barth, *KD*, I/2, 187:

> Es könnte ja auch sein, daß es um das Verständnis dieses ἐγένετο gerade keine Ruhe geben, daß es über die Rangordnung dieser beiden Anliegen innerhalb der evangelischen Theologie gerade zu keiner gütlichen Übereinkunft kommen darf, daß es hier, damit sie evangelische Theologie sei – und in der Einsicht dieser Notwendigkeit vielleicht erst recht werde – ein statisches und ein dynamisches, ein ontisches und ein noetisches Prinzip, nicht in schönem Gleichgewicht, sondern als gegenseitigen Ruf und als gegenseitige Frage (und also Lutheraner und Reformierte) immer geben muß: nicht im Schatten einer Einheitstheologie, sondern als zweifache theologische Schule. Um der Wahrheit der Wirklichkeit Jesus Christus willen, die sich von keiner Einheitstheologie einfangen und begreifen läßt, die aller Theologie – und darum vielleicht notwendig einer zweifachen Theologie Gegenstand sein und bleiben will: Gegenstand im strengsten Sinn des Begriffs. Es könnte ja sein, daß sich in der Einheit und Verschiedenheit der beiden evangelischen Theologien innerhalb der einen evangelischen Kirche nicht mehr und nicht weniger als das eine Geheimnis selbst spiegelt, um das sich beide einst bemüht haben und immer neu bemühen müssen: ὁ λόγος σάρξ ἐγένετο.

4.9 Barth and the Johannine tradition

By now, the circle has been closed. We started with the Barmen Declaration in its interpretation of CD II/1, seeing how Barth suggested that it was Jesus Christ himself who established Christocentrism in the Confessing Church of the 1930s, doing away with a theology of Christ and culture, faith and reason. Having recognized this interpretation of Barmen as a later rereading of the original events, we began a journey through Barth's earlier work to explore ways in which Christocentrism, the Gospel of John and alternative theological trajectories played a role in his earlier work. What we found was a Christocentric interest that is as old as the origins of his dialectical theology, providing already many of the building blocks for his later Christocentrism. Nevertheless, we also found explorations of ways of doing theology that were still not as strictly Christocentric as his expressions in CD II/1 and I/2 would suggest.

I hope that my argument has contributed to a reading of Barth's work that emphasizes the adventurous and creative nature of his theology, much in line with what the later Barth describes as his way of doing theology: saying the same things all over again, but every time in response to new questions and theological challenges, circling around the truth, hoping to touch the 'Mitte', but never being able to master it or to give the final answer. It is theology more as rhetoric (in the positive sense of the term) than 'systematic theology', as Barth himself criticizes that term in the basic patterns article.

What we have seen is an increasingly Johannine concentration in Barth's theological approach. Increasingly, he develops a Christological exclusivism that is primarily found in the Gospel of John. Mentioned first as a possible key verse, Jn 1.14 came to take centre stage in CD I/2. Likewise, Jn 14.6 initially was a prooftext for the first Barmen thesis suggested by others, but was subsequently used by Barth as a rather associative scheme for the setup of the basic patterns of theology, and reconceived as Jesus' own proclamation of Christocentrism in the interpretation of Barmen in CD II/1.

With a view to Barth's reception of the Gospel of John in terms of a Christocentric approach to the whole of dogmatics, I would like to propose an alternative. My contention is that Barth in this reception deviated considerably from the mainstream of the Christian tradition, a tradition that moderated the Christological exclusivism which can be found in the Gospel of John through an appeal to other voices in Scripture. Of course, there is as such no reason to follow the theological tradition in something, not even in moderating the radicality of the Gospel of John. As I will argue at greater length in the rest of this book, however, the tradition did so for all sorts of good reasons. Barth seems to be so one-sidedly concentrated on the risk of a Neo-Protestant anthropologization of the Christian faith that he applies John's Christological exclusivism to a refutation of it in the strongest possible way. As one might argue, however, heresies and theological problems mostly emerge from an overly radical concentration of one biblical voice over all the others, and it is this risk that Barth seems to overlook.

In fact, as I have argued before, Barth had an excellent opportunity to bring in a controlling voice that could moderate the Christological exclusivism of John, namely the Decalogue. As the earlier Barth was well aware, the old theology had good reasons for speaking about natural law and natural theology, even though this implied the presence of authorities and voices of revelation apart from the person of Jesus Christ. It was precisely because of what was written elsewhere in the Bible that these theologians had to acknowledge that the Gospel of John's radical Christocentrism had to be read in the context of Scripture as a whole.

Chapter 5

CONTRA ET PRO *SOLA SCRIPTURA*

5.1 Introduction

In Chapters 3 and 4, I have shown how the Law-Gospel distinction can be helpful for elucidating the role of Scripture in theology. The forms of Scripture management that interpreters of Scripture use in their work, even when they do not make them explicit, can be fruitfully understood in terms of the distinction. The current chapter brings the insights on Scripture management gathered in the previous chapters to bear on the locus in systematic theology that undergirds appeals to Scripture: the doctrine of Scripture. This chapter is also the first of the remaining chapters of the book that take on concrete loci from systematic theology to illustrate how systematic theology in terms of the Law-Gospel distinction works concretely. The place of the topic in the overall structure of the book is fitting in two ways. First, it follows immediately from the previous chapters which dealt with the way in which Scripture reception in systematic theology can be analysed through the Law-Gospel distinction, and second, the doctrine of Scripture has often been put at the beginning of dogmatics because it is alleged to provide the foundation of theology.

The problem that I want to take on in this chapter, concerning the Reformation principle of *sola scriptura*, is well illustrated by Baruch de Spinoza in his *Tractatus Theologico-Philosophicus*, at the beginning of chapter 7, where he deals with the interpretation of Scripture:

> On every side we hear men saying that the Bible is the Word of God, teaching mankind true blessedness, or the path to salvation. But the facts are quite at variance with their words, for people in general seem to make no attempt whatsoever to live according to the Bible's teachings. We see that nearly all men parade their own ideas as God's Word, their chief aim being to compel others to think as they do, while using religion as a pretext. We see, I say, that the chief concern of theologians on the whole has been to extort from Holy Scripture their own arbitrarily invented ideas, for which they claim divine authority.[1]

---

1. Benedictus de Spinoza, *Complete Works*, ed. Michael L Morgan, trans. Samuel Shirley (Indianapolis, IN: Hackett, 2002), 456.

In the first part of this chapter, I will argue that Spinoza was right.[2] I will argue that the *sola scriptura* principle, especially in the Reformed rendering of it which Spinoza aims at with his criticism, suffers from intrinsic problems because it obscures the selection processes that unavoidably accompany appeals to Scripture, so that the idea that only Scripture directs theological claims cannot be upheld because the hand of the interpreter is inescapably present in every appeal to Scripture's authority. My argument takes the following steps. First of all, I will try to clarify what we mean by the *sola scriptura* maxim. Subsequently, I will illustrate how the *sola scriptura* principle obscures the selection process involved in Scriptural interpretation through an example from contemporary theology. Building further on this example, I will suggest that *sola scriptura* makes theologians lazy. Making the transition from pragmatic to material-theological arguments, I will finally argue that central to Christian theology is a balance between the appropriation of salvation on the basis of God's incarnation in Jesus Christ on the one hand, and the otherness of God as commanded by the Decalogue on the other: the Law-Gospel distinction. This balance, then, will lead to a final defence of the *sola scriptura* because of the singularity of the incarnation, while still upholding that our dependence on the witness of Scripture to God's revelation to Israel and in Jesus Christ does not do away with theology's obligation to take responsibility for its selective use of Scripture and the prices to be paid for this.

5.2 What do I mean by sola scriptura?

If we want to plea against or in favour of the *sola scriptura* principle, we have to become clear about what we mean by it. The complexity of such an endeavour is that we cannot just define the concept however we want, because what we are talking about is 'the Reformation principle' of *sola scriptura*. Hence, our use of the concept must be sufficiently consonant with historical usage if we want to avoid refuting a strawman that has never existed in history. On the other hand, this actual history is by no means obviously coherent or diachronically consistent, and therefore, we have to systematize our use of the concept in order to make clear what we mean, and which use of the concept we want to criticize and which we want to affirm or tolerate. Taking these conditions into account, I think it is helpful to distinguish between the meaning of the catchphrase *sola scriptura* on different levels.

Let me start with the more strict, theological meaning of the term. First of all, the phrase *sola scriptura* points to a fundamental theological principle. Scripture

---

2. Although I would by far not agree with the drastic consequences that Spinoza draws from this statement, cf. the discussion of Spinoza in Arnold Huijgen, *Divine Accommodation in John Calvin's Theology: Analysis and Assessment* (Göttingen: Vandenhoeck & Ruprecht, 2011), 31–2.

is, quoting Gisbertus Voetius and others, *principium fidei*, axiom of faith.[3] In terms of this principle, one might define *sola scriptura* as follows: *sola scriptura* denotes the conviction that Scripture is the one and only criterion for Christian faith and living and beliefs and practices are true and truthfully Christian if and only if they correspond to the witness of the whole of Scripture. The notion of 'Scripture as a whole', *tota scriptura*, is important. According to the Reformed tradition, Scripture has to be interpreted by itself, well in line with Augustine's rule that more difficult passages should be explained with the aid of clearer passages. *Sacra scriptura sui interpres*, it is its own interpreter, is another typical Latin phrase that represents this insight.[4] *Sola scriptura* is no license for biblicism, the arbitrary use of Bible verses to claim that one's own religious convictions are Scriptural. If so, any heresy could be defended on the basis of Scripture.

At the same time, it is characteristic of the Reformed interpretation of *sola scriptura* that it is, basically, unqualified.[5] This means, different from the Lutheran Reformation, there is no extra criterion that qualifies the appeal to Scripture, a filter on the basis of which the data from Scripture can be ordered and prioritized. With Luther, this is Christ. For Luther and the Lutheran tradition, the *solus Christus* qualifies the *sola scriptura*.[6] In my view, it is typical of the Reformed tradition to implicitly reject and practically ignore such a filter. Theological reasoning should lead to a balanced view of Scripture in which the various parts and claims are brought into harmony with each other (*analogia Scripturae*). The Reformed tradition did not succeed completely in a unanimously agreed balance between the Old and the New Testament. One might think of the struggles between Voetius and Cocceius about the fourth commandment, or about the place of the Law between antinomians or neonomians. Even Socinianism can be seen as a more drastic way of diverging from the mainstream ways of balancing out the Old against the New Testament in biblical interpretation.[7]

So far so good for the principle. The principle can be applied to concrete expressions of theological reasoning. One might write a dogmatic handbook in

---

3. Willem J. van Asselt, T. Theo, J. Pleizier, Pieter L. Rouwendal and Maarten Wisse, *Introduction to Reformed Scholasticism* (Grand Rapids, MI: Reformation Heritage, 2011), 225-47.

4. John V. Fesko, 'The Doctrine of Scripture in Reformed Orthodoxy', in *A Companion to Reformed Orthodoxy*, ed. Herman J. Selderhuis, Brill's Companions to the Christian Tradition 40 (Leiden: Brill, 2013), 434-5.

5. It is true that there are additional hermeneutical rules for interpreting Scripture, such as the rules of faith and love, but such rules will never be admitted as necessary prerequisites for Scripture to have a unified and clear meaning in and of itself.

6. W. J. Kooiman, *Luther en de Bijbel*, 3rd edn (Baarn: Ten Have, 1977), chapter 17-19; cf. Christoph Schwöbel, *Gott in Beziehung: Studien zur Dogmatik* (Tübingen: Mohr Siebeck, 2002), 323-4, although Schwöbel does not explicitly note that this is just Lutheran rather than Protestant.

7. Cf. Chapter 7.

which one aims to base oneself through and through on Scripture and, therefore, refer to or discuss Scriptural passages. It might also find expression in a biblical commentary in which the interpreter abstains from criticizing the literal sense of biblical passages under discussion, or an interpretation in which one aims at respecting the historicity of the events narrated in the Bible as long as possible. It goes without saying that the *sola scriptura* principle forbids one to let one's own theological judgement be a critical and decisive factor in weighing the different aspects in the witness of Scripture. Accepting genuine contradictions within Scripture seems to be incompatible with the principle, because they would entail that the interpreter be forced to intervene and choose which part of the contradiction to disagree with. Even in the relationship between the Old and the New Testament, the interpreter does not really intervene, because, in practice, the New Testament prescribes how the Old Testament has to be read, although even there, it has become a good custom among Reformed theologians to let the Old Testament speak for itself as much as possible. Here too, a complete theoretical reflection that covers the actual practice of the interpretation of the Old Testament in the Reformed tradition has never been developed.

I do not deny that the description so far is to some extent systematizing, generalizing and, therefore, one-sided. Scholars have pointed to various aspects of the Reformation *sola scriptura* that add to its dynamic character. Richard Muller, for example, has pointed to a number of ways in which the post-Reformation approach to Scripture is in continuity with the medieval tradition.[8] This is true of figurative interpretation of Scripture, and of the necessary role of the church or of doctrine. In the Dutch context, Henk van den Belt and Arnold Huijgen have drawn attention to the pneumatological character of the Reformed doctrine of Scripture.[9] The Reformation did not see Scripture as a neutral deposit of timeless truths that only need to be uncovered by an equally neutral interpreter. The God-given character of Scripture can only be seen and appropriately received by believers who are directed in this by the Holy Spirit.[10] Finally, one might nuance the *sola scriptura* by pointing to its origin in the Reformation as a critical slogan. Thus, *sola scriptura* is a critical instrument for criticizing power structures and

---

8. Richard A. Muller, *Post-Reformation Reformed Dogmatics*, vol. 2, Holy Scripture: The Cognitive Foundation of Theology (Grand Rapids, MI: Baker Academic, 2003), chapter 7.

9. Henk van den Belt, *The Authority of Scripture in Reformed Theology: Truth and Trust* (Leiden: Brill, 2008), 333–6; Henk van den Belt, 'The Problematic Character of Sola Scriptura', in *Sola Scriptura: Biblical and Theological Perspectives on Scripture, Authority and Hermeneutics*, ed. Hans Burger and Arnold Huijgen, Studies in Reformed Theology 32 (Leiden: Brill, 2017), 38–55; Arnold Huijgen, 'Alone Together: Sola Scriptura and the Other Solas of the Reformation', in *Sola Scriptura: Biblical and Theological Perspectives on Scripture, Authority and Hermeneutics*, ed. Hans Burger and Arnold Huijgen, Studies in Reformed Theology 32 (Leiden: Brill, 2017), 79–104.

10. Van den Belt, *Authority of Scripture*, 316–24.

giving Scripture back into the hands of ordinary people. This has certainly been its primary function in the early Reformation.

I do not deny these aspects, but they do not do away with the fact that, especially in the context of an ongoing polemic with Christians of other confessions, the Reformed tradition saw Scripture as a weapon in the hands of believers and theologians to claim that their tradition was most true to the whole of Scriptural witness.[11] This makes it inevitable to downplay or reinterpret those parts of Scripture that run counter to the key interests of the Reformed tradition, and what is worse, it makes it inevitable to hide those parts in the interest of upholding one's own identity. If one would admit that Scripture can be legitimately read otherwise as the Reformed tradition would do, this would immediately open the door to those competing confessions such as Roman Catholics, Lutherans and particularly Anabaptists to claim the legitimacy of their way of being church.[12] This can be amply illustrated by a few questions from Gisbertus Voetius' Catechism, written down by one of his pupils and reissued by Abraham Kuyper in the nineteenth century:

> Q. But all those religions that name themselves after the Christian name, are they the true religion? A. No.[13]
> Q. Which religion among Christians then is the true religion? A. The religion of the Protestants and Reformed.
> Q. Why is the religion of the Reformed the only true religion, and not the others? A. Because the Reformed religion alone accords with God's Word in everything, and the other contradict it.[14]

Ultimately, as this example illustrates, the *sola scriptura* is part of an appeal to absolute religious power. To this extent, it hinders a truthful, responsible way

---

11. My argument here is roughly in line with Alister E. McGrath, *Christianity's Dangerous Idea: The Protestant Revolution: A History from the Sixteenth Century to the Twenty-First* (New York: HarperOne, 2007), chapter 2–3 and 9.

12. Cf. Chapter 4 in this book.

13.
> V. Maer alle die Religien, die haer selve bekleeden met den Christelicken naem, zijn die de ware Religie? A. Neen. V. Welcke Religie onder de Christenen is dan de ware Religie? A. De Religie der Protestanten ende Gereformeerden. V. Waerom is de Religie der Gereformeerden alleen de ware Religie, ende de andere niet? A. Om dat de Religie van de Gereformeerde alleen in alles met Godts woort accoordeert ende over-een-komt, ende de andere daer-en-tegen tegen Godts woort zijn strijdende.

14. Gisbertus Voetius, *Voetius' catechisatie over den Heidelbergschen Catechismus: naar Poudroyen's editie van 1662 op nieuw uitgegeven, bij ons publiek ingeleid, en met enkele aanteekeningen voorzien*, ed. Abraham Kuyper (Gebroeders Huge, 1891), 57.

of dealing with one's own uses of Scripture, because these motives must remain hidden for the sake of upholding one's own claim to power.

Apart from being a principle, however, the *sola scriptura* is also the basis of religious practices. One might say that the *sola scriptura* is the critical governing principle that directs the life of churches and families in (mostly conservative) evangelical Protestantism. One can see the principle at work in all sorts of contexts. First of all, we find it in worship services, where we do not read Augustine, Calvin or Karl Barth, but Scripture (except for the Heidelberg Catechism). Ultimately, the question of truth about a sermon is: is it according to the Scriptures, or not? The same goes for all other aspects of the life of the community of faith. If the leadership of a community of believers asks itself a question, it will turn to Scripture, all complexity of answering those questions in practical contexts included. A synod that finds itself confronted with proposals for renewal of the life of the church appoints a committee that is asked to answer the question: is this biblical? In fact, the community has no other official standard for evaluating the legitimacy of church life than the Bible.

In line with this, one might see a third layer of *sola scriptura* in the sense that it is the powerful basis of the catechetical culture and spirituality of the Reformation. *Sola scriptura* is the basic presupposition and driving force behind religious reading practices. In that sense, it is the principal religious rite and, hence, sacrament of the Reformed tradition. If we take typical devout Christian youngsters as an example, they will start their day with a moment of devotion, reading the Bible. In the family Scripture will be read one or more times, during church events for youngsters Bible readings will take place and during worship services they will hear from Scripture again.

Before I will attack the principle of sola Scriptura, it is important to note that my critique of the principle does not include every religious practice that is prompted or vindicated by this principle. A critique of a principle does not necessarily lead to the demise of every religious practice that is based on it. My critique, if it finds resonance among believers, will possibly qualify and transform religious practices, but it will not do away with them, nor is this my intention.

5.3 It's dogmatics and preaching, stupid!

In this section, I will pursue my critique of the *sola scriptura* maxim further by taking a very concrete example. Often, a shift away from a traditionally Reformed *sola scriptura* theology has been motivated by doubts about the historical reliability of the Bible. However, this has often led to an easy juxtaposition of those who would accept the Bible as a whole, and would thus be truthful Bible readers, and those who are modern and critical towards the Bible, and so were no longer faithful. This obscures the fact that there is a problem with the application of *sola scriptura* in every Bible use, not just in the denial of the historicity of a passage. 'Biblical doctrine' is a claim that raises a question of what this is in every case in which the claim is being made, and I would say that there is always, in every appeal to 'biblical teaching', a leap to one's own context that is hidden in that claim.[15]

I want to show this in terms of a concrete example: John Piper in his bestseller *Desiring God*.[16] I do not at all intend to stigmatize Piper here as an abuser of Scripture. What I aim to do is to sketch a paradigmatic example of how in evangelical circles appeals to Scripture are being made and discern the argumentation processes that play a role in such appeals, be they made in sermons, theological treatises or Bible reading groups.

Needless to say, Piper claims to be a Calvinist and a biblical Christian. Therefore, it is obvious that he aims to find warrant for his Christian hedonism in Scripture, although he has been realistic enough to situate his interest in the topic in his own biography already in the introduction. Subsequently, in the first chapter, he finds the roots of it in Scripture. On the page preceding the first chapter, the bridge between Piper's hedonism and the alleged biblical basis become clear, when he mentions on top of the page: 'Our God is in the heavens; he does all that he pleases' (Ps. 115.3). At the bottom of the page, we find Piper's own statement: 'The climax of God's happiness is the delight He takes in the echoes of His excellence in the praises of His people.'[17] God strives after pleasure, happiness and delight and he finds it not in us, but in his own glory, so Piper argues on the next page.

There is no space here to delve extensively into the exegesis of Psalm 115 or the role of the theology of Jonathan Edwards in the argument of Piper. What I want to suggest is that between Piper's Christian hedonism and the Scriptural material that he brings together to support it biblically, there are many steps that are not taken into account by Piper at all, at least not in terms of references to Scripture. One might summarize the explicit and implicit chain of reasoning between Psalm 115 and Piper as follows:

1 God does all that he pleases. This emphasizes that God is free and sovereign, which is indeed in Psalm 115, although in a totally different context, but
2 here, in Piper's argument, it also suggests that God is heading towards something, strives after things, which is definitely not obviously Reformed or Christian and
3 that God is emotionally involved in this ('pleases' is linked up to 'pleasure') and
4 is freely moved in this by human beings who
5 experience a similar sort of 'pleasure' by enjoying God's 'pleasure'.

---

15. I have made an honest attempt to select a fair and not too esoteric example. For a similar example, but then in Calvin, see Maarten Wisse, *Scripture between Identity and Creativity: A Hermeneutical Theory Building upon Four Interpretations of Job*, Ars Disputandi Supplement Series 1 (Utrecht: Ars Disputandi, 2003), http://dspace.library.uu.nl/handle/1874/294105, chapter 4.

16. John Piper, *Desiring God* (Sisters, OR: Multnomah, 2003).

17. Ibid., 30.

Piper constantly adduces biblical passages that support the notion of God's sovereignty and power (Psalm 33, Daniel 4, Job 2 and 42, Lamentations 2 etc.), but he does not seem to pay any attention to the other four steps in his argument. However, these steps are the ones that provide the added value and thus constitute the distinctive spirituality that is typical of his Christian hedonism.

What I do not want to suggest is that Piper should at last start to develop an interest in reading Scripture as he ought, namely without prejudices, and according to the single true historical sense of the text. My conviction is that this is not possible. You cannot read Scripture without having your own present-day agenda. My problem is that the idea of biblical *sola scriptura* Christianity precludes him from admitting this personal agenda, admitting that his Christian hedonism is either not in the Bible at all (which would be a harsh evaluation of it) or is a rather particular approach to certain biblical passages that runs counter to or competes with other selections of biblical material. Thus, we see how an appeal to Scripture because of a willingness to be biblical always has to face the way in which this appeal to Scripture fares against the whole of Scripture. In the Reformed tradition at least, there is no *sola scriptura* without *tota scriptura*. But this also blows up the *sola scriptura* in the sense that any proof that aims to justify that a particular claim is biblical has to justify this claim against any other verse of Scripture, which, practically, implies an endeavour ad infinitum.

5.4 The sola scriptura *makes theologians lazy*

This example from Piper's work illustrates the next point that I want to make against the *sola scriptura* maxim, namely that it makes theologians lazy. It is easy to trace a widespread scepticism towards abstract theology, towards 'dogmatics' in many circles of believers. If we would just be 'biblical', we could get rid of much 'theology' that leads us astray from the simplicity of the biblical message. Is it not Jesus who told us to become like a child? Well, children do not do theology, so better do theology as little as possible.

The problem is: the *sola scriptura* maxim sanctions this widespread line of reasoning. Theological reflection, so it seems, is basically superfluous. And this is why it makes believers and theologians lazy. It makes theologians lazy because it provides them with a free card for not making their selection processes of biblical material and the reasons for those selections visible. They are stimulated to hide why they downplay or reinterpret one verse and privilege another. Believers likewise are stimulated to 'just read the Bible' without being aware of the reasons why they constantly focus on, for example, the Gospel of John, or read John in terms of Paul or the Old Testament in the light of the New Testament (cf. Chapter 3 for illustrations of this). Let the texts speak for themselves, so the mantra goes, whereas in fact texts are adapted or even forced to align with contemporary interests and tacit presuppositions of religious communities.

In fact, the difficult position of dogmatics in theology since the Enlightenment can be understood in the light of the *sola scriptura* maxim. If only Scripture is normative for faith, and Scripture is to be interpreted in its historical context and according to its primary historical meaning, dogmatics should best strive for its own removal. If it is still worth something, it should restrict itself to a collection of biblical material. A stronger awareness of the diversity of material in the Bible only increased this effect, because if the Bible is diverse and heterogeneous, then a systematizing approach to biblical material as we find it in dogmatics leads us away from the richness and diversity of Scripture. Thinking along these lines, one might argue that Protestant theology prepared its own demise in modern theology.

However, if the *sola scriptura* maxim is false, and if in fact Protestant dogmatics, just like all the others, did never live up to its own principle, this might open a new perspective on what dogmatics is and on the way in which it has been practiced over the centuries.[18] Dogmatics used to be the discipline that controlled access to biblical material and hide its motives and arguments for granting, limiting or even forbidding access to the different biblical passages. Therefore it seemed very sensitive to cramp or an exaggerated search for consistency, as there were always heretics on the horizon who would challenge their procedures for control. But if we look at dogmatics as those ways of managing access and instead of hiding these processes of control, bring them into the open, both in the past and today, dogmatic discourse is the ongoing documentation of 'Scripture management', of prescribed and forbidden routes that made people encounter the right Bible verses at the right moment, the theologians being the policemen who directed the traffic.

Of course, those theological motives determining the directions could not be brought into the open, because this would imply that they were in fact contingent upon certain interpreters' lines of reasoning that could be different, and therefore not intrinsic to the biblical message itself. This is why one did not need to argue for them. But if we do bring them into the open, all at once this seemingly static discipline of dogmatics turns out to be much more dynamic than it seems. And all at once, this debate about taking the right route through the Bible verses becomes much more relevant to theology and homiletics than it is often alleged to be. Dogmaticians turn out to give answers to the challenges and questions of their time under continuously shifting circumstances through a conversation with the diverse material that Scripture contains. Charismatic gifts, a decrease in piety, political domination, increase of welfare, the treatment of illnesses and mental and bodily handicaps or the independence of religious experts, they are all part of the challenges that theology responds to as part of an ongoing reading community and tradition.[19]

---

18. Cf. Maarten Wisse, 'Doing Theology through Reception Studies: Towards a Post-Postmodern Theological Hermeneutics', *Nederduits Gereformeerd Theologisch Tijdschrift* 53, no. Supplement 3 (2012): 239–49, https://doi.org/10.5952/53-0-237.

19. Cf. Maarten Wisse, 'Towards a Theological Account of Theology: Reconceptualizing Church History and Systematic Theology', in *Orthodoxy, Process and Product*, ed. Mathijs Lamberigts, Lieven Boeve and Terrence Merrigan, BETL 227 (Leuven: Peeters, 2009), 351–74.

Seen in this way, dogmatics is not only a historical reconstruction of a practice from the past, but also an ongoing weighing of the arguments and choices from the past in the present. Every argument that leads to a neutralizing or privileging of a biblical passage offers arguments for an old but also a new debate. Not only then, but also now, believers have to take decisions in a dialogue between Scripture and their own context.

In the meantime, the nature of the task of the policemen has changed. They can no longer act as direct representatives of the Most High. They know that both practically and theologically, such a position is no longer at their disposal. As I will argue shortly, such a position would be in direct contradiction with a proper reading of the Scriptures. The frame of reference from which we read the Scriptures is no longer absolute. It is a chosen frame of reference, and because it is chosen, it is contingent. That it is contingent does not mean that it is arbitrary: we can argue for it (as I will do below), but we indeed have to argue for it. If anyone nevertheless decides to take another route through the biblical texts, the policeman may warn for the ravine that is near, or point to the beauty of his own route, but the policeman has no more than the weakness of words.[20]

5.5 Scripture between Law and Gospel

Up to now, I have pleaded against the *sola scriptura* for pragmatic or even secular reasons. The use of *sola scriptura* is part of a power structure of religious communities, cannot live up to its own standards and is therefore to be rejected. However, for me as a theologian, this is only half of the story. The pragmatic objections are embedded in a theological point of view. This theological standpoint has originated in a dialogue with the Bible, the tradition in which I grew up and the post-Marxist Western tradition by which I was influenced during my PhD studies.[21] Over the years, I have discovered that there are resources for the management of religious power in Christianity itself, resources that could be seen as the intrinsic Christian critique of religion.[22] Such a critique of religion is prominently present in the experientially Reformed tradition in which I grew up, although it is not

---

20. Cf. Maarten Wisse, 'De integratie van theologie en religiewetenschap in Stefan Paas' Vreemdelingen en priesters: De Utrechtse theologische faculteit in de jaren '90', *Soteria* 35, no. 1 (2018): 19–31.

21. Wisse, *Scripture between Identity and Creativity*, chapters 2 and 6.

22. On the internal critique of religion in contemporary theology, see Wolfgang Huber, '»Keine anderen Götter.« Über die Notwendigkeit theologischer Religionskritik', in *Gott, Götter, Götzen: XIV. Europäischer Kongress für Theologie (11.–15. September 2011 in Zürich)*, ed. Christoph Schwöbel (Leipzig: Evangelischer Verlagsanstalt, 2013), 23–35; for concrete examples of developing theological critiques of religion, see Christoph Schwöbel, *Gott im Gespräch: Studien zur theologischen Gegenwartsdeutung* (Tübingen: Mohr Siebeck, 2011), 355–405.

generally seen as such. In this tradition, the question is crucial: are your religious experiences or narratives the result of God's work, or are they your own deceitful construct? Is your religious commitment sincere and God-given or is it in your own interest?

Later on, I learned to ask the same questions concerning the appropriation of religious power from a post-Marxist philosophical frame of reference. However, the more I bring this post-Marxist frame of reference in conversation with the Christian tradition of which I study the history, the more I come to the conclusion that the history of theology is moving back and forth between two poles, two extremes in the management of religious power, both individually, collectively and institutionally. The one pole is the appropriation of salvation in Jesus Christ, both personally, as part of religious communities and as part of religious institutions. The other pole is the conviction that this salvation is nevertheless not ours. It is a gift and even after it has been given, it remains someone else's, the Most High whose place we can never take.[23]

The thesis to which this chapter pays tribute and which is central to the book as a whole is that the attempt to find a responsible balance between these two poles is the toolbox of Christian dogmatics, both *de jure* (this chapter) and *de re* (Chapters 3 and 4). Such an attempt does not lead to one possible outcome, neither *de jure* nor *de re*. Christian communities in the history of church and theology have made very different choices in finding a balance between the two poles, even mutually excluding choices, but there is a shared consciousness that neither of these two poles can be given up. Thus, the two poles function as the defining matrix of the limits and possibilities of theological conversation.

I see these poles symbolized by the two major units in the Bible, the Old and the New Testament, or what is classically phrased as the Law-Gospel distinction.[24] It is rough, but I think even historically, a case can be made for the thesis that the diversity of opinions within the Reformation can be linked up to the various ways in which strands in the Reformation conceived of the relationship between the Old and the New Testament.

It is from this perspective of the balance between the appropriation of salvation and the distinction between God and creation that I would like to evaluate the *sola scriptura*. Of course, to some extent, this is a case of circular reasoning. First,

---

23. One way to oversimplify this notion of the two poles is to reduce it to well-known pairs such as 'transcendent' versus 'immanent' or 'extra nos' and 'intra nos'. I cannot go too deeply into this, but they are oversimplifications because they are generalizations that apply to everything, Scripture e.g. but the characteristic of the two poles mentioned is that at least one of the two poles, Christology, is unique and as such particular rather than general. In one of these poles, Christians hold that they have their ultimate salvation, and so the dynamics of the Christian faith around this pole is unique and particular, and as such cannot be extrapolated to other contexts.

24. Cf. Chapter 2 for a more precise analysis of the Law-Gospel distinction and how it relates to Old and New Testaments.

I select a specific approach to what Scripture has to say, and subsequently, I evaluate Scripture itself in those terms. But what if I would choose another perspective on Scripture? Such a case of circular reasoning seems inevitable, but it becomes bearable to the extent that I manage to give reasons for the way in which Scripture should be positioned in between these two poles. Those reasons are an invitation to readers and dialogue partners to assess them, accept them or give other reasons that change the position of Scripture between those poles. In such a way, theology is a form of conversation around the shared conviction that our salvation is in Jesus Christ, but remains God's free gift that cannot be made ours at the same time.

In formulating the balance between Law and Gospel, I opt for a rather strong emphasis on the critical voice of the Decalogue. From the Decalogue, the first commandment sounds as a constant reminder of the absolute unicity of the one true and transcendent God, creator of heaven and earth. There is no human being who may claim to be God. From the second commandment (Reformed numbering), I hear a strong reminder against human appropriations of God's presence or will, traditionally part of polytheistic traditions. Based on these reminders, nothing in the created order can be the direct means for evoking God's presence or will.

Christology shows us how crucial the right balance between appropriation of salvation and maintaining the difference between the divine and the created order is for theology, especially Reformed theology.[25] Especially in Christology, it is crucial to uphold the truly interrupting nature of the incarnation, in which God and a human being become inseparable in the unity of one person.[26] On the other hand, it is equally crucial to uphold the distinction between two natures: only God can save and only to God we pray, not to a human being. The salvation that is in Jesus Christ's incarnation, cross and resurrection is in a human being truly and fully, but still remains divine and does not as such shift from this particular human being to humanity as a whole. This Christological tension played a key role in the Reformation, and especially Reformed theology put much emphasis on maintaining the distinction between the two natures against the Lutherans.

From this Christological point of view, it is crucial to maintain the singularity of the incarnation.[27] God has become human in Christ but is now present among us through the Spirit. The taxis of God's Trinitarian actions leave us with a beneficial problem. Although God has really come among us in Christ, tangible and visible, God is no longer among us in this way. In spite of the incarnation, God is still

---

25. Cf. Maarten Wisse, *Trinitarian Theology beyond Participation: Augustine's de Trinitate and Contemporary Theology*, T&T Clark Studies in Systematic Theology 11 (London: T&T Clark International, 2011), chapter 3.

26. Cf. Lieven Boeve, 'Theological Truth, Particularity and Incarnation: Engaging Religious Plurality and Radical Hermeneutics', in *Orthodoxy, Process and Product*, ed. Mathijs Lamberigts, Lieven Boeve and Terrence Merrigan, BETL 227 (Leuven: Peeters, 2009), 334–6.

27. By 'incarnation', I do not mean just the beginning of the life of Christ, but the whole of his life as God on earth, so including the crucifixion and resurrection.

transcendently present among us. This transcendence is beneficial because it interrupts our religious powergames. This is the theological reason why I argued against the *sola scriptura*, because constructively, as a stable basis on which a single true theology can be formulated, it turns into an extension of the incarnation, in which God is no longer among us in Jesus, but nevertheless present through his speech and will in Scripture. This is to be denied. Scripture witnesses to the incarnation, but it is not in itself incarnational.

5.6 *Pro* sola scriptura

And this is then what finally leads to a positive affirmation of the *sola scriptura* maxim. In the previous section, I have suggested that both the doctrine of Scripture and Christology have to be controlled by the first and second commandment, and that Christology indeed did function as such in the history of dogma. In this argument, the singularity of the incarnation plays a key role. The incarnation can never be 'extended' to the church, the ministerial office or Scripture. Only Christ is God on earth and even in the case of Christ, the distinction between two natures in one person precludes a creature from becoming venerated as if he was God.

It is this singularity of the incarnation that finally leads to an affirmation of the *sola scriptura* maxim. The argument runs like this: if our salvation is in a singular event, or a singular life of a specific historical person from the past, Jesus Christ, then our salvation is historically mediated, and radically so. If there were no Scripture or no oral report about Jesus Christ being transmitted to us, we would not know about the Gospel. Therefore, the singularity of the incarnation implies the necessity of a stable transmission of the Gospel message throughout the ages and so, Scripture is a necessary means through which the Gospel message is received by us.

In line with this, we cannot avoid accepting *scriptura*. If God deals with us in a historical manner and by becoming human in one particular person, to our salvation, then our faith is essentially historical and scriptural. By analogy, the same goes for Israel and the revelation in the Old Testament. God's election of Israel is the election of a particular people with a particular history and as such, still constitutive for the identity of those who believe in Jesus Christ. God's becoming a human being in Jesus Christ is preceded by the singularity of God's election of Israel. Ultimately, the singularity of God's action in Christ has consequences for the whole of creation, because this singularity of God's acts makes clear that God deals with a creation that has its own value, its own history, its own sequence of moments with a beginning, middle and end. None of these moments are just as mediatory of God's being or will as all the others, but everyone has its distinct being and role in God's plan with creation.

Of course, one may ask: *scriptura*, yes, but does it have to be *sola scriptura*? Should we not better say that the whole history of Christianity and Judaism contributes to this transmission of the singularity of the incarnation equally, given that I have argued above that there is no Scripture without its reception in particular times and contexts. Is not the community of believers co-constitutive of revelation, as postmodernism has taught us? Can we do without the 'sola' part of the maxim?

I do not think so. The *sola* is infinite, in the sense that it will never be fulfilled and that it has to acknowledge and discover its own situatedness, but it is also a *sola* that can never be satisfied with its *locus* in the community or a sacramental church, exactly due to this singularity of the incarnation. This singularity cannot be extended or paralleled to the community of believers or the enactment of them in a sacramental presence, and therefore it is the exact nature of this singularity that is crucial to our salvation. The sources that tell us about God's acts in history are the criterion for the nature of our salvation, and so, the content of these historical sources is really at stake. The way in which we have dealt with these sources or what an authoritative representative of Christ claims about them in the here and now does not suffice. What is really said or what really happened in the there and then of history matters.

This is also the reason why an appeal to the role of the Spirit as the Trinitarian person who warrants the continuity between the singularity of the incarnation and the Christian community in the present does not suffice. Such an appeal to the Spirit would turn that appeal into an incarnational phenomenon of its own. If in the here and now anyone can claim the authority of the Spirit without any external critical reference, such claims become absolute and as dangerous to the nature of the Christian community as popes, infallible scriptures or whatever means we use to get God's will into our hands. The singularity of the incarnation and the unique history of God's actions in creation, Israel (election!) and ultimately in Jesus Christ are the particular critical references that relativize any appeal to divine authority in the present, and it is in this way that the singularity of the meeting-point between heaven and earth in Jesus Christ is retained.

5.7 Consequences of this step

It might sound like a conversion. After a passionate critique of the *sola scriptura* a sudden and passionate turn to a defence. But the change is less radical than it seems. What we win by this step is that we discern a very clear distinction between the Scriptures and other scriptures. The Scriptures derive their special status from the witness to God's unique acts in the history of Israel and in Jesus Christ. This is why Augustine's works, however great things they might contain, are not normally the subject matter of a Christian worship service. And this is also why we do painstaking exegesis of single words or passages from Scripture, an approach to texts that is normally rather to be discouraged in interpretation processes. This is why we still write new commentaries on Scripture and develop new approaches to it. From a secular perspective, the amount of attention paid to this particular collection of texts from antiquity must unavoidably count as extremely exaggerated, but from a Christian perspective, it is more than natural. The distinction between Scripture and other texts is crucial.

The singularity of the incarnation as the basis of Scripture makes us see why the change is less radical than it seems. The singularity of the incarnation leads immediately to a strong emphasis on the human nature of Scripture. If Rome extends the incarnation through the doctrine of the church, the Reformation should not do so through the doctrine of Scripture. This would immediately undo the singularity of the incarnation. Scripture, therefore, is radically human. Scripture is our only witness to the singularity of the incarnation, but it is a radically human witness. This does not mean that we have to deny that it is inspired by God. Our confession of faith can or even should be that everything that is written in it is written to our salvation because God wanted it to be as it is, and therefore, it is as such necessary and sufficient to our salvation (cf. *Confessio Belgica*, article 7).

This sounds very orthodox, but it is intended more heterodox than it sounds. Less piously phrased: even if it turns out that the Bible is a very diverse collection of chunks of very human witness to God's acts in history, even then it remains the witness to God's acts that has been given to us. God has given us those chunks, and we have to deal with them. There might be historical inaccuracies in them, points of view that are inconsistent with each other, theologically problematic passages, problematic views of women or homosexuals, you name it, these are the Scriptures that God gave us.[28]

I would say, this is indeed the case. The internal differentiation of the witness of Scripture is indeed of such a kind that it is impossible to accept everything it contains. We have to choose constantly, and for this reason, my argument against the way in which the *sola scriptura* has been used in the past, remains valid.[29] Whoever believes in *sola scriptura* constantly has to take responsibility for his way of dealing with Scripture, because accepting Scripture as a whole is, exactly because of the nature of Scripture itself, an impossibility. And this is because of the sort of Scripture that God gave us, and so, it is God's will.

What this calls for is a specific understanding of the Christian community of believers. As far as I can see, the consequences of the understanding of the *sola scriptura* for ecclesiology are more profound than those for the doctrine of Scripture. If Scripture is fundamentally open to different interpretations, not only *de re*, but also *de jure*, then this has much to say about conflicts in the church and of doctrinal divergences. Brutely stated: it means that we have to accept the

---

28. See e.g. Eep Talstra, 'Text, Tradition, Theology: The Example of the Book of Joel', in *Strangers and Pilgrims on Earth Essays in Honour of Abraham van de Beek*, ed. A. J. G. van der Borght and Paul van Geest (Leiden: Brill, 2012), 309–28; Eep Talstra, *De Éne God is de andere niet: theologie en rolverdeling in Jeremia 5:1-9* (Amsterdam: VU University Press, 2011).

29. This goes much further than the common insight that we will never manage to fully understand the true meaning of Scripture, and so to uphold the *sola scriptura*, but use it in a merely critical sense, in the sense that the *sola scriptura* will always point us beyond what we think Scripture means. What I mean to admit is that Scripture is indeed such that one can never accept all that it claims, because its claims are heterogeneous.

plurality of the church insofar as it reflects the plurality of the Bible. This does not mean that anything goes. There are arguments for certain sets of selective uses of Scripture, and in fact, such sets are always already in place and form a part of stable confessional or ecclesial traditions. Discussions about sets of selective uses do not start from scratch but are always in conversation with existing traditions and the ways in which they function within the life of the church.

Moreover, if the argument that I have developed so far has something to offer, it implies that in this ongoing conversation within the church, there is a shared sensitivity towards the reality of the incarnation and the saving work of Christ on the one hand, and the fundamental distinction between God and creation on the other. This does not mean that every believer, theologian or church community agrees on how this sensitivity has to be turned into practice, but it means that they have an idea of what has to be held in creative tension and what kind of common ground they have at their disposal to remind each other of what cannot be given up without jeopardizing the integrity of the Christian faith.

Ultimately, however, they have no warranty that the Christian community in the here and now is exactly on par with God's will or with divine truth. To have this would imply an imbalance of the two poles to be held in tension. The warranty for the future of the Christian gathering in the past, present and future is the saving work of the Father, Son and Holy Spirit, of God alone.

Chapter 6

IN DEFENCE OF DOUBLE PREDESTINATION

6.1 From Law and Gospel to predestination and the other way around

In Chapter 2, we have seen that the development of the distinction between Law and Gospel emerges from, and is closely interrelated to, the doctrine of grace as Augustine, Luther and Melanchthon see it. This chapter is about the doctrine of grace, focusing on a retrieval of the classical doctrine of double predestination. Because it offers an account of the doctrine of grace, it is in a certain way the core of this book. Here I make decisions that decisively determine the way in which I interpret the distinction between Law and Gospel. However, the distinction between Law and Gospel occurs in the flow of the argument only to a very limited extent, precisely because here it almost completely takes the form of the distinction between God and the world, between divine and human action. At the same time, my view of the doctrine of grace and predestination is also decisively influenced by the way in which I enriched the distinction between Law and Gospel with insights borrowed from twentieth-century power analysis, introduced in Chapter 2 and previously applied in Chapters 3–5. This is particularly evident from two aspects of my argument: first, the way in which Scripture plays a role in my argument; and second, the role that a post-Marxist power analysis plays in my argument on predestination.

Different from others before me, I will make no attempt to show how my view of predestination and grace provides the best representation of the witness of Scripture. Quite the contrary, every now and then I will try to show how different views of predestination all find considerable support in Scripture, and how even my own view requires reading certain passages from Scripture against the grain in order to uphold my claims. What determines my view of predestination is not so much the support of a maximum amount of material from Scripture that corresponds to it, but rather the distinction between God and the world, divine and human action, and intimately related to it, the distinction between Law and Gospel. This corresponds to what I have shown in earlier chapters regarding how the appeal to Scripture has functioned in the theological tradition, even when the selection mechanisms that were operative in the tradition were mostly not explicitly expressed.

In addition, I have already indicated that I have enriched the distinction between Law and Gospel with insights from the post-Marxist tradition. In this way, the distinctions between Law and Gospel, God and the world, and divine and human action are reconceived in terms of the question of who speaks on behalf of whom. Hence, although the distinction between Law and Gospel has its origin in the doctrine of grace, I reinterpret the doctrine of grace and predestination in terms of a power analysis, similar to the way in which I have developed the distinction between Law and Gospel.

6.2 Why predestination matters today

In contemporary mainstream systematic theology, a universalist soteriology is commonly accepted.[1] The doctrine of double predestination is often seen among mainstream theologians as a horrible doctrine, a residue of old-fashioned and deplorable forms of Christianity. Apart from being seen as horrible or old-fashioned, soteriological universalism has become deeply intertwined with the doctrine of God and Christology.[2] If God's being is in Christ, in his condescension to human beings, as an expression of what has become the most important divine attribute, love, then it belongs to God's essence to forgive and to save all. For this reason, it is very hard for contemporary systematic theologians to avoid universalism, since this is implied by what they commonly say about who God is.

For quite a few contemporary theologians, especially those in line with twentieth-century liberation or feminist theology, matters of eternal life are even further beyond their field of interest. Why bother with questions of eternal bliss or damnation at all? Why care about questions that only made sense from a medieval frame of reference, a frame of reference that is no longer ours? If our destiny is no longer heaven, but this life, and if hell and heaven might not even exist, why bother about predestination? Would it not be better to fight for justice in the world or for the environment?[3]

Among those who still defend predestination or a particular view of salvation, the appeal to the Bible and the tradition often plays an important role, and

---

1. To mention a few recent accounts: David Bentley Hart, *That All Shall Be Saved: Heaven, Hell, and Universal Salvation* (New Haven, CT: Yale University Press, 2019); Gregory MacDonald, *The Evangelical Universalist*, 2nd edn (Eugene, OR: Cascade, 2012); Tom Greggs, *Barth, Origen, and Universal Salvation: Restoring Particularity* (Oxford: Oxford University Press, 2009); Hartmut Rosenau, *Allversöhnung: ein transzendentaltheologischer Grundlegungsversuch* (Berlin: W. de Gruyter, 1993).

2. MacDonald, *The Evangelical Universalist*, chapter 1, and in many other places as it is clearly the key to his argument.

3. Cf. Dorothee Sölle, *Suffering*, Twentieth Century Religious Thought (Philadelphia, PA: Fortress, 1975). Sölle's argument, of course, goes much further than simply downplaying the importance of predestination.

understandably so. In response, American evangelicals, primarily, have presented attempts to defend universalism on the basis of Scripture, such as MacDonald,[4] Talbott[5] and Hart.[6] Whether they are convincing or not is beyond the scope of this chapter, but what it has led to is a rather 'dogmatic' or 'intellectual' approach to the question of universalism. Either the discussion has centred around authority and the possibility of justifying a universalist position on the basis of Scripture, or the question of universalism is debated in philosophical theology. In addition, the discussion seems rather limited to the evangelical and Reformed world.

In what follows, I offer a fresh perspective on the doctrine of double predestination. In doing so, I draw inspiration from both the confessionally Reformed and evangelical traditions and the postmodern critical awareness of power structures. In a way, I will apply a power analysis to the traditional confessional debate about universalism. The core of my argument will be that as human beings, we must refrain from claiming the right to pronounce the ultimate verdict on our own existence. I will reread the traditional doctrine of double predestination and its universalist counterpart in terms of maintaining the distinction between God and human beings. The doctrine of predestination is not so much to tell us who is going to heaven and who is going to hell, but rather to ensure that the ultimate verdict on our life does not rest in our own hands. It aims at underscoring the freedom of God and the freedom of grace.

Predestination is about salvation, about one's ultimate fate in life. If, as liberation or feminist theologies generally claim, all theology is political, then the idea that predestination is trivial and that universalism is obviously true is surprising, because being absolutely certain about the positive outcome of the ultimate verdict about one's life makes one quite open to an attitude of power. From this perspective, the widespread acceptance of various forms of universalism in post–Second World War theology is surprising. The psychological and existential implications of ignoring the question of whether I am okay in the eyes of the Most High seem attractive. These motives for advocating universalism are comprehensible against the background of images of the Divine that brought people to perturbations of religious anxiety and despair. However, the background of our increased awareness of the way in which religious views support power structures also makes these lines of reasoning very counter-intuitive. Soteriologically, the question of whether we are predestined is about the most profound question of our human existence, and an affirmative answer to it thus sets us free at the highest possible level. This also makes such an affirmative answer liable to the highest possible sin of cheapening grace and thus to severe levels of injustice and abuse of the earth. And so, I argue, it

---

4. MacDonald, *The Evangelical Universalist*.

5. Thomas Talbott, *The Inescapable Love of God*, 2nd edn (Eugene, OR: Wipf and Stock, 2014).

6. Hart, *That All Shall Be Saved*; Hart, however, needs his own translation of the Bible to make this work: David Bentley Hart, *The New Testament: A Translation* (New Haven, CT: Yale University Press, 2019).

is naive to suggest that discussions about predestination are outdated and limited to a medieval frame of reference.

A few limits have to be set, because the topic is wide, and the areas of controversy abound. First of all, as a retrieval, it will not be a straightforward or full-scale defence of the traditional doctrine. I will not try to convince the reader through a knockdown argument of the truth of the doctrine. I even doubt whether an attempt at a knockdown argument would be possible or useful. Inevitably, it seems that the discussion of predestination and universalism strikes an existential chord. Talbott, for example, in his article in the *Oxford Handbook of Eschatology*, opens with a biographical note.[7] Another example is the recent defence of universalism by David Bentley Hart, *That All Shall Be Saved*, which, again, is written from a strongly existential point of view.[8] The present chapter will be no exception, although I hope that it is more sensitive to counterarguments than Hart's book. If our ultimate destiny is at stake, a detached approach is difficult to maintain. Moreover, when it comes to one's evaluation of universalism, many considerations from a wide range of dogmatic loci come together and play a role in the choice of one view or another. Therefore, it is difficult to convince everyone by means of a one-dimensional rational argument. Against this background, I will attempt to demonstrate the strength of the doctrine vis-à-vis the present theological, pastoral and cultural contexts. Also, I will offer a retrieval of it by revising it against the background of objections that have been raised against it.

The argument runs as follows: first, terminological issues will be discussed. Subsequently, two alternatives to double predestination will be evaluated in terms of upholding the distinction between God and human beings. In Section 6.5, I will develop my account of double predestination as a way in which the perspective of God and the perspective of human beings are distinguished although not entirely separated, and I will attempt to safeguard double predestination against some of the charges that have been levelled against it. In Section 6.6, I will discuss two dimensions of my account that I consider a retrieval of the traditional doctrine, and in the final section, I deal with the question of double predestination and the assurance of faith.

6.3 Definition of terms

What do we mean by 'predestination'? Predestination is, according to the handbook tradition from the period of Reformed orthodoxy, God's eternal decree concerning the eternal destiny of (fallen) human beings.[9] Whether these human beings are

---

7. Thomas Talbott, 'Universalism', in *The Oxford Handbook of Eschatology*, ed. Jerry L. Walls (New York: Oxford University Press, 2010), 446–61.

8. Cf. e.g. the opening of part 1: Hart, *That All Shall Be Saved*, 10–13.

9. Cf. e.g. Johannes Wollebius, *Compendium Theologiae Christianae*, 2nd edn (Amsterdam: Aegidius Janssonius, 1655), chapter 4.

considered as 'fallen' is a matter of debate between infra- and supralapsarians. I take my starting point in a moderate version of the 'Calvinist' view,[10] Calvinist in the sense that this decision on God's part is independent from any foreseen faith on the part of the elect, and moderate in the sense that the damnation of the reprobate is a matter of justice because of their actual sins, sins which are not to be attributed to God's eternal decree, but to their own responsibility as responsible and considerably free human agents. In the context of a contemporary retrieval and in order to circumvent the difficult questions about 'eternal destiny', I would like to note that we should not necessarily interpret the word 'eternal' as pointing to an infinite expansion of time, but to the nature of the decision, namely as definite or ultimate.

The question of whether this version of predestination deserves the label 'double', I answer with the claim that any version of predestination that includes this aspect of a decision about humans' ultimate destiny in a way that is totally independent of their actions in life implies a predestination that is 'double' in the sense that it implies two alternative destinies. In other words, any Calvinist version of the doctrine is to a significant extent a 'double' version. It is of considerable consequence to characterize the decrees of God as asymmetrical, as the Canons of Dordt describe the decrees of election and reprobation. The Canons represent reprobation in a largely negative way, as God's passing over or not choosing to save some persons from among fallen humanity, rather than a positive decision to designate some persons for eternal suffering in hell with no respect to their guilt or deserving. There are many good theological reasons for doing this, but doctrinally, this remains a version of 'double' predestination. There will always be an aspect of the will of God involved in the act of not-choosing. Any pastorally formulated view of predestination includes a 'double' aspect.

Predestination is thus primarily concerned with soteriology, not with the doctrine of divine omniscience or providence, although the tradition called it a matter of *decretum* or *providentia specialis*.[11] I acknowledge why they did this, but in our time this is confusing, given that it could be construed to support the idea that predestination is, in one way or another, engraved in the structure of reality, so that belief in predestination would imply a belief in hard determinism, and I agree with Oliver Crisp who argues in *Deviant Calvinism* that it does not.[12] I would even like to argue that a proper Reformed doctrine of predestination presupposes a world in which real contingency is possible, as God created the world not as a machine, but as an open system in which defect and free moral agency are possible.

---

10. 'Calvinist' is put between parentheses because I am well aware that it is an anachronistic term and that various thinkers before Calvin held such a view. I nevertheless use the term because it is common among theologians to refer to this view with that name.

11. Ibid., and many other handbooks.

12. Oliver Crisp, *Deviant Calvinism: Broadening Reformed Theology* (Minneapolis, MN: Fortress, 2014), chapter 3.

6.4 Three basic options in soteriology

The reason why I argue in favour of a version of 'double' predestination can be more easily understood when we explore the consequences of alternatives to my thesis that the ultimate verdict about our life should not be in our own hands. In other words, the argumentative power of my contention in the rest of this chapter depends to a considerable extent on the plausibility of my claim in this section, namely that there is a limited set of consistent options regarding soteriology and eternal destiny and that only the predestinarian option is sufficiently able to avoid the risk of putting our ultimate destiny in our own hands.

6.4.1 Hard universalism

This argument regarding the limited set of soteriological options runs like this, assuming that predestinarianism as defined above is one option. My thesis is that if consistency is a requirement, apart from predestinarianism, there are only two remaining options. I call them 'hard' and 'soft' universalism. I will discuss hard universalism in this subsection and soft universalism in the next. Hard universalism means that God elects us all no matter what our response would be. This amounts to the view that God saves everyone, period. God may accomplish this by pleading endlessly with sinners (as defended by John Hick, for example), or by infusing grace into everyone, or by letting certain people go through purgatory and allowing them to go to heaven afterwards. Regardless of the means, hard universalism entails that no one ends up in hell in the end, nor will anyone be annihilated. God loves every human being up to the end. A term that has become popular for this view is '*apokatastasis (pantoon)*' as it was ascribed to the church father Origen.

Hard universalism raises serious problems in view of my concern that one's ultimate verdict should not rest in one's own hands. It implies a reversal of the order between God and humanity. If believers claim to know what everyone's ultimate destination is, they put themselves in God's place and free themselves from any judgement whatsoever. In this regard, hard universalism, whether we try to defend it on the basis of Scripture or deduce it directly from God's nature of love, ultimately rests on a confusion of the *opus Dei* and *opus hominum*. One can never put oneself in the position of declaring everyone's sins forgiven. That would be an exceptional form of hubris.

The reversal of the order of God and humanity is the main problem of hard universalism. This reversal leads to other problems. One might summarize these problems using Bonhoeffer's concept of 'cheap grace'. The concept of cheap grace can be elaborated further by distinguishing various dimensions implicit in it. One of them is the nature of grace. Grace, traditional theology holds to be certain, can only be freely given, and therefore, it can never be assumed or taken for granted. We will discuss this point below when we consider MacDonald's objection to it. Grace also becomes 'cheap' because even before we commit evil, it is evident that

God will forgive us. A concept of God emerges in which God indulges us all the time, like a kind of Santa Claus. It seems that God does not really care about evil.

However, this line of reasoning also has other, and perhaps unexpected, consequences for the psychology of believing in forgiveness, for example. Of course, hard universalism is intended to convince even the most hardened sinner of God's love and forgiveness. However, when forgiveness is assumed before we commit evil, it becomes psychologically harder to believe in it because forgiveness is so general that it does not seem to correlate with the actual life circumstances in which serious evil was committed. In order to be able to forgive oneself serious evils, it is essential to be convinced that the evil committed is really taken seriously by the one who forgives. Therefore, forgiveness can never be a given, not only from the perspective of the victim but also from the perspective of the perpetrator.

One might also approach the matter not so much from the perspective of the perpetrator as from the perspective of the victim. To offer a very practical example: hard universalism has led to many Christian funerals in which the deceased are unconditionally declared to be in heaven with God, and in which their life is sketched during the funeral in predominantly positive terms. This happens notwithstanding the fact that many funerals are moments in which those who remain behind have to deal with not only the positive aspects of the lives of their beloved but also the negative. And such aspects can be very serious, and they may have wounded those who remain behind in very profound ways. The problem of a Christian funeral in which universalism is assumed is that it has to start from the fact that all of these negative aspects have no serious place in the divine economy. In God's perspective, these negative aspects have been washed away, but they remain in the consciousness of those who are left behind.

What this means in more general terms is that a universalist concept of God and salvation encounters difficulty in adequately accounting for the nature of evil in the world. The severity and impact of evil are hard to measure. And evil should have a significant enough place in our theology that we consequently hesitate to claim that all sins will be forgiven, or to preach God's goodness as the reason why all shall be saved. It is easy to point out that a God who arbitrarily sends people to a place of eternal torment is a monster,[13] but the straightforward alternative to a God who must save all because he is good is perhaps another sort of monster, an almighty clown who simply grins at everyone. It is in any case not a God who takes fallen humanity, including all the atrocities that humans of flesh and blood commit in their sometimes very civilized and educated lives, sufficiently seriously. Evil is so serious that one cannot say whether it can be forgiven in some cases. How much punishment, how much correction, how much therapy does a father who abuses his child deserve? How much does a soldier who rapes a woman in a war deserve? Particularism can leave these questions open because they are questions for the most High to answer, not for us. Such a limitation in our theologies benefits

---

13. MacDonald, *The Evangelical Universalist*, chapter 1; Hart, *That All Shall Be Saved*, pt. 1.

both perpetrators who begin to show signs of repentance as well as victims who desperately ask themselves whether there is Someone who listens to their cries.

In recent years, Gregory MacDonald has made an attempt to counter various points made here in his *The Evangelical Universalist*.[14] One finds relevant counterarguments particularly when MacDonald argues against 'Calvinism' in various ways. First, he argues against the idea that claiming that God saves everyone leads to hubris.[15] In the preface to the second edition, he remarks:

> As an aside, I would add that this is precisely why I do *not* think it hubris to claim that God *will* save all people. Many theologians would assert that while we may hope that God *may* save all we cannot know that he *will*. To move beyond the mere hope that all will be saved is to go beyond what God has revealed. I beg to differ. The supreme revelation of God is found in Christ – the Word made flesh. And it is precisely *there*, in the climactic events of the gospel story, that we see God's revelation of the future of humanity. A hope grounded in the resurrection is not just an expression of what we'd *like* to see happen; it is, rather, a hope that does not disappoint.[16]

In the first chapter, he continues along these lines by linking up his 'hopeful dogmatic universalism' ('dogmatic universalism' is his term that is roughly equivalent to my term 'hard universalism') to the witness of Scripture, or at least to divine revelation:

> But why may we not be certain? Two kinds of argument tend to be given. Some universalists appeal to human freedom as the complicating factor, but we have already seen that freewill reasons for rejecting universalism are seriously wanting. Others appeal to God's sovereign freedom. 'Who are we to say that God *must* save all? In the end the decision is God's alone and he has not revealed it to us.' In no way would I wish to deny God's mystery or his sovereign freedom, but I must confess to finding this argument perplexing. As I argued in the Calvinism section above, not saving all people seems utterly out of character with the kind of God revealed to us in Jesus Christ.[17]

Hence, MacDonald rejects the accusation of hubris through an appeal to divine revelation in Jesus Christ, through Scripture. We are certain because God lets us know that we can be certain. In Chapter 5 of this book, on the doctrine of Scripture, I have already argued against the *sola scriptura* maxim because it runs the risk of turning Scripture into an idol, granting us infallible access to God's will and, therefore, giving us power that belongs to God alone. What leads to 'hubris'

---

14. MacDonald, *The Evangelical Universalist*.
15. Ibid., xx–xxi, 33.
16. Ibid., xx–xxi; original emphases.
17. Ibid., 33; original emphasis.

in soteriology aligns with a similar 'hubris' in the doctrine of Scripture and, as a consequence, in ecclesiology, because a church that claims to know God's truth through an infallible divine revelation in Scripture forgets about its own fallibility.

But there is another reason why MacDonald's confident statements about universalism in Scripture are problematic. When he deals with the question of the biblical basis for belief in hard universalism, he makes two types of statements that contradict each other. On the one hand, he claims – and this is the main thread running through the book – that the whole of Scripture is best understood in universalist terms. On the other hand, he explicitly admits that there are parts of Scripture that do not support universalism, and his aim is, as he explicitly notes, to reinterpret them in such a way as to make them compatible with universalism. In an appendix to the second edition, he makes the most explicit claim in this regard when he says: 'Remember too that my proposal was *not* that all the biblical authors or all New Testament authors believed in or taught universal salvation. In fact, I was very explicit that some biblical authors did not.'[18] There is no passage in the earlier chapters that is as explicit as this, although he says that 'virtually all the key Christian beliefs have some texts that seem to run against them'.[19] The sentence that follows, however, suggests that this is because we do not properly understand these texts: 'We may well maintain that, properly interpreted, they do not actually contradict what we take to be the clear teaching of other texts.'[20] In practice, the bulk of MacDonald's book consists of an attempt to show that the Bible can be read as supporting hard universalism, based upon the idea that

> the biblically minded systematic theologian is looking for theological grids, or stories, or doctrines that are *taught clearly in some biblical texts and are broad enough to serve as organising categories for considering the teachings of other biblical texts (without doing violence to them).*[21]

How one evaluates the result will probably strongly depend on one's view of the Bible and one's theological commitments. To me, MacDonald's reading of the Bible is too selective and too strongly predisposed to his own theological commitments to convince me of universalism. MacDonald explains at various places in his book why he does not want to go with a Bible that really contradicts itself,[22] but to me a self-contradictory Bible is the more convincing option.

With respect to the role of the Bible in MacDonald's argument, so far, so good. MacDonald touches on various other aspects of arguments that I have mentioned above. I do not only suggest that hard universalism leads to hubris, putting us in the position of God, I also suggest that it opens up the risk of producing a 'cheap grace'.

---

18. Ibid., 212; original emphasis.
19. Ibid., 37.
20. Ibid.
21. Ibid.; original emphasis.
22. Ibid., 210–14.

One element of this is that it deprives grace of its gratuitous nature because it turns God's grace into the 'default'. God must forgive, and this is why this forgiveness is 'cheap'. MacDonald argues against this in conversation with Paul Helm:

> I suggest that Helm is correct in seeing a certain asymmetry between justice and mercy but mistaken in claiming that if God *has* to show mercy then it cannot be true mercy he shows. It could be that it is in God's nature that he desires to show mercy to all. After all, Christians claim that God is love and that he loves his enemies. For God to be love, it would seem to be the case that he has to love all his creatures. This is because if it is God's very essence to love, then God cannot but love, in the same way that if God's essence is to hate evil, then he cannot but hate evil. And if God loves all he has created, then he will want to show saving mercy to all his creatures.[23]

My problem with MacDonald's argument here is that he merely repeats his claim but does not provide an argument for why he is right. MacDonald states that if love is God's nature, God has to forgive because of his nature as love and that this does not take away God's freedom. Later on, in an appendix to the second edition, MacDonald seems to argue that for every positive attribute we assign to God, God is forced to act in every case according to this positive attribute.[24] Therefore, if God is love, God has to act accordingly. However, this claim is problematic. If God is love in the relational sense of the word, as MacDonald and many other modern theologians claim, God is not only essentially love of some kind, but because God's actions in history are essential to his nature, God has to act according to this nature. In a different concept of God, a pre-modern Augustinian concept, for example, the divine attributes do not force God to act in a certain way. That God is merciful in Godself, the classic attribute that comes closest to divine love as an attribute, does not force God to be merciful to everyone everywhere, because God is also fully just, and it is God's wisdom and creativity to be both merciful and just in God's actions.

In addition, later on in one of the appendices to the second edition, MacDonald appeals to Barth's famous key thesis in the doctrine of God: God is the one who loves in freedom:

> Even if we grant that God does not *have* to love or save people, as soon as we confess that (i) God, in his freedom, has indeed chosen to love people and desires to save them (and the critic above *does* confess this), and that (ii) God is *able* to bring this salvation about (and the critic above also confesses this), then it *does* follow that (iii) all will be saved. In other words, this notion of radical divine freedom is universalist-compatible. The critic is wheeling divine freedom in the argument at the wrong point.[25]

23. Ibid., 22; original emphasis.
24. Ibid., 203–4.
25. Ibid.; original emphases.

Those who take Barth at his word will also believe that this solves the problem. This key thesis in Barth's concept of God reflects, in fact, a tension between God as being essentially with humans in Christ on the one hand, and being free to be the God who chooses to be with us in Christ on the other. It is very hard to see how one can be essentially with others on the one hand and free to be (or not be) with them on the other.

There is a third aspect of MacDonald's argument that affects my claim that hard universalism leads to cheap grace, namely the idea that evil would not matter because God will ultimately forgive everyone and everything. MacDonald denies this because he distinguishes between God's wrath and punishment as a corrective measure against evil and damnation as everlasting punishment. The first, he argues, is compatible with universalism, whereas the second is not. All passages in Scripture where God is said to punish, be angry, condemn and so forth are explained by MacDonald in temporary, transitive terms.

Another aspect of MacDonald's view is that he argues against the 'cheap grace' objection by suggesting that God does indeed punish, but not with eternal punishment. 'Covenant love is not a soft, sentimental love, but it does guarantee grace *in the end*.'[26]

> A theology that allowed both heaven and hell to be equally acts of divine love and justice is what we need. Those in hell are experiencing the wrath of God, but such wrath is not the *absence* of divine love but the *severity* of a divine love that allows the obstinate to experience the consequences of unwise lifestyles with the aim of ultimately redeeming them. God's justice is loving and his love just, and all the divine attributes cohere without any tension. The universalism that I have defended in this book promoted this coherence of the divine nature.[27]

Let me say first that the view of predestination that I defend in this chapter does not make eternal punishment an inevitable consequence of predestination. As God is free, God may also choose to save all. The point is that we do not know and should not claim to know whether he does. Moreover, I do not see it as the obligation of a Christian to believe that, if God does not elect certain people to salvation, God must consequently torment them eternally in some version of a medieval hell. I do not want to form an opinion about these forms of punishment because it is not up to me to decide on them.

This being said, I see more problems in MacDonald's view of punishment and the wrath of God. First of all, I think that his reinterpretation of all instances of the wrath of God in the Bible in terms of therapeutic correction and signs of the intensity of God's love are less than convincing. The wrath of God in the Bible is too frequent and too unpredictable to make such a model work.

---

26. Ibid., 102; original emphasis.
27. Ibid., 163–4; original emphases.

Also, my main question to MacDonald would be how this divine wrath fits into his concept of God as love. It is one thing to claim that both divine love and wrath are coherent aspects of MacDonald's soteriology, but it seems to me that to combine the two convincingly is more difficult than MacDonald suggests. Why would a God who is self-giving love and who showed that self-giving love in the death and resurrection of Jesus Christ still punish and do harm to people? How does that fit into the divine economy or, perhaps more importantly, into the human psychology of moral improvement that is implied by the concept of God as self-giving love? In any case of the commission of evil is the harmless confrontation with divine love not more helpful for improving the sinner than any harm or punishment done to them? If there is some truth in this, it is more than just arbitrary that, in many of the mainstream Christian universalist contexts, the punishment or wrath of God no longer plays a significant role. A more fundamental question, perhaps, is whether the relational God of MacDonald and others is so much on the same level with an idealized loving human being of some specific Western kind (daddy/mommy) that an authoritarian almighty punishment becomes altogether inconceivable? This is to say nothing of the question of how the promise of eventual forgiveness would affect the experience of punishment on the part of the sinner.

6.4.2 Soft universalism

Let me now briefly explore the second alternative to 'double' predestination. I call it 'soft universalism'; it is popularly phrased as 'Arminianism'. According to soft universalism, God did everything that one could possibly think of to save human beings. God will, however, in some significant way, respect human freedom. Although Arminians differ in their view of what counts as 'significant', this significance is of such a kind that if human beings persevere in refusing to accept God's offer of salvation, God will respect this decision and not save them in the end. Classically, Arminianism construed this significance in terms of so-called 'middle knowledge'.[28] Nowadays, various forms of so-called 'open theism' also come to mind as defences of soft universalism, although some of them could also count as examples of hard universalism in the sense that God will unceasingly entice people to give in to God's offer of salvation until all ultimately accept it.

Whereas in hard universalism, one of the key problems is cheap grace, soft universalism appears to be located at the opposite side of the spectrum by tending towards works righteousness. I need to 'do' something, although, at least theoretically, the main emphasis will still be on God helping me through his grace. Whereas defenders of hard universalism may draw all kinds of support from passages in the Bible where the absoluteness of God's grace is emphasized, soft universalists draw support from all of those passages where we seem to be

---

28. Eef Dekker, 'Was Arminius a Molinist?' *Sixteenth Century Journal* 27, no. 2 (1996): 337–52, https://doi.org/10.2307/2544137.

invited to be co-workers with God and where a strong appeal is made to human responsibility and indispensable acts of faith.

When we look closer at soft universalism, we will see that here too, the ultimate verdict on a person's life rests in their own hands. God becomes significantly dependent on the response of human beings, and although proponents of soft universalism are ready to add that God made Godself freely dependent on us, this does not really solve the problem. As Augustine already knew, soft universalism opens up a fundamental possibility of 'pride'. If God preaches the Gospel to everyone in my surroundings and most do not accept it, but I do, who is to be praised for this? I am. And through my conscious decision to be a believer, I arrive in a position where I can determine my own ultimate destiny.

The rest of this chapter will be a defence of the predestinarian view introduced above. As a form of soteriology, and in contradistinction to the two forms of universalism, I will call it 'particularism'. Most of the discussion of particularism will be continued in the next sections. Particularism is a view in which salvation depends on God alone. God chooses who will be saved independent of any human merit or foreseen faithful response to the preaching of the Gospel. In addition, by implication,[29] Christ died for the elect only, so that there is no room for a universal proclamation that Christ died for you.

This has significant implications for the nature of the Gospel message. The preaching of the Gospel can and should aim at everyone, but it is an invitation to believe in Jesus Christ with the promise that whosoever does this will be saved. As I will argue at length in the next section, this does not mean that the preaching of the Gospel or a faithful response to it becomes superfluous.[30] God is not depending on our faithful response in an absolute way, but on the other hand, quite to the contrary, God ordains the execution of God's sovereign will such that the elect will hear the Gospel and be enabled to faithfully respond to it with acts of faith.

Historically, we can confidently say that the tenability of particularism has always hinged upon the question of whether this option can be upheld without collapsing the whole of salvation history into the divine decree, as if salvation is no more than a getting to know one's election or reprobation. Thus, it would boil down to fatalism, and human responsibility would not receive its due place in theology. It would include the possibility of cheap grace or 'cheap condemnation' in the sense that as soon as I know that I am on a certain side, it no longer matters

---

29. For those who may doubt that this implication holds true: definite atonement is an implication of soteriological particularism because in particularism, not only the possibility of salvation must be in Christ salvific work, but also the actual faithful response by the believer. Because this faithful response is the actualization of the predestination decree, the work of Christ can only be applicable to the elect.

30. For a more elaborate argument in favour of this, see Maarten Wisse, 'The Inseparable Bond between Covenant and Predestination: Cocceius and Barth', in *Scholasticism Reformed: Essays in Honour of Willem J. Van Asselt*, ed. Maarten Wisse, Marcel Sarot and Willemien Otten, STAR 14 (Leiden: Brill, 2010), 259–79.

what I do. Consequently, the key question about particularism is whether it can avoid the pitfalls of either hard or soft universalism. In addition, it needs to uphold a significant level of concern about the knowledge of election or reprobation; otherwise, this option too will suffer from blurring the distinction between God and human beings. This is to say: if I know with certainty who is going to be on the right or the wrong side, I am in no better position than a hard universalist, because I assume the role of God. If, for example, church membership, or the performance of a certain ritual, is a guarantee of election, this makes it possible to determine my own salvation. In the rest of this chapter, I will come back to these risks in various ways.

6.5 Understanding double predestination

So far, we have not gone much further than an argument against hard and soft universalism. In this section, my aim is to explain in a bit more detail how I understand the practical implications of accepting the idea of double predestination in the face of the most basic objections that are brought forward against it. Again, in line with the main thread running through this chapter, the key to a proper understanding of double predestination is a careful distinction between the domain of God and the domain of human beings. In the tradition, this point is often made with reference to Deut. 29.29: 'The secret things belong to the Lord our God, but the things that are revealed belong to us and to our children forever, that we may do all the words of this law' (ESV). In the Reformed tradition, this verse was connected with the distinction between the hidden and the revealed will of God.[31] In the tradition, the use of this verse was part of a confessional frame of reference, as a way of making a truth-claim. I am using it not primarily as a truth-claim but as an interpretive key to the doctrine of double predestination as a whole, and even as part of the way in which the pre-modern method of thinking about predestination can be freed from the aberrant iterations of the doctrine.

Most problems raised concerning the doctrine of predestination are related to a failure to distinguish between the domain of God and the domain of human beings. Take such common objections as: well, if I am predestined, I do not need to care about how I live, because God will save me anyway; or, phrased differently: double predestination will make God the author of sin. These objections do not hold as long as one properly distinguishes between the domain of God and that of human beings. Human beings, as long as they are in this life, do not have access to a God's eye point of view regarding their election or reprobation, so they have no clue whatsoever about it. The only thing that belongs to their domain is: 'Whoever believes in the Son has eternal life' (Jn 3.36; ESV), or 'Assuredly, the evil man will not go unpunished' (Prov. 11.21). The only point of contact between the two domains,

---

31. Wilhelmus à Brakel, *The Christian's Reasonable Service*, ed. Joel R. Beeke, trans. Bartel Elshout (Ligonier, PA: Soli Deo Gloria, 1999), I, 3, 114.

and the reasons why it makes sense for believers to know about predestination (not: their own predestination), is at the point where predestination meets faith. A believer who believes, following this doctrine, knows that this is God's work in the believer, preceding the believer's own actions.

This leads the tormented believer to worry about whether God did his work in her or not, but again, this is a confusion between the domain of God and that of humans (I will deal with this particular concern more extensively below, in Section 6.7). Believers are kindly and sincerely invited through the preaching of the Gospel to embrace Christ offered to them, and the only thing that the doctrine of predestination adds to this is that believers are reminded that they do not embrace Christ from their own power, but that it is by the grace of God that they do so, if they do so. Thus, the doctrine of predestination, properly understood, does no more than underline the nature of faith as the result of grace, but it does not in any way directly interfere with human action.

In this respect, it is similar to the (traditional) Christian doctrine of providence. That God foresees and ordains everything in the future to keep me alive does not make me wait with taking my food and drink until God intervenes to ensure his providential care for me. Quite the contrary, it is through my taking my food and drink that God's providence is effectuated. Technically, the tradition phrased this by saying that the means were included in the divine decree of predestination.

The problem is that, apparently from the beginning of the doctrine as it was developed and propagated by Augustine, it has been open to misunderstandings based on a confusion of the two domains. This point was, clearly enough, one of the biggest concerns for those who argued against predestination in the seventeenth century and onwards. This is the reason why I propose a modern retrieval of the doctrine of predestination in what follows, although one might also see it as a proper interpretation of what the classical doctrine was supposed to mean. How one reads it depends partly on the reader's frame of reference.

6.6 Innovating double predestination

As we have seen above, one of the most common objections against double predestination not only in twentieth-century theology but also in spirituality is the claim that it is incompatible with the nature of God as love. If God is love, not just accidentally but essentially, as the famous verse from the Johannine tradition has it (1 Jn 4.8), then God cannot but be forgiving, as any fear is incompatible with love. As Barth 'defines' God in volume II/1 of the *Church Dogmatics*, God is the one who loves in freedom. This freedom aspect is a weak point in twentieth-century theology, because how can anyone be free to forgive if forgiving is one's essence? And what about other attributes such as justice?

Here my first modernization of the classical notion of double predestination comes into play. I do not think that it is entirely opposed to most historical forms of predestinarianism, but traditional theologians would probably not hold or propagate it in the form in which I do, nor for the same reasons. I believe that the freedom aspect is the key to the doctrine of double predestination, but in a way that is different from Barth. It means that God is free to choose who is going to be saved. Theoretically, this could include every single human being. There are even good biblical grounds to be added for believing so, although there is also quite a bit of biblical witness against it. I would hope for universal salvation, but the key point is: it is not my job to determine who is going to be saved or not.[32] This is God's business, as the doctrine of predestination serves the doctrine of God in which God is God and we are fallible and limited human beings.

The basic problem in the theological tradition defending predestination, especially the modern Calvinist one, is the fact that it identified too easily those who are going to heaven and those who are going to hell. And because it did so, it also knew what one had to do, what one had to believe or of what one had to be a member of in order to be on the right side of the spectrum. If not in theory, this was often the case in practice. Thus, predestination no longer functioned as an instrument for maintaining the distinction between God and humanity, between a divine and a human perspective, but quite the contrary, it tended to confuse the two domains.

The basic reason for this may be anthropological in the sense that human beings have a deep inner desire for identity markers and for controlling their ultimate end, but it is also motivated by the support that the tradition found for this in Scripture. Especially in Romans 9, a classic in the history of predestinarian thought, Paul openly speaks about Jacob who was loved by God, while Esau was hated (Rom. 9.13). Notwithstanding nuanced explanations of the word 'hated' in this context, here it seems clear that it is known to human beings who is on the right and who is on the wrong side. There are similar passages elsewhere in the Bible.

In spite of this, I still think that it is possible to find a good deal of support for my modernized version of the doctrine of predestination in the theological tradition. The idea that we cannot know who has been chosen and who has been reprobated is implied by the idea of double predestination itself, because if God chooses sovereignly, irrespective of any human actions or merit, then it is possible for God to choose anyone and, less explicitly noted, everyone. The predestinarian tradition indeed drew this implication. As early as Augustine, we find references to pagans during the times of the Jews who lived piously because they were predestined by God to eternal life in Christ, even while not knowing it.[33] Later, we find the same notion in the Westminster Confession, when it speaks about the

---

32. This is why I do not count myself among so-called 'hopeful universalists'. This hopeful universalism generally takes the form of trusting and proclaiming God's universal love such that one is a universalist without being completely certain. Although the position defended here may theoretically count as 'hopeful universalism', my emphasis on the distinction between God and humanity keeps it closer to particularism and double predestination. And again, as I argued in Section 6.3, as long as one has to maintain God's freedom, one's notion of predestination retains a double element.

33. Augustine, *De civitate Dei*, III, 1, and XVIII, 47.

work of the Spirit apart from the preaching of the Word (pagans or anyone who is chosen by God even without knowing the Gospel).[34]

In this respect, my modification is more an amplification than a complete departure from what is already present in the tradition, but it is present in a different way, under different circumstances and with different practical conclusions to be drawn from it.

Another modification of the traditional understanding of predestination concerns the question of eternal damnation, of 'hell' so to speak. I stress that I do not want to claim too much knowledge about hell or about the nature of 'eternal' damnation; this corresponds to my emphasis on the distinction between God and the world and the possibility of God saving everyone. What Scripture has to say about it, I would suggest, is meant as an incentive to do good, not necessarily as an accurate description of a state of affairs. What hell is like, if something like this exists, is God's business. I do not want to put anyone in hell, apart from my worst moments, and I do not think that it belongs to the core of my faith to say anything straightforward about it. My argument does not forbid anyone to do so; rather, it invites other people to join me and to leave eternal punishment to God and not form an opinion about it. This is, of course, different from the tradition, parallel to what I said above about knowing who goes there and who does not. All of this depends on a more nuanced hermeneutic with regard to what we find in Scripture.

6.7 Predestination and assurance of faith

Finally, in this section, I will address an issue that highlights the cost of accepting my account of double predestination. This cost has to do with the emphasis on the distinction between the domain of God and that of human beings. I have argued that human beings have neither the ability nor the need to inquire about their predestination in any direct way, because the order of salvation in time does not provide immediate access to the decree of predestination, but rather an indirect knowledge of one's salvation through a faithful response to the Gospel message. There is one important consequence of this, and this is both an innovation and something deeply rooted in the tradition, namely the fact that an absolute certainty about one's salvation, an access to God's knowledge, so to speak, is impossible. What I know in this life is that God welcomes sinners and promises sinners to be saved by embracing Jesus Christ as their Saviour, but I do not know whether I am among the elect or not.

One might ask: why not? If I believe, my act of faith in Christ is the fruit of God's grace, so if I believe, I perform that act of saying yes to the Gospel, I have received grace and therefore, I belong to the elect. But the tradition has not put it in such an easy way, and this is because it is aware, both from Scripture (the

---

34. 'Westminster Confession of Faith' (1646), 10, 3.

parable of the sower is famous and notorious!) and from pastoral practice, that not all faith is sincere. An example from the tradition is William Perkins who writes the work *A Treatise Tending unto a Declaration, Whether a Man Be in the Estate of Damnation, or in the Estate of Grace*, where the first chapter bears the telling title: 'How farre a Reprobate may goe in Christian Religion'.[35] Many others follow in his footsteps.

Theologically, therefore, one has to distinguish between assurance of faith and assurance of one's election, because assurance of faith depends on the sincerity of one's faith. Subsequently, one has to distinguish different levels of assurance of faith. If Christ died for the elect only, as I have suggested above, it is impossible to preach to everyone: 'Christ has died for you.' The message of the Gospel cannot be that Christ died for you; rather, it must be that everyone who believes in Jesus Christ, will be saved.[36] In the post-Reformation Reformed tradition, this leads to discourse about assurance of faith that recognizes various levels of assurance. Differing from John Calvin, who emphasized that assurance belongs to the nature of faith, post-Reformation Reformed theologians acknowledge that there are different acts of faith, some more direct and others more indirect. The direct and proper act of faith is embracing Christ as present and proclaimed in the Gospel (and the sacraments) and in this act, there is assurance because the believer is united with Christ.

However, there are also indirect acts of faith that bring with them certain levels of assurance. As William Perkins notes in his little work *A Graine of Mustard-Seed: or, the Least Measure of Grace That Is or Can Be Effectuall to Salvation*,[37] an act of faith can be as small as 'longing for faith' and so it will be rather distant from assurance at that point. Nevertheless, Perkins uses the recognition that one longs for faith to comfort terrified believers in their hope for salvation, since it is God who brings them to faith. Likewise, as the Heidelberg Catechism acknowledges (Question and answer 86), there is a more steadfast and mature indirect form of assurance that involves recognizing the grace God has given us in our relationship with God in Christ and the good works that come with it. As to the condition of assurance, this is a condition that results from reflections on, and so is subsequent to, the direct act of embracing Christ. The believer's conscience comes to this conclusion on the basis of the recognition that one is united to Christ, and therefore, assured of salvation, but only in accordance with the measure of their faith.

This of course raises worries among believers based on the signs of true faith that they find (or do not find) within themselves. This has led to what is often perceived as the worst spiritual consequences of the Calvinist tradition, because it can result in believers who do not feel free to enjoy the salvation that Christ has

---

35. William Perkins, *Works* (London: Legat, 1600), 574ff, https://archive.org/stream/gol denchaineorde00perk.

36. For a more elaborate account of this point, see Wisse, 'Inseparable Bond'.

37. Perkins, *Works*, 1046ff.

accomplished for us, but who only worry internally about the question of whether they can trace within themselves the signs of God's work. The reply is that such a conclusion does not follow from the doctrine, because believers should turn to Christ and find security in him rather than within themselves. Calvin's famous dictum 'Christ, then, is the mirror wherein we must, and without self-deception may, contemplate our own election'[38] is still valid in the later tradition. The major problem that later pietists create concerning assurance of faith is not caused by the doctrine of predestination as such but by making the invitation to embrace Christ preached in the Gospel in faith dependent on the recognition of certain signs of election in one's spiritual life.

Assurance of faith is what it says: assurance of faith, and faith is in the believer and therefore relative to the believer's relationship with God in Christ. Thus, there is assurance of faith, but this assurance of faith cannot be taken out of the believer's actual relationship with God in Christ and, therefore cannot be absolutized. Faith can be insincere, and as such, it may and does err. One might raise eyebrows about this and ask how on earth one might subscribe to such old-fashioned ideas. However, what we find behind this, religiously and anthropologically, is a deep concern about displacing God's verdict about one's life, and consequently, a deep religious concern about proper behaviour and about the abuse of the teaching in the form of cheap grace. Apart from a concern about concrete proper behaviour, it includes a concern about an appropriate form of humility that helps to cultivate virtues such as modesty, openness to others and a healthy attitude towards questions of power. And in this regard, I think that one has to take these consequences much more seriously in contemporary theology than has often been the case. Although most liberation theologians and postcolonial thinkers would never imagine it, these old-fashioned ideas are part of an internal Christian critique of religion that comes close to their own concerns.[39]

And therefore, I am defending the propositions that this consequence of not having access to the ultimate verdict about one's life in this life is appropriate.

> And therefore it is the duty of every one to give all diligence to make his calling and election sure, that thereby his heart may be enlarged in peace and joy in the Holy Ghost, in love and thankfulness to God, and in strength and cheerfulness in the duties of obedience, the proper fruits of this assurance; so far is it from inclining men to looseness.[40]

---

38. Cf. Calvin, *Institutes (1559)*, ed. John T. McNeill, trans. Ford Lewis Battles (Kentucky: Westminster, 1960), III.24.5.

39. At this point, there is a similarity with the argument developed in Susannah Ticciati, *A New Apophaticism: Augustine and the Redemption of Signs* (Leiden: Brill, 2015), who argues that Augustine's late predestinarian works should not be read as accounts of what God does, but rather as attempts to stimulate proper ways of being human.

40. 'Westminster Confession of Faith', 18, 3.

Chapter 7

ATONEMENT: SOCINUS AND OWEN IN CONVERSATION

7.1 Two theses

Two theses posed by Christoph Schwöbel provide the context for this chapter. One thesis occurs time and again in Schwöbel's work and was mentioned repeatedly during sessions of his doctoral seminar when I was a fellow in Heidelberg and Tübingen: the conviction that in theology the concept of God is decisive for one's overall view of the Christian faith.[1] The other thesis is an oral remark in a conversation about the relationship between God and the world in which Schwöbel remarked that all speech about God's actions in the world would have to follow the distinction between Law and Gospel.[2]

In this chapter, I would like to bring these two statements into dialogue with each other. Having learned from Schwöbel to think through the Christian faith in its inner dynamics, seeing how the Christian confession of the Triune God plays a decisive role in the shaping of every Christian doctrine, I have gradually become interested in the way in which the Law-Gospel distinction plays such a role as well.

In what follows I will explore these two approaches in terms of a very concrete dialogue: the dialogue on the nature of Christ's atonement between Faustus Socinus (1539–1604) and John Owen (1616–1683). After giving a brief account of their positions on atonement, I will argue that, in spite of the strong difference between the two with regard to the doctrine of atonement, both have a common target. That is, both are interested in justice. They differ with regard to the path

---

1. Christoph Schwöbel, 'Die Trinitätslehre als Rahmentheorie des christlichen Glaubens. Vier Thesen zur Bedeutung der Trinität in der christlichen Dogmatik', in *Gott in Beziehung: Studien zur Dogmatik* (Tübingen: Mohr Siebeck, 2002), 25–51; Christoph Schwöbel, 'Einleitung', in *Gott, Götter, Götzen: XIV. Europäischer Kongress für Theologie (11.–15. September 2011 in Zürich)*, ed. Christoph Schwöbel (Leipzig: Evangelischer Verlagsanstalt, 2013), 11–20.

2. It would be interesting to compare my way of bringing the two in dialogue with Schwöbel's own Trinitarian way, but there is no space here to go into this. See also: Christoph Schwöbel, 'Law and Gospel', in *Religion Past and Present*, ed. Hans Dieter Betz, 4th edn vol. 3 (Tübingen: Mohr Siebeck, 2006–13), 862–67.

towards it, but their intention is the same. Somehow, one might say that my reading is an attempt to bring Socinus and Owen into a retrospective ecumenical conversation, a dialogue in which they learn to understand each other's motives for holding their beliefs. In organizing this conversation posthumously, primarily, we will not pragmatically strive towards common ground or mutual agreement, but the understanding of God operative in the dialogue will take centre stage.[3]

Finally, I would like to defend Owen's point of view and subsequently see what the analysis of Socinus and Owen might tell us about the theological rationality at work within the conversation. This will show us how the doctrine of God and the Law-Gospel distinction shape the way in which they develop their views of atonement.

7.2 Socinus' critique of substitutionary atonement

When *De Jesu Christo Servatore*, one of Socinus' groundbreaking works, appeared in 1594, it caused a theological earthquake. Here was someone who dared to say that Christ did not and even could not die for our sins. If God forgives, God forgives without satisfaction.[4] In his work, Socinus gives us various arguments for this position. I will address the key reasons given in part three of his work, the part in which Socinus attacks the doctrine of substitutionary atonement.

Socinus' first reason is that if God could not forgive without satisfaction, God would be less powerful than human beings (Socinus, 221). Human beings are able to forgo our right to punish, and indeed it is this that we mean when we say that someone forgives someone else. The one who forgives was within his rights to punish or to require compensations but forgoes this right. This is what forgiveness means, and, therefore, this is what it should mean for God too. Otherwise, God would lack a capability that humans have.

In the next paragraph, Socinus immediately adds another argument. If God would be obliged to punish, and therefore executes this punishment on his Son, God would be too similar to a human judge. A human judge punishes because he has to obey a law that has been given to him and on which he is dependent. But it is impossible to compare God to such a judge, because, Socinus says, 'God should be considered a Lord and supreme Leader, whose will alone is law in everything and is the absolute perfect standard because he has to act from his own right alone.'[5]

---

3. Thus, programmatically: Christoph Schwöbel, 'Gottes Ökumene. Über das Verhältnis von Kirchengemeinschaft und Gottesverständnis', in *Christlicher Glaube im Pluralismus. Studien zu einer Theologie der Kultur* (Tübingen: Mohr Siebeck, 2003), 107–32.

4. Faustus Socinus, *De Jesu Christo Servatore* (Alex Rodecius, 1594). Page numbers are to this edition and mentioned in the English translation used: Alan W. Gomes, 'Faustus Socinus' de Jesu Christo Servatore, Part III: Historical Introduction, Translation and Critical Notes' (Fuller Theological Seminary, 1990).

5. 'sed tamquam dominus & princeps, cuius sola voluntas, cum de ipsius iure tantùm agatur, omnium rerum lex est, & perfectissima norma.'

Therefore, the good is not something that exists independent from God. What is good wholly depends on God's will (Socinus, 222). Something is not righteous because it is righteous but because God wanted it to be so. And so, God can forego his right to punishment because God is not bound to the rules of justice.

On the contrary, asking for satisfaction for our sins would degrade God's right and power enormously. Suppose that a human king had various debtors and went to a rich man to ask him to pay back the debt of all of the poor people and, in the meantime, went to the poor to declare that they were free from debt. Would we praise the king for absolving the debts? Quite to the contrary, we would hold him for a robber because the king is rich and does not need such compensations at all. Likewise, Socinus argues, would it be if God would find satisfaction for our wrongdoings through the death of his own Son (Socinus, 237).

Nevertheless, there is a snag that has to be considered. This becomes clear when Socinus starts using the phrase 'true satisfaction' (*vera satisfactio*). When he explains why he uses this phrase, the snag becomes apparent:

> I said 'true satisfaction' because God no doubt has always demanded something from people whom he has forgiven. Perhaps we could even go so far as to say that this 'some-thing' takes the place of satisfaction. (228)[6]

For Socinus, repentance and improvement of life is a precondition of forgiveness. Right at the moment in which we hoped to receive forgiveness without any effort from our side, the true form of satisfaction emerges: God does not do something for us, but we have to do something for God, namely repent and better our lives (Socinus, 228). Here also we see a marked difference between those who feel sympathetic to Socinus in our time and Socinus himself. Present-day critics of substitutionary atonement will suggest that God's forgiveness concerns all, without any preconditions on our side to be fulfilled. To Socinus, on the contrary, the acts of repentance and improvement of life are the cornerstones of his teaching on satisfaction.

7.3 John Owen's reply

In 1653, about fifty years after Socinus' death, one of the many responses to his work appeared. John Owen (1616–83) published his *Dissertation on Divine Justice*, initially in Latin.[7] The English theologian and puritan John Owen, who

---

6. 'Dixi autem, Vera satisfactione, propterea quòd dubium non est, quin Deus in iis, quibus peccata condonavit, semper aliquid requisierit, quod fortasse satisfactionis loco fuisse dici potest.'

7. John Owen, *Diatriba de Iustitia divina* (Oxford: Thomas Robinson, 1653). Quotations from and references to: John Owen, 'Dissertation on Divine Justice', in *The Works of John Owen*, ed. William H. Goold, vol. 10 (London: Johnstone & Hunter, 1850-5), 482–624.

was a professor at the University of Oxford at the time of this work's publication, addressed extensively Socinus and those who followed him. This was because Socinianism and subtle derivations of it were enormously popular in England. This was not only true of people who Owen saw as heretics, but equally so of some of Owen's dear colleagues such as the Scottish divine Samuel Rutherford. After having set out his view of vindicatory justice, Owen makes his argument on the basis of the Bible and non-Christian sources, and finally refutes the opinions of others, Socinus' among others.

Owen's focus is not so much on atonement as on justice. The reason for attacking Socinus and others at this point, however, is Socinus' suggestion that satisfaction is not necessary. So, rather than attacking Socinus in the field of atonement, Owen addresses his view of justice.

The key to Owen's argument is that vindictive justice (*iustitia vindicatrix*) belongs to God's nature. This is to be understood as those things that we can say about God because they are an essential part of his way of acting (Owen, 498–99). Given that God does something, it is an integral part of this acting to act justly, and necessarily so. In Socinus, God as the supreme Lord was free to choose what is just or unjust. To Owen, this is a mistake because God is intrinsically just and so cannot arbitrarily choose what is just or not.

This idea that God is intrinsically just and so, sin presupposed, is obliged to punish was Socinus' main reason to suggest that God, who is infinitely just, must infinitely punish any sin committed by human beings. This charge provides the background for the second key aspect of Owen's view of vindicatory justice, namely that God is free how to exercise it:

> Let our adversaries, therefore, dream as they please, that we determine God to be an absolutely necessary agent when he is a most free one, and that his will is so circumscribed, by some kind of justice which we maintain, that he cannot will those things which, setting the consideration of that justice aside, would be free to him; for we acknowledge the Deity to be both a *necessary* and a *free* agent. (Owen, 510; original emphases)

Hence, Owen's key concern is to maintain the integrity of divine action as being integrally embedded in the divine nature, but given that the Triune divine nature intends to save human beings freely through the death of Christ as the second person of the Trinity incarnate, God is not forced to punish in a certain way but freely chooses to punish sin through the death of his Son Jesus Christ. That God must punish means that God cannot be indifferent, but it does not imply that God has to punish in a specific way (510).

7.4 Owen's use of the Bible

As is well known, and modern biblical exegesis has made amply clear, biblical discourse about the salvific meaning of Jesus' death and resurrection is much broader than the concept of substitution.[8] In the Gospels, discourse about substitution is quite rare. The Gospel of John uses the metaphor of Jesus as the Lamb of God who carries away the sins of the world. In Paul, we find the notion of substitution, but the notion of Jesus' death as a punishment for the sins of believers is not so common. Socinus would have been happy with these results. In the second part of his work, he deals extensively with passages from Paul in order to interpret them in such a way as to not say that Christ has died for our sins on our behalf.

An illuminating aspect of Owen's work on divine justice is that he deals with the biblical evidence in a way that is markedly different from what one might expect. Owen in particular is known for his emphasis on the infallibility of Scripture, even up to the vowel signs of the Hebrew script.[9] As is often supposed about pre-modern theologians, one would expect him to give proof-texts, *dicta probantia*. One would perhaps expect him to deal with Isa. 53.5: 'But he was wounded for our transgressions, he was bruised for our iniquities: the chastisement of our peace was upon him; and with his stripes we are healed' (AV). But surprisingly, he does not deal with any passage from Scripture in order to argue that it directly supports his position.

Quite to the contrary, Owen's discussion of Scripture starts and ends with the statement that his view is supported by Scripture all over the place (Owen, 510 and 516–17). Initially, this might sound as an easy generalization that saves him from the pain of having to prove his point. However, one might also read it differently. One might say that, according to Owen, what the whole of Scripture has to say can be understood only in terms of the idea that anyone who transgresses the Divine commandments has to do with God himself, with the essence of who God is. And God can do nothing but react to this with anger and punishment. How God has to react is still to be seen, but it is unavoidable that God will react because, indeed, God and his justice are one and the same. In line with this, Owen discusses all sorts of verses from the Bible that affirm the righteousness of God and God's liability to punishment.

7.5 Anthropology as an argument

Another very interesting aspect of Owen's use of the Bible is the place that the Bible has in his overall argumentation. When it comes to 'proving' theological claims, Owen is still in a quite different world from ours. The Bible is still part of a broader frame of reference in which other sources of wisdom from extra-biblical

---

8. Cf. Jörg Frey and Jens Schröter, eds, *Deutungen des Todes Jesu im Neuen Testament* (Tübingen: Mohr Siebeck, 2005).

9. Carl R. Trueman, *The Claims of Truth: John Owen's Trinitarian Theology* (Carlisle: Paternoster, 1998), 64–75.

antiquity have a legitimate place.[10] The Bible is important, but his method is not yet influenced by the Enlightenment idea that the Bible is a separate source of truth against which all theological statements have to be verified. As we will see below, his appeal to Scripture goes smoothly together with appeals to human civilization, and he reserves more space for these than for the argumentation on the basis of Scripture.

This is evident from what follows. Owen continues with an anthropological argument, arguing that all of us have been created with the inner conviction that God punishes injustice. We know this from Scripture, but various pagan authors show an awareness of this as well. Pagan cultures of sacrifice show that the desire for satisfaction of our guilt is deeply rooted in our human condition. Rather than interpreting these cultural phenomena as mere signs of human behaviour, Owen interprets them in the context of the Christian doctrine of creation. God has given us basic knowledge of his essence and for this reason, Christians and non-Christians alike have an innate desire for compensation of their wrongdoings, even when they lose the appropriate means through which God takes them away.

Under different hermeneutical and cultural circumstances, we might make Owen's point in this way: compensation of evil is not only necessary for God but equally for us as well. In order to enable us to begin anew, both in our relationship with God but also in our relationships with fellow humans and with ourselves, we have to be reconciled with ourselves. This reconciliation with ourselves does not and cannot replace our reconciliation with God. Quite to the contrary, it is the anthropological corollary to it. Being reconciled with oneself is complicated, because one always knows oneself only partially, and this makes us anxious. Who are we? And what and how much evil did we commit? There is always something to worry about. Sometimes, we pass by those feelings with extravagance and an overload of worldly pleasure, but all too often it leaves us with a debilitating feeling of anxiety. Did I do well enough with my children, or my partner? Was this business transaction really responsible? What if I had done this or that? And this is why we ask for punishment ourselves. What is more, we in fact punish ourselves with feelings of obligation, depression or anger. We might also punish others by overruling them and do even more evil to them than we did before.

The cult of sacrifice is a way in which human beings effectuate their desire for compensation and punishment. One wants to make sacrifices because one feels unable to go on with one's life without it. This, Owen argues, is not arbitrary; it is given by God (Owen, 545). The ultimate soteriological target of this theological statement is beautifully rendered towards the end of the tractate:

---

10. Hans W. Frei, *The Eclipse of Biblical Narrative; A Study in Eighteenth and Nineteenth Century Hermeneutics* (New Haven: Yale University Press, 1974), 2–3, and more extensively chapter 2.

As, then, the perfection of divine justice is infinite, and such as God cannot by any means relax, it is of the last importance to sinners seriously and deeply to bethink themselves how they are to stand before him. (623)

This is what Owen is after: we have to ask ourselves fundamentally and profoundly who we are *coram Deo*. And such a question to ourselves has to be strong enough to block easy escapes such as quickly reminding ourselves of God's loving kindness. Life is too serious to be lived in this way up to the highest level of our existence.

Anyone who wants to find peace will have to face himself or herself. The Gospel message is *Gott sei Dank*; we do not need to find an escape. God has decided to be satisfied with the death of his only Son, Jesus Christ. Socinus is right: God is no marionette of his own justice, as if he is bound to his own character to be eternally punishing to an infinite extent. God is free in the way in which God makes satisfaction for our wrongdoings. Nevertheless, God takes our actions seriously at every moment of our life. God asks for something to be done by way of recompense. And we do well to realize this as we take our next step.

7.6 How Socinus and Owen share the same concern

In Faustus Socinus and John Owen we meet two extremes. Both go for a radical way of putting the matter. Owen tries to get as close as possible to the thesis that God must punish. That the guilt of those who belong to Christ is taken away is more than just an arbitrary aspect of the economy of salvation; Scripture teaches that Christ had to suffer and then enter his glory (Lk. 24.26). Faustus Socinus, on the other hand, makes an honest attempt to maintain that Christ did not suffer at all for the sins of others. He argues why this is not necessary and even impossible. The only satisfaction that God asks from us is our repentance and change of life. These are two extremes of which it seems there is no way in between.

There is a shared concern, however. As we have seen, Owen's fundamental concern is how we live *coram Deo* and that God's justice has the highest priority in this, not only for God but also for us. What is at stake is that God's good news of salvation does not shut down God's justice. His fundamental concern is how our appropriation of salvation links up with our concrete way of living. This has been an ongoing concern in the Reformation. Part of this concern is the question of to what extent the commandments spoken of in the Old Testament still remain valid within a Christian frame of reference. Does God do something radically new in Christ, or do old structures remain, albeit in a modified form? These are questions that have bothered Christianity from the very beginning, and they are given with the complexity of its canonical tradition.

Exactly at this point, Socinus and Owen might learn to appreciate each other's concerns. If Socinus has to give a moral reason why he rejects the idea of substitutionary atonement, he would express the same concern as John Owen, except for the fact that their solutions are opposite. Is it not far too easy, Socinus would say, to put the guilt of all you have done wrong at the feet of someone else and say that he made satisfaction for it? Is that not a license for going on with your life as if nothing happened? What does it mean for the future? Is this not a license for cheap grace?

Socinus' solution to the perceived problem is radical: the doctrine of substitutionary atonement must be completely abolished. What has to be done to make forgiveness on God's part possible, we must do. And this is what Jesus shows us: how you can and must do justice, and so we have to follow!

Yes, Owen replies, this is true, we have to follow him and, indeed, justice has to be done from the beginning to the very end, in Christ or not. What we see all around us, however, is that we cannot follow Christ. We will only be brought on the way towards following Christ if he is not only our example, but if he is also the one who died for our sin. Only then, living in communion with the living risen Christ and participating in him through the sacraments, only then will we manage, albeit partially, with trial and error, to accomplish what God asks from us. If we only try to take a single step on our own, we will never make progress. Christ's work for us goes before our doing his will.

Oh yes, Socinus mumbles, we know that: 'with trial and error'. You simply do not try hard enough! You believe that in those things in which you still fail Christ will come to help and forgive, and this is why you keep being imprecise in keeping God's commandments. Socinus and Owen will probably not find agreement. There was harsh criticism from followers of both sides in the sixteenth and seventeenth centuries. But their concern, the big danger that they see in front of them, is the same.[11]

7.7 Diagnosing the Fall

From an initial description of Owen's and Socinus' positions on substitutionary atonement, we have made a gradual transition towards bringing these two positions into dialogue with each other. Now, I want to make one additional step and argue why Owen has to be preferred over Socinus. One of the main reasons why Owen has to be preferred over Socinus is the latter's anthropology. We have already seen that for Socinus, although he denies that God needs satisfaction for being able to forgive, there is still something like a satisfaction required, namely our repentance. Of course, requiring repentance from human beings as their satisfaction for their wrongdoings presupposes that they can and do repent. Otherwise, it would not constitute a viable path towards salvation. And indeed, Socinus' anthropology is considerably more optimistic than Owen's, too optimistic I would say.

---

11. In Chapter 3, I presented a similar argument in terms of the range of interpretations of the prologue to the Gospel of John, showing how all varieties of the Reformation, including the radical varieties, shared the same concern about the good life and the well-being of society.

In the context of his argument in favour of our repentance as a condition for forgiveness, Socinus presents the following straightforward anthropological scheme. According to him, there are two types of humans:

1 Human beings who make small mistakes every now and then. They are regarded by God as pure and, therefore, they do not need forgiveness.
2 Human beings with deep rooted evil habits. They have to convert themselves and show genuinely new behavior in order to become liable to forgiveness. If they change their minds, they with be forgiven without recompense. (Socinus, 228–9)

There is a third type, namely those who 'stubbornly persist in sin', that Socinus does not speak of explicitly, but which he mentions in passing. God remains angry with them, although Socinus does not specify for how long (235). Basically, conversion is something that one has to accomplish for oneself. After having converted oneself, the help of the Holy Spirit is available to remain on the right track.

I consider Socinus' anthropology to be the best reason for not accepting his position. First of all, as I suggested above, repentance as a condition to forgiveness is in tension with Socinus' own argument that God forgives without recompense. It is true that God forgives without recompense if your sins are minor, but on the other hand, God demands something for being able to forgive. Ironically, in arguing so, Socinus exactly confirms Owen's point, namely that it is very difficult to conceive of divine forgiveness without recompense!

Furthermore, the anthropological scheme is so straightforward that it is difficult to imagine a reality in which the scheme can be successfully applied. What are these 'minor sins'? What is 'minor' to one is 'major' to another. And what about repentance and permanent change of mind? How does it work to simply intrinsically change one's mind if one has deep-rooted evil habits? Socinus seems to overlook the complexity of the layered and tragic reality of evil. He cannot elucidate it, let alone have a solution to it. At this point, Owen digs much deeper. The deep-rooted reality of evil in our lives requires the depth of God's grace rather than a sudden moral change of mind.

Evil goes deep, and a change is needed that reaches to that depth. From Owen's view of atonement the psychological complexity of guilt and forgiveness can be much more convincingly elucidated than from Socinus'. I cannot simply undo my sins by starting anew and never do it again. Even children know that, and Socinus knew so himself by speaking about deep-rooted evil habits. In order to start anew, forgiveness is already required, and, therefore, it cannot just be the consequence of my conversion. This is partly because evil feels, psychologically, irreversible. The idea 'once a sinner, always a sinner' is part of our psychological setup. And this is, among other reasons, why satisfaction is necessary.

Speaking about the believer who has received forgiveness, Owen manages more convincingly to show that the believer remains a sinner, and thus, copes with the fact that the deep-rooted evil habits do not fade away overnight. This should not lead the sinner to become overly easy-going, but it should strengthen him or her to keep going and recover when sin creeps in again.

7.8 God as the lord of Florence

Next to the worry about Socinus' anthropology, one of the main reasons for concern about his position is the way in which he speaks about God. To some extent, it might seem that Socinus has a point when he says that God can never become the servant of justice.[12] God has to be free to choose what is right. Nevertheless, Owen is particularly concerned about the images of God that play a key role in Socinus' view of atonement. We have to be concerned as well, but we live after modernity, after Marx who made us particularly conscious of the ways in which theologies may serve the interests of those in power.

Such a post-Marxist consciousness is possibly awakened by Socinus' way of speaking about God. Socinus describes God as follows: 'God is the highest lord and leader, whose will alone is law and the highest norm of all things' (Socinus, 221). What sort of God is this? In this definition, God does not seem far away from a dictator who does whatever pleases him. There is another aspect of Socinus' argument that catches the post-Marxist eye: the concept of merchandise. In Socinus' theology, justice and merchandise become linked up with each other. Satisfying God's justice after sin has been done begins to sound like buying justice and using it to satisfy God's desire for punishment. If not carried out by the perpetrator, then by one who substitutes for him. On the one hand, Socinus criticizes the metaphor of paying for sin by the death of the innocent Jesus, but, on the other hand, these are the metaphors that determine his discourse.

With Socinus, God becomes like the Di Medici lords in Florence who determined almost wholly independently who was to make their next brilliant sculpture. The sculptures are still admired by us, but what about the principles of justice? A certain nobility of character cannot be denied of God, Socinus says about the essence of God, but in God there is apparently no such thing as inherent justice. The Di Medici lords also had quite a good taste, so this nobility of character cannot be denied of them either, but as we know from quite a few of their other actions, this was still far removed from an intrinsic justice.

The problem is: if it is true of God that justice is the result of the arbitrary decisions of the Most High, this has crucial ramifications regarding the status of justice in us and the world around us. We will thus regard the principles of justice as expressions of God's arbitrary preferences. Things are good or bad because God wants it to be so, but their moral qualities are not intrinsic to the things themselves. And because they are arbitrary, they can be negotiated.

Owen helps us to understand the question of justice at the most fundamental level, namely on the level of God. We do not relate to God in a contractual way, as if God is our partner on the same level as we are. And likewise, the law of God is not arbitrary; they are not useful rules that have been fixed sometime, waiting to be taken up for modification under new circumstances. Neither are they rules that

---

12. Cf. Vincent Brümmer, *Speaking of a Personal God: An Essay in Philosophical Theology* (Cambridge: Cambridge University Press, 1992), chapter 4.

can be negotiated every time we think we need this, ensuring some moral flexibility on God's part that we could not count on before. Justice is not a commodity. God and creatures are not related as equal merchandising partners.

Such is also the case with our position in creation. We cannot move God into our way of operating with good and evil, as if we can opt for evil one time and for good at another. Indeed, God is the highest justice and so God cannot choose what justice is. And therefore, God does not choose the good because it is good, nor can God choose what he wants to be good. God is the highest justice, not because we can prove this to be the case, but because by definition, we are God-made. We belong to a lower order. We are creatures of God; we can only trace God's ways; we cannot determine God's nature.

And this is why Socinus' story about atonement is also fundamentally flawed. Socinus tries to reorganize the relationship between God and the world in a revolutionizing way by changing the point of departure, albeit probably partly without realizing it himself. Socinus starts thinking about the relationship between God and us as a neutral relationship that we can arbitrarily organize. God has something to choose, and we have something to choose. God is infinitely more powerful than we are, but, fundamentally, God plays the same game as we do. Within this game, the rules of just play can be freely negotiated between the two partners. Justice is a commodity whose shape is freely determined, but one can even sell it between partners if one of the partners happens to violate the rules agreed upon. In this same context, one might negotiate whether, in case one of the partners breaks the contract, compensation is necessary or not.

Owen does not understand anything of this. The misunderstanding is not such that Owen and Socinus disagree in the context of the same frame of reference. The real problem is that, although unconsciously, they have started to speak different languages. For Socinus, justice is a commodity that one might buy or sell, whereas for Owen, justice is not a product but the backbone of the system itself. Justice is not a package that you can transfer from one place to another, but the prerequisite of the traffic. As soon as we change our understanding of justice, the whole system collapses. Our world is upheld by the life-giving justice of God, flowing to us through creation, and recreating us according to Christ's image through the saving work of the Holy Spirit.

This is why what God does in Christ cannot be put in terms of negotiating satisfaction for our guilt. Socinus frames the traditional doctrine of atonement in those terms and refutes it, but this framing is a redescription of old concepts in terms of his own new frame of reference. What God does in Christ is not simply a way of 'resetting the system' as if nothing happened and as if one can always begin anew. Owen sensed this even when he might have had difficulties to put it into terms. Atonement is the restoration of the system in substantial ways. It is, to formulate it more theologically, the recreation of creation in its fundamental direction towards God. Atonement, not just as personal salvation but as a more encompassing restoration of the shape of the world, is a cosmic process. It restores the foundation of our existence. In Christ, God restores the fundamental 'rightness', the backbone of our existence, without which we cannot live or at least not live as we ought to and as we are destined to. We touch this in our flesh and bones, in the despair in which we find ourselves and in the anxiety that drives us forward.

The suffering of Jesus Christ is an indispensable link in the chain of the restoration of this brokenness. It is not the only link, but an indispensable one. The other crucial link is the Holy Spirit, who is poured out in our hearts and who makes us do justice again and restores our proper orientation towards God, our fellow humans and ourselves. Three moments in one direction: the Father who creates us as directed towards justice, the Son in whom we find our justice while being sinners and the Spirit who is poured out into our hearts as just love.[13]

7.9 God, Law and Gospel

Finally, we may ask ourselves what our research into Owen's and Socinus' views on atonement means for the methodological questions with which we started this chapter: which notions are leading in this exploration of dialogical rationality? Was it the concept of God or, rather, anthropology? And how do they relate to the concepts of Law and Gospel?

The concept of God turned out to be crucial when we chose between Owen and Socinus. With Socinus, God's position becomes like ours. God becomes superman. And because God becomes superman, we have to be supermen, too. Socinus asks more from us as human beings than we can do. The concept of God as we use it to rebut Socinus is not leading or determinative in the sense that our understanding of the way in which God is, our description of his true nature, is normative for the way in which we think about us as human beings. To the contrary: we have rebutted Socinus' heresy by showing that God's position in our theological language game is different from that of all of us. God is not even a position in a language game. God is the fundamental First without whom there is nothing at all. God is always already there, given that we are and the world is. In this sense, the concept of God is determinative of theology, and this is why Socinus' theology suffers from a theological defect. Also, if theology goes wrong, anthropology follows, because humans have to bear a heavier moral and soteriological burden than they can live up to.

---

13. It would be interesting to compare this to Schwöbel's way of putting this in terms of love (*schöpferische Liebe*). I would like to suggest that the difference is smaller than one might think. Cf. Christoph Schwöbel, *Gott im Gespräch: Theologische Studien zur Gegenwartsdeutung* (Tübingen: Mohr Siebeck, 2011), 265–7. Here, Luther is quoted in the context of the Trinitarian giving of God in creation, reconciliation and completion of God's works. Luther, however, speaks of 'justice' and not of 'love'. This once more suggests that the determining question is not how we describe God, but the way in which we keep the Law-Gospel distinction in speaking about God, namely by distinguishing carefully between the *opus Dei* and the *opus hominum*.

And thus, we have used the Law-Gospel distinction as an instrument for upholding the right doctrine of God. The concepts of Law and Gospel do not refer to the language about God as terms that refer to realities but as grammatical rules that direct our use of language about God. The Law-Gospel distinction functions as a means for safeguarding theology from mixing up the work of God with the work of human beings.[14] The Law does this by warning us at any moment when we tend to ascribe something to human beings that only belongs to God. Also, the Law calls for our obedience to God's commandments as in accordance with and rooted in God's essence as justice. The Gospel does so by inviting us to accept God's grace in Jesus Christ as the sole ground of our righteousness and pointing us to God as the only source and aim of our being in the world. As such, our obedience to God's justice can only be fulfilled by God who is the true giver and fulfiller of our life, in Jesus Christ and through the Holy Spirit.

However, someone may ask: where do we find theology as a description of the reality of God and of the world? The reality of God is between and underlying those in conversation. Following the line of my argument, theology does not intend to describe the nature of God and derive the nature of reality from God's nature. What it aims to do, instead, is to respect God as the ground and object of faith and call us to live in accordance with it.[15] Insofar as theology deals with being, it is merely critical; insofar as it identifies and calls God by his name, it is primarily doxological. However, in making this move, we have probably taken major steps beyond both Socinus and Owen.

---

14. Cf. Schwöbel, 'Law and Gospel', 863.

15. At this point, my argument is in line with Koch's argument for hermeneutical realism: Anton Friedrich Koch, 'Rationalität im Gespräch. Grundlegendes aus philosophischer Perspektive', in *Rationalität im Gespräch – Rationality in Conversation*, ed. Markus Mühling, Marburger Theologische Studien 126 (Leipzig: Evangelischer Verlagsanstalt, 2016), 11–22.

Chapter 8

HOLY SUPPER: RETRIEVING ABRAHAM KUYPER

8.1 Introduction

As we have seen in previous chapters, the distinction between Law and Gospel leads to an emphasis on the distinction between God and the world, God and human beings, God's works and human works. It is obvious that such an approach to dogmatics creates the greatest tensions in the theological loci that deal with the mediation of salvation. It is true that Christology is already the primary field in which the mediation of salvation is at stake, but the Christ-event is an event in the past, and it is only available to us in a mediated way in the present. Loci that relate to this mediation of salvation in the here and now are ecclesiology, pneumatology, ordained ministry and the sacraments. For this reason, it is appropriate to test my approach to systematic theology by using it as a key for understanding the sacraments. This chapter provides a preliminary investigation of the theology of the Lord's Supper to demonstrate what a retrieval of the Reformed doctrine of the Lord's Supper might look like if it is pursued through the distinction between Law and Gospel.[1]

Basically, one might have low expectations for a sound and helpful doctrine of the sacraments based on the distinction between Law and Gospel. My understanding of the distinction is to be comprehended from the perspective of the Reformed tradition, more than the Lutheran, and the Reformed tradition is notorious for its lack of sacramentality. The Reformed tradition is supposedly full of 'Zwinglian' tendencies; 'Zwinglian' means a view of the sacraments in which there is a lack of divine presence.[2] There are not that many intense controversies about the understanding of the Lord's Supper in Reformed theology. Rather, the problem is

---

1. My other explorations in the field of the theology of the Lord's Supper so far have been: Maarten Wisse et al., 'Promoting Priestly Christianity: The Role of Scripture in Max Thurian's the Eucharistic Memorial', *Questions Liturgiques/Studies in Liturgy* 101 (2021): 202–20; Jelmer Heeren and Maarten Wisse, 'Reprioritizing the Lord's Supper among the Reformed', *Calvin Theological Journal* 54, no. 1 (2019): 91–122; Maarten Wisse and Fabian Eikelboom, 'Alle gelovigen zijn gelijk, maar sommigen meer dan anderen: Een verkenning van de relatie tussen avondmaal en ambt', *Kerk en Theologie* 68, no. 1 (2017): 64–83.

2. Cf. Heeren and Wisse, 'Reprioritizing the Lord's Supper among the Reformed'.

that often the Lord's Supper plays only a minor role in Reformed spirituality. The frequency of the celebration of the Lord's Supper in many Reformed congregations is low, often only four times a year. Even when Abraham Kuyper claimed, as in the quotation at the beginning of the chapter, that the Lord's Supper is the focal point of our religion, Reformed believers generally do not see it that way. In pietistic circles, there are still many who do not receive the bread and wine during the Lord's Supper, and even outside of pietism, this is a common practice. Even in ecumenical Protestantism, where the Liturgical Movement invested much energy into strengthening the role of the Lord's Supper in the life of the congregation, this was not successful.

From the beginning of the twentieth century onwards, and in fact even earlier, there have been various attempts in Reformed theology to 'upgrade' the significance of the Lord's Supper and the sacraments more generally for Christian faith. These attempts occurred more in theology than in practical piety and were closely linked to developments in the ecumenical movement. Among those who were strongly engaged in the ecumenical movement, this happened in line with the liturgical renewal that is now generally labelled as 'the Liturgical Movement'. One scholar who has become particularly well known for this in the Netherlands is the theologian and phenomenologist Gerardus van der Leeuw.³ For those who were more traditionally Reformed and critical of the Liturgical Movement, this renewal took place through a *ressourcement* of the classical Reformed tradition, in which John Calvin took pride of place.⁴ The result of this *ressourcement* was a new attention to what we might call 'the Reformed answer' to the question of the Lord's presence in the sacrament. One could describe this Reformed approach as the affirmation of *praesentia realis*, though the 'real presence' refers not to a physical presence or the omnipresence of Christ's body but, instead, to Christ's presence through the Holy Spirit.

As Kees van der Kooi and others have argued, the Reformed tradition after Calvin has followed the line of Huldrych Zwingli more than that of Calvin.⁵ This Zwinglian approach led to a neglect of the sacraments and of the Lord's Supper in particular. The theology of Calvin provides insights that can help to reverse this development and place the Lord's Supper once again at the center of Christian worship.⁶ At the same time, the pneumatological approach to Christ's real presence and the appeal to Calvin are not without problems.⁷ Wim Janse, for instance, has

---

3. Cf. Gerardus van der Leeuw, *Sacramentstheologie* (Nijkerk: G. F. Callenbach, 1949); Gerardus van der Leeuw, *Liturgiek* (Nijkerk: Callenbach, 1940).

4. Cf. e.g. G. C. Berkouwer, *The Sacraments*, trans. Hugo Bekker, Studies in Dogmatics (Grand Rapids, MI: Eerdmans, 1969), chapter 11.

5. Van der Kooi, *As in a Mirror*, 190, 198–9.

6. Ibid., 213.

7. In contemporary literature on the Reformed view of the Lord's Supper, it is common to speak about Calvin's view of the Lord's Supper as a view that endorses 'real presence'. Therefore, I will do this in this chapter as well. Cf. Michael Allen, 'Sacraments in the Reformed and Anglican Reformation', in *The Oxford Handbook of Sacramental Theology*,

pointed out that Calvin's view of the Lord's Supper is much broader and more ambiguous than the pneumatological approach suggests.[8] In fact, in addition to the Calvin who holds to real presence, there are Zwinglian and Lutheran aspects in Calvin. This variation depends largely on the particular party Calvin is engaging in conversation or polemicizing against at any given time.[9] In a recent article, Hugo Meijer and I have explored the history of pneumatology in Reformed scholasticism.[10] We found that the role of a pneumatological approach to Christ's presence is, in fact, rather minor in the post-Reformation Reformed tradition. The Reformed tradition quickly departed from Calvin's view of the Lord's Supper, and the notion of *praesentia realis* faded into the background.[11]

So far, the role that the tradition of neo-Calvinism may have played in this development remains an open question. Does neo-Calvinism, as its name might suggest, also rediscover Calvin's view of real presence? In this chapter I would like to address the reception of the pneumatological approach to Christ's real presence in the first stage of the neo-Calvinist tradition. Because of the space available and the research that has already been done,[12] I will focus on the work of Abraham Kuyper, comparing him with Herman Bavinck. I will focus on three aspects: first, I will ask to what extent Kuyper advocates a pneumatological view of the Lord's Supper and, if so, how he relates this view to the Reformation period. Subsequently, I will address how Kuyper relates this view to the distinction between spirit and body.

---

ed. Hans Boersma and Matthew Levering (Oxford: Oxford University Press, 2015), 283–98; Scott R. Swain, 'Lutheran and Reformed Sacramental Theology: Seventeenth–Nineteenth Centuries', in *The Oxford Handbook of Sacramental Theology*, ed. Hans Boersma and Matthew Levering (Oxford: Oxford University Press, 2015), 362–80. For the discussion of the term 'real presence' in Calvin, see Joseph N. Tylenda, 'Calvin and Christ's Presence in the Supper – True or Real', *Scottish Journal of Theology* 27, no. 1 (February 1974): 65–75, https://doi.org/10.1017/S0036930600059056. Calvin usually speaks about 'true presence'. Cf. J. Todd Billings, *Calvin, Participation, and the Gift: The Activity of Believers in Union with Christ* (Oxford: Oxford University Press, 2009), 128–9. I owe this point to Raymond Blacketer.

8. Wim Janse, 'Calvin's Eucharistic Theology: Three Dogma-Historical Observations', in *Calvinus Sacrarum Literarum Interpres: Papers of the International Congress on Calvin Research*, ed. Herman J. Selderhuis (Göttingen: Vandenhoeck & Ruprecht, 2008), 27–69.

9. Bavinck's article from 1887, see below, comes close to the same observation. Van der Kooi does not address the problem explicitly.

10. Maarten Wisse and Hugo Meijer, 'Pneumatology: Tradition and Renewal', in *The Brill Companion to Reformed Orthodoxy*, ed. Herman J. Selderhuis (Leiden: Brill, 2013), 465–518.

11. Ibid., 509–14.

12. For literature on Bavinck, see below. On Kuyper, see Willem Hendrik Velema, *De leer van de Heilige Geest bij Abraham Kuyper* ('s Gravenhage: Uitgeverij Van Keulen, 1957), 201–18. Unfortunately, Velema's discussion of Kuyper is strongly determined by normative convictions about the tenability of Kuyper's views.

Subsequently, I will examine the distinct aspects of Kuyper's view by comparing his thought with that of Herman Bavinck. I will address the differences between them, and, based on this comparison, I will investigate what questions still remain unanswered in the light of our present-day challenges in understanding and rediscovering the significance of the Lord's Supper for theology and spirituality.

This chapter is no more than a preliminary exploration of the role of neo-Calvinism in the development of the theology of the Lord's Supper in the Reformed tradition. It is also a step towards a contemporary theology of the Lord's Supper. As we will see, the account of the Lord's Supper in neo-Calvinism is strongly informed by the doctrine of grace and, thus, by the distinction between Law and Gospel. Moreover, Abraham Kuyper uses the distinction between Law and Gospel in his explanation of the meaning of the Lord's Supper, and the pressing question will be what this means for the mediation of salvation in his theology, as well as in my own.

8.2 Abraham Kuyper on the Lord's Supper

We have various resources for Kuyper's theology of the sacraments and, more precisely, the Lord's Supper. His earliest elaborate exposition is in *E voto Dordraceno* (*EV*), his exposition on the *Heidelberg Catechism*, issued as articles in the *Heraut* and published as a whole in 1893. Subsequently, in 1897, students' notes from his lectures on dogmatics at the VU were published as the *Dictaten Dogmatiek* (*DD*).[13] Although it was authorized by Kuyper himself, the *DD* must be used with some care. The last elaborate discussion of the sacraments can be found in *Onze Eeredienst*, which began as a series of articles and was published in 1911.[14] The articles on the Lord's Supper in *Onze Eeredienst* never appeared in the *Heraut*. They were written for the published version of the collection as a whole.[15] We will not discuss *Onze Eeredienst* because it does not offer an additional theological account of the Lord's Supper, and from a liturgical perspective, Kuyper changed his mind only at minor points. In *EV*, Kuyper offers an extensive doctrine of the sacraments. A rough comparison with the *DD* shows that in the latter, the material is presented in a more intellectual way. However, in terms of content there is not much difference between the two. Often the same scheme is visible, even when *EV* follows the flow of the Heidelberg Catechism.

When we ask whether Kuyper proposes a pneumatological approach to Christ's real presence in the Lord's Supper, the answer must be affirmative, although it must be nuanced immediately. A thoroughly Trinitarian view of the sacraments is important to Kuyper. In this view, the work of the Spirit is important, but it is

---

13. Abraham Kuyper, *Dictaten dogmatiek: College-dictaat van een der studenten* (Grand Rapids, MI: J. B. Hulst, 1910).
14. Kuyper, *Onze eeredienst*.
15. Ibid., 5.

not more, and perhaps is even less, important than that of the Father and the Son. Kuyper does explicitly situate his view of the sacraments in the Reformed tradition and especially in Calvin.[16] Calvin figures as a middle way between Rome and the Lutherans on the one hand, and Zwingli on the other. Kuyper notes that the mode of Christ's presence in the Lord's Supper is a pneumatological one, but he pays rather little attention to this and, as we will see, he speaks about real presence primarily from a Christological perspective. Regularly, Kuyper simply appeals to Calvin by mentioning his name to indicate that Calvin's view is to be preferred over Rome, Luther and Zwingli. Rome and Luther are near each other, whereas Kuyper locates Zwingli on the same trajectory as modern theologians of his own time. Unlike Bavinck,[17] Kuyper makes no attempt to rehabilitate Zwingli.[18] Zwingli is an example of how the Reformed perspective on the means of grace can go wrong, because with Zwingli, grace is given so directly that the means of grace become superfluous.[19] Kuyper is careful to avoid this extreme, and he gives the means of grace a substantial role in spite of how much stress he puts on distinguishing between divine and human action in the mediation of grace.

Kuyper certainly fits into the pattern of those who appeal to Calvin for a renewal of the theology of the sacraments and who especially appeal to Calvin's pneumatological view of Christ's presence in the Lord's Supper. Nevertheless, Kuyper stresses the Trinitarian character of God's activity in the sacraments.[20] He explicitly regrets that the doctrine of the Lord's Supper was not formulated from this perspective.[21] In *EV*, the role of the Father, the Son and the Spirit in the Lord's Supper is discussed in three chapters. In the chapter on the Father, Kuyper speaks extensively about the work of the Father in creation, from which the signs that are used in the sacraments have been taken.[22] Elsewhere, he had previously linked these signs of water, bread and wine phenomenologically to our created nature.[23]

---

16. Kuyper, *E voto*, II, 430-1, 483, III, 127-9; Kuyper, *Dictatendogmatiek*, IV, Locus de Sacramentis, 231-6.

17. Herman Bavinck, 'Calvin's Doctrine of the Lord's Supper', trans. Nelson D. Kloosterman, *Mid-America Journal of Theology* 19 (2008): 129, http://www.midamerica.edu/uploads/files/pdf/journal/bavinkkloosterman19.pdf; Herman Bavinck, 'Calvijn's leer over het Avondmaal', in *Kennis en Leven: Opstellen en artikelen uit vroegere jaren*, ed. C. B. Bavinck (Kampen: J. H. Kok, 1922), 166-7; Herman Bavinck, *Gereformeerde Dogmatiek*, 2nd edn (Kampen: J. H. Kok, 1911), IV, 609-11; Herman Bavinck, *Reformed Dogmatics*, ed. John Bolt, trans. John Vriend (Grand Rapids, MI: Baker Academic, 2003), IV, 557-8.

18. Kuyper, *E voto*, III, 126.

19. Kuyper, *Dictatendogmatiek*, IV, Locus de Sacramentis, 229: 'Zijn geheele stelsel is dus, dat God immediaat op het hart werkt door den Heiligen Geest.'

20. Kuyper, *E voto*, III, 135-54; Kuyper, *Dictatendogmatiek*, IV, Locus de Sacramentis, 32-40.

21. Kuyper, *E voto*, III, 136.

22. Ibid., III, 135-8.

23. Ibid., II, 457-62, III, 87-92.

At this point, Kuyper gives nature a prominent place in Reformed theology, thereby renewing the Reformed doctrine of the sacraments. Similarly striking are the many examples from technology that appear throughout his discussion of the sacraments in *EV*.

Nevertheless, the work of the Son receives most attention. It is already present in the discussion of the work of the Father, who sends the Son. A separate chapter is devoted to the Son, and, in the same way, the pneumatological chapter is not so much a discussion of the work of the Spirit as it is a discussion of the mode of Christ's presence in the Lord's Supper.[24] The pneumatological view of Christ's presence is advocated from within a strongly Christocentric view of the Lord's Supper in which the *unio mystica* with Christ takes centre stage.[25]

In *DD*, where the discussion of the Trinity is a part of the general doctrine of the sacraments, Kuyper pays even less attention to the work of the Spirit.[26] There, he merely formally affirms that Christ is present in the community of faith and in the soul of the believer through the Spirit. That Kuyper's major work on the Holy Spirit, published in 1888, pays no attention to the work of the Spirit in the sacraments further reinforces the impression of a pneumatological deficit in Kuyper's doctrine of the sacraments.[27]

8.3 Comparison and further analysis

We can more easily grasp the specific aspects of Kuyper's view of the Lord's Supper and the role of pneumatology within it when we compare them more explicitly to those of Herman Bavinck, represented primarily in his *Reformed Dogmatics* (*RD*) and an early article on 'Calvin's doctrine of the Lord's Supper', published in *De Vrije Kerk* in 1887.[28] George Harinck says that for neo-Calvinism, Kuyper and Bavinck should not be seen as individuals but as a common brand name, such as Goldman and Sachs, Mercedes and Benz, and so on.[29] This is certainly true, but it does not mean that they always agree with each other. Theologically, they are further from each other than their close cooperation might lead us to expect. A select comparison of their views of the sacraments and the Lord's Supper in particular will shed more light on their respective ways of construing the pneumatological character of Christ's presence in the sacraments.

---

24. Ibid., III, 147–54.
25. Ibid., III, 143–5, 162–7, 169–75.
26. Kuyper, *Dictatendogmatiek*, IV, Locus de Sacramentis, 36.
27. Abraham Kuyper, *Het werk van den Heiligen Geest* (Amsterdam: Wormser, 1888); Velema, *De leer van de Heilige Geest*, 203.
28. Bavinck, 'Calvin's Doctrine'; Bavinck, 'Calvijns leer'.
29. George Harinck, 'Herman Bavinck and Geerhardus Vos', *Calvin Theological Journal* 45 (2010): 18, found in James Eglinton, *Trinity and Organism: Towards a New Reading of Herman Bavinck's Organic Motif* (London: T&T Clark International, 2012), 19.

As previous research has already shown,[30] and as Bavinck himself made amply clear in an article from 1887 on 'Calvin's Doctrine of the Lord's Supper', Bavinck agrees with Kuyper on the significance of Calvin's pneumatological approach to Christ's presence for a Reformed understanding of the Lord's Supper. The first remarkable difference has to do with the role of the Trinity in Kuyper's doctrine of the sacraments and the absence of that doctrine in Bavinck's account. Bavinck does not pay specific attention to the doctrine of the Trinity in his account of the sacraments. Kuyper makes an attempt to use the doctrine of the Trinity as a regulative principle in the doctrine of the sacraments.[31] In doing so, he operates within a classical Trinitarian frame of reference, in which the incomprehensibility of God and the strict indivisibility of the works of the persons in the Trinity, *ad extra*, have a decisive role. Because the work of the Trinity *ad extra* are undivided, Kuyper continually qualifies his theological language as figurative.[32]

There is another interesting difference that I cannot discuss at length. Both Kuyper and Bavinck put a major emphasis on the *unio mystica* in the doctrine of the sacraments. Kuyper, however, explicitly connects this with the notion of the church as the body of Christ. Whereas in Bavinck's account of the Lord's Supper, the mystical union is primarily an individual phenomenon, in Kuyper the mystical union with Christ is primarily a collective and social notion, particularly in the general account of the sacraments in *EV* volume II.[33] In Kuyper's description of the Lord's Supper, later on in *EV*, the mystical union is described in both individual and collective terms.[34]

However, the most fundamental difference between Kuyper and Bavinck is to be found in their views on the relationship between Word and Sacrament and, in close connection with this, the relationship between Word and Spirit. On this point, Bavinck roughly follows the *Heidelberg Catechism* which posits a hierarchical relationship between Word and Sacrament.[35] The Word produces faith. The sacrament is nothing without the Word, whereas the Word without the sacrament still brings about salvation.[36] In the essay from 1887 Bavinck stresses communion with Christ in the Lord's Supper to such an extent that he seems to give the Lord's Supper an independent status over and against the Word of God. In *RD*,

---

30. Ronald N. Gleason, 'Calvin and Bavinck on the Lord's Supper', *Westminster Theological Journal* 45 (1983): 273-303; Ronald N. Gleason, 'Herman Bavinck's Understanding of John Calvin on the Lord's Supper', 2009, http://www.richardsibbes.com/_hermanbavinck/hermanbavinck.org-Gleason2.pdf; Hans Burger, *Being in Christ: A Biblical and Systematic Investigation in a Reformed Perspective* (Eugene, OR: Wipf and Stock, 2009), 119-25.

31. Kuyper, *E voto*, III, 135-6.

32. Ibid., III, 135, 155.

33. Ibid., II, 479-84; cf. Van der Kooi, *As in a Mirror*, 189-90, who uses the same insight when interpreting Calvin.

34. Kuyper, *E voto*, III, 115-16, 119-20, 162-7, 169-75.

35. Bavinck, *Reformed Dogmatics*, IV, 448-9; Bavinck, *Gereformeerde Dogmatiek*, IV, 490.

36. Bavinck, *Reformed Dogmatics*, IV, 479; Bavinck, *Gereformeerde Dogmatiek*, IV, 524.

however, he repeatedly emphasizes the hierarchy between Word and sacrament.[37] As the Word makes us partakers in Christ's person, so does the sacrament.[38] He also says this once in the 1887 article,[39] but there the lively communion with Christ in the sacrament plays such a large role that it seems to give the sacrament its independent function in the mediation of Christ. The emphasis on the hierarchy between Word and sacrament raises the question of the nature of the specific roles played by the sacrament and the materiality of the sign. Bavinck does not raise this issue. While most of the emphasis in the essay is on mystical union with Christ, in *RD* the emphasis seems to rest on the mode of Christ's presence, namely a presence mediated through the Spirit and the spiritual character of the sacraments.[40] In the sacraments God gives nothing that God could not give otherwise.[41]

Behind this lies a view of the relationship between Word and Spirit that is different from that of Kuyper. Bavinck acknowledges that the Spirit needs to join the Word for the Word to effectively unite us with Christ preached in the Gospel,[42] but he is very insistent on binding the Spirit as tightly as possible to the Word of God. The Word is never without the Spirit, even when the Spirit does not always use the Word to the same purpose.[43] Where the Word is, whether or not in connection with the sacraments, there is also the Spirit. To be sure, at the very beginning of his exposition on the means of grace in *RD*, Bavinck acknowledges the possibility of God working salvation through the Spirit *without* the Word, but he does not want to give this insight any substantial theological significance.[44]

This is markedly different in Kuyper. Right from the beginning, Kuyper construes a strict relationship between Word and Spirit, aligning it with the relationship between God and human beings, noting the distinction between divine and human action.[45] Framed in terms of the present study, one might say that Kuyper thinks through the doctrine of the sacraments in terms of the distinction between Law and Gospel. Kuyper formulates it like this:

> The confession of God's free, all-powerful sovereignty (*vrijmachtige souvereiniteit*) does not allow the work of God to be bound to the service of human beings. And this is why one [the Reformed lay people in Kuyper's time] could not be led away from this confession that there are means of grace that the Holy Spirit uses in

---

37. Bavinck, *Reformed Dogmatics*, IV, 479, 569; Bavinck, *Gereformeerde Dogmatiek*, IV, 523, 634.
38. Bavinck, *Reformed Dogmatics*, IV, 479; Bavinck, *Gereformeerde Dogmatiek*, IV, 523.
39. Bavinck, 'Calvin's Doctrine', 132; Bavinck, 'Calvijns leer', 170.
40. Bavinck, *Reformed Dogmatics*, IV, 569; Bavinck, *Gereformeerde Dogmatiek*, IV, 634–5.
41. Bavinck, *Reformed Dogmatics*, IV, 479; Bavinck, *Gereformeerde Dogmatiek*, IV, 523.
42. Bavinck, *Reformed Dogmatics*, IV, 460; Bavinck, *Gereformeerde Dogmatiek*, IV, 504.
43. Bavinck, *Reformed Dogmatics*, IV, 459; Bavinck, *Gereformeerde Dogmatiek*, IV, 502–3.
44. Bavinck, *Reformed Dogmatics*, IV, 446–8; Bavinck, *Gereformeerde Dogmatiek*, IV, 486–9.
45. Kuyper, *E voto*, II, 485–6.

the work of grace, but that what is accomplished through these means, is by no means the whole of the work of the Holy Spirit; that the Holy Spirit *also* works without means: and that, particularly, re-creation from death to life, like creation itself, excludes any use of means.[46]

Thus, the relationship between Word and Spirit is strictly aligned with the doctrine of grace. On the basis of this starting point, Kuyper concludes that the work of the Spirit is always primary and basically unmediated as long as it is concerned with the gift of grace.

> In this, we have to hold on to the view that the Holy Spirit, insofar as he uses means of grace, is bound to them only to the extent as God has ordained this, so that we do not exclude or restrict the direct working of the Holy Spirit in addition to[47] the mediated one. This statement has to be made explicit, because many think they can conclude from this very question 65 and answer that the Reformed church also denies the direct and unmediated work of the Holy Spirit. If the whole of salvation depends on sincere faith, they reason, and it is stated here that the Holy Spirit works and strengthens this, but in such a way that he brings it about through the Word as a means of grace and strengthens it through the use of the Sacraments, then it is clear that, here too, everything happens in a mediated way. This misunderstanding has to be precluded in advance. The Catechism clearly states that the Holy Spirit effects faith, *not* in an unmediated way, through the proclamation of the holy Gospel, and afterwards strengthens this faith through the use of the Sacraments.[48]

God may use means, but God need not do so. If God acts in a salvific manner, God primarily acts independently from human actions, and, therefore, Kuyper agrees with Zwingli and various Reformed scholastics who argue that God may and indeed does save people who had never heard the Gospel.[49] In Kuyper's view, given that children are often born again before they have any ability to act or think consciously, this is in fact God's ordinary way of action. The germinating of the seed of faith always precedes our conscious response to the Gospel.[50] Obviously, we see here the basis of Kuyper's doctrine of presumptive regeneration (*veronderstelde wedergeboorte*), but it is important to note that Kuyper's view of the sacraments is not the product of this doctrine. Instead, this doctrine is the product of a much more rigorous way of thinking through the relationship between divine

---

46. Ibid., II, 406, my translation.
47. This translation of 'naar' as 'next to' comes down to an emendation of the Dutch original. The Dutch, as *EV* in this print has it, does not make sense. I have changed the 'naar' to 'naast'. This corresponds to Kuyper's argument at this point.
48. Ibid., vol. II, 403–4; original emphasis.
49. Kuyper, *E voto*, II, 403–6.
50. Ibid., III, 70–4.

and human action than was usually the case in the Reformed tradition before him, especially in the era of the Reformation, the tradition to which Bavinck primarily appeals, as we have seen.[51]

Kuyper does not state it explicitly, and although *EV* is an exposition of the *Heidelberg Catechism*, he nonetheless basically disagrees with the Catechism's statement about the Word effecting faith and the sacraments only strengthening faith. His conviction is that neither the Word nor the sacraments produce faith.[52] Kuyper paraphrases the passage from the Heidelberg Catechism as follows, after he has elaborately discussed various answers to the question of whether the Catechism means the unconscious, God-given power to believe (the *habitus fidei*) or our conscious actual response to the proclamation of the Gospel (the *actus fidei*):

> From the Holy Spirit, who in regeneration implants the power to believe within us, and evokes the conscious act of faith in our hearts through the proclamation of the holy Gospel, in the same way, [the Holy Spirit] confirms the implanted power to believe through the Sacrament of infant baptism, and strengthens conscious faith through the Baptism of adult persons, and through the Sacrament of the holy Supper.[53]

Only God can bring forth faith; the means of grace cannot do so. Kuyper uses the scholastic distinction between the habit and the act of faith to explain the nature of faith.[54] As to the seed of the habit of faith, the Word or Sacraments cannot produce this. The means of grace can only function as just that: the means through which the God-given seed can be brought to growth and flourishing. But the means of grace cannot give us the seed of faith.[55]

As I said above, Kuyper's view of *baptism* is based on this understanding and leads to his much-contested concept of presumptive regeneration, though this is not the place to reflect on that. Instead, I would like to examine what this view of the role of the means of grace means for Kuyper's view of the Lord's Supper. There, too, Kuyper starts from a strict distinction between the *opus Dei* and the *opus hominum*. Now that Kuyper has concluded that neither the Word nor the sacraments bring about salvation, it becomes possible to ascribe to the sacraments a role as a distinct means of grace, apart from that of the Word. Although both strengthen faith, they do so in different ways. This is not possible for Bavinck, because in Bavinck the function of the Word wholly determines the function

---

51. Ibid., II, 470–5.

52. Ibid., 403–6, 470–2.

53. Ibid., 405, my translation; quotation marks and unusual capitalization are in the original.

54. For a history of these concepts in theology, see Maarten Wisse, 'Habitus Fidei: An Essay on the History of a Concept', *Scottish Journal of Theology* 56, no. 2 (2003): 172–89.

55. Kuyper, *E voto*, II, 425–6.

of the sacraments, and according to Bavinck, the function of the Word, strictly bound as it is to the work of the Spirit, is to effect faith. Thus, in Bavinck, the role of the Word and that of the sacraments are intimately connected to the question of salvation and bound to predestination. In Kuyper, the sacraments are now separate from the question of salvation as such. Salvation is a work of God; thus, believers cannot bring about their own salvation. Kuyper explicitly works with a distinction between the divine perspective, in which the means of grace have no place because God effects faith directly through the Spirit, and the human perspective, in which the means of grace are crucial, because they evoke and strengthen the active side of faith and bring it to maturity.[56] This is why we hear the Word of God, and this is also why the Word of God calls us to conversion, not in the sense of bringing grace into our hearts but turning us consciously to God in faith.[57] Neither the Word nor the sacraments have to do with the gift of the habit of faith, because only God can implant this in us. Both Word and sacraments operate on the level of evoking acts of faith in those who have already received the gift of grace.

Thus, the sacrament of the Lord's Supper receives its own place in strengthening faith. Through it, we are in communion with Christ in a bodily way, not only individually but also corporately as the mystical body of Christ that is the church, the community of believers:[58]

> If one would ask what is this special, this peculiar, this extraordinary and distinguishing character of the strengthening of our faith through the sacrament, this should no doubt be sought in communion with the Body of Christ. Holy Baptism leads our faith into this communion, and Holy Supper feeds and nourishes this communion.[59]

Kuyper's construal of this specific role of the sacraments reveals a concern about the theology and spirituality of the Lord's Supper that is different from that of Bavinck. For Bavinck, the concerns around the Lord's Supper are particularly theological, related to Roman Catholic, Lutheran and Zwinglian 'errors' with respect to the mode of Christ's presence. For Kuyper, those concerns about such errors are present as well, but he is much more concerned about the practical neglect of the sacrament among believers. This neglect may be because believers have become so modern that they cannot see any benefit in the sacrament or because they are so anxious about approaching the Lord in the sacrament with the right disposition and spiritual experience of regeneration that they stay away from it.[60]

---

56. Ibid., II, 464–5.
57. Ibid., III, 74–6, 220.
58. Kuyper has a peculiar preference for the two senses of hearing and seeing, although one might think that feeling and tasting are equally important in the sacraments: ibid., II, 407, 426–8.
59. Ibid., II, 479, my translation.
60. Ibid., III, 211–19.

From this perspective, Kuyper puts considerable emphasis on the actual celebration of the sacrament.[61] In the 1890s, he still argues in favour of weekly communion, and he deplores the low frequency that is usual in most Protestant churches. Although this changes over time,[62] he aims to bring Word and Sacrament to a more equal level of importance as means of grace. More than once he notes that the Reformed view of the sacraments developed in the direction of Zwingli soon after the Reformation.[63] As we have seen above, the attempt to present Word and Sacrament as equally important means of grace is rooted in his fundamental view of the *opus Dei* and *opus hominum*: Word and Spirit or, maybe more accurately, Spirit and Word. For Kuyper, baptism, confession and the Lord's Supper belong inextricably together. This is why he so strongly opposes believers refusing to partake in the Supper. This does not mean that Kuyper has no eye for the experiential side of faith.[64] An experiential thread is present throughout his discussion, in which he repeatedly notes the sweet experience of the children of God when they partake in the Lord's Supper.[65]

8.4 Preliminary conclusion

So far, we have seen that Bavinck and Kuyper differ considerably in their views of the sacraments. Bavinck remains rather traditional. His view of the Lord's Supper is primarily concentrated around an appraisal of Calvin's notion of real presence and mystical union with Christ. What exactly the specific role of the sacraments is in strengthening this union and what the differences are between the sacraments and the Word of God remain unclear. Also, Bavinck does not rethink the relationship between Word and Spirit, and he tries to keep them as closely together as possible, but at the same time he is forced to admit that the salvific work of the Spirit is distinct from the Word.

Compared to this, Kuyper's contribution is much more creative and radical. Kuyper does not merely follow the Reformed tradition but also assesses its strengths and weaknesses. He diagnoses the relationship between Word and Spirit as a problem in the Reformed tradition. The efficacy of the Word depends on the work of the Spirit, who remains free to give grace to whomever God wants. This opens the possibility that there will be hearers of the Word who will not receive grace, and it also opens up the possibility that some will receive grace who never heard the Gospel.[66] Thus, Word and Spirit cannot be held together

---

61. Ibid., 74–6, 219–42.
62. K. W. de Jong, *Ordening van dienst: Achtergronden van en ontwikkelingen in de eredienst van de Gereformeerde Kerken in Nederland* (Baarn: Ten Have, 1996), 41–8, 78–9.
63. Kuyper, *E voto*, II, 431, 483, III, 126.
64. Ibid., III, 225.
65. Ibid., II, 414, 423–4, 487.
66. Cf. e.g. 'Westminster Confession of Faith' (1646), 10, 3.

to the extent in which the Reformation sometimes suggested and as Bavinck maintains. He also sees the problematic consequences of this in the doctrine of the sacraments, and he proposes a way ahead from a more consistent point of view.

As far as I can see, Kuyper has taken very significant steps towards rethinking sacramentology from a Reformed perspective. He saw that the relationship between Word and sacrament needed renewal. He also rightly diagnosed the *Heidelberg Catechism* as part of the problem here with its distinction between working and strengthening faith in Word and sacrament. He rightly concluded that this idea is not fully consistent with the Reformed doctrine of grace, in which God alone can save, so that the means of grace can only be necessary for us but not for God.

On the basis of his implicit criticism of the tradition, Kuyper develops his own view of the sacrament. He astutely sees that the Reformed scholastic distinction between the habit and act of faith helps us to construe a consistent relationship between divine and human activity. Within the realm of our actions, the sacraments can be perceived as ways in which believers grow in communion with Christ and one another through the bodily dimensions of the Lord's Supper and the coming together of believers in the church.

8.5 In search of a new paradigm

However, one may ask to what extent Kuyper gives us a view of the sacraments that is suitable to the questions of the twenty-first century. In the context of this essay, we have to stay close to his theology, and we can by no means offer a full-scale doctrine of the Lord's Supper or address all of the challenges that we face when we develop a contemporary doctrine of the Lord's Supper. The question that Kuyper leaves unsolved is how to construe the role of the means of grace when God's grace is fundamentally unmediated. In the context of baptism, Kuyper tries to keep the sign and thing signified together through his teaching of presumptive regeneration, a very controversial issue already in his own time. This solution is not convincing, because it runs against Kuyper's own careful distinction between God's work and ours. By presenting the work of God as something that we can *presume*, Kuyper turns the divine perspective into something that is under our control. The distinction between *opus Dei* and *opus hominum*, which is intended to teach us humility, is rendered meaningless because of the presumption that God is on our side.

Another open question is to what extent the Reformed approach to real presence is tenable. As mentioned above, Kuyper and Bavinck follow Calvin, claiming that Christ's person is bodily present through the Spirit – if that was indeed Calvin's view is another matter. This, however, is problematic because the Reformed tradition claims that bodies are located at a certain place. Kuyper and Bavinck want to be consistent; they have to maintain that Christ's human body is in heaven, at a place which we perhaps do not know of, but at a certain place and not everywhere.[67] At the same time, they claim that this body, which is at a certain place and not everywhere, can be really present through the Holy Spirit in a mysterious way.

At this point, one reaches the limits of the use of 'mystery' language in theology. I do not want to claim that speaking about mysteries in theology makes no sense. Quite to the contrary, I have defended elsewhere that we have to speak about a 'mystery' in theology in the doctrine of the Trinity and Christology.[68] However, some ways of speaking about a mystery are more helpful than others. The mystery that Calvin, Kuyper and Bavinck think they see is primarily a consequence of problems they have created themselves and which lead them to not saying anything meaningful at all. They have strong reasons to maintain that Christ, according to his human body, is in heaven, but if so, one cannot with the same strength maintain that Christ, according to his human body, is on earth, and even so in a *bodily* way.

I argue, however, that this is not necessary. The denial of Christ's bodily presence in the Lord's Supper is motivated by the concern about confusing God's work with ours, rooted in the distinction between Law and Gospel. The priest cannot bring about what is only the work of God, God's free presence among us in Christ. However, Kuyper is the only one of these three theologians who has already made room for this concern by maintaining that neither the Word of God nor the sacraments can constitute salvation as such. In line with the tradition that he inherits, he incorporates this concern again at a different level by denying the claim that Christ is bodily present in the sacrament. Thus, he exaggerates his concern and, thereby, gets into theological problems. As soon as it has been established that the bodily, physical presence of Christ in the sacrament is not about the work of God as the determination of one's ultimate salvation, but about growing in faith as the human response to God's work, and thus, about the mediation of the saving presence of Christ to believers, it can be safely claimed that Christ is present in the Lord's Supper in a bodily way. Of course, this presence is effectuated by the Holy Spirit, because it is a presence freely given by God and to the believer, but it is nevertheless a bodily presence.

And in fact, this is what Kuyper does. Neither the Word of God nor the sacraments are about something that only God can do, giving saving grace to human beings. With this decision he creates theological space to examine the role of the sacraments from another angle than the approach used ever since the Reformation. The sacrament is not there for God, to enable God to give us divine grace, but it is there for us, to grow in faith through Word and sacrament. The

---

67. See e.g. Girolamo Zanchi, *De Religione Christiana Fides = Confession of Christian Religion*, ed. Luca Baschera and Christian Moser (Leiden: Brill, 2007), I, 308–9, who claims exactly this.

68. Cf. the motto to that book, taken from Francis Turretin: Maarten Wisse, *Trinitarian Theology beyond Participation: Augustine's de Trinitate and Contemporary Theology*, T&T Clark Studies in Systematic Theology 11 (London: T&T Clark International, 2011), vii.

specific feature of the sacrament, over against the Word, is that it mediates Christ's presence in a bodily way. In this way, Kuyper creates space for a symbolic view of the presence of Christ which sees this presence in a performative way. At the same time, any magical understanding of such a performative view of the sacrament has been precluded from the very start. The priest or the believer cannot organize anything on God's side through their behaviour since their mediation of salvation is possible only because God brings something about freely.

In these previous paragraphs, we attempt to reshuffle the pieces of a sacramental paradigm that have been in place at least since the Reformation. This paradigm prevailed not only among the Reformed but just as much in the Roman Catholic and the Lutheran traditions, in which the efficacy of the sacraments on God's part was seen as inextricably bound to the sacrament. Although the Reformed tradition made a desperate attempt to dispense with this paradigm, it remained dependent on it in the sense that its own line of thinking was wholly dependent on the opposition to the prevailing paradigm, thereby unwillingly supported it. The Reformed did this because they were at pains to avoid a magical or automatic correlation between divine and human actions in the sacraments and because their doctrine of predestination precluded them from positing such a magical correlation.

If we strictly follow Kuyper's distinction between God's saving work and our use of means of grace to grow in faith, then we can say that our communion with Christ in the Lord's Supper is bodily real but not in the sense that Christ is bodily present in a way that jeopardizes his location in heaven according to his human nature. The bodily (i.e. physical) presence that counts for us is the specifically material character of the signs under which God is present to us and through which God nourishes and feeds us. In the Lord's Supper, different from the hearing of the Word, God is present in a bodily way. Participating in it is not automatically linked to eternal salvation. Such linkage would be the divine perspective. Our perspective, while ordained and effected as it is by God through the Spirit, is that we grow in faith. In partaking of the sacrament, God effects this by allowing us to grow through bodily means, that is, by eating and drinking rather than by hearing. This bodily presence makes us grow in faith and righteousness through the Spirit.

Thus, the 'bodily' in the bodily presence does not point to a special magical or automatic way in which the body of Christ is present where it cannot be present, but it points instead to the nature of the means through which God makes us flourish and grow in faith. Thus, we can and must claim that Christ is bodily present in the Lord's Supper, even when this does not mean that we receive grace *ex opere operato*. Through these bodily signs and through performing this rite we enjoy communion with God in Jesus Christ, because it is the Holy Spirit who decided to strengthen us in this particular way, a way which particularly suits our bodily existence. Not only this, but we experience communion with one another as the body of Christ. This communion with one another is already salvific, but it is also a means for transforming us into the image of Christ, because the community of faith is the body of Christ. Is Christ present in the Lord's Supper? Yes, he is. Is he bodily present? Yes, in the sense that he is present according to bodily means, through which means the Holy Spirit unites us more and more with Christ and with one another.

From this point of view, we can also see why the sacraments are of the utmost importance; indeed, they are as important as the proclamation of the Word of God. They are necessary for us because they make us grow in faith in a way that the proclamation of the Word of God can never do, since the Word of God is an intellectual means of communicating with us. Word and sacraments are the two ways in which God chose to be with us and transform us on our way towards the heavenly Kingdom.

8.6 A Zwinglian point of view?

So far so good, someone might say, but this is really no more than a repetition of the 'Zwinglian' point of view. I deny that Christ is present in the sacrament in a real way. He is present 'for believers' but not 'from the perspective of God'. Therefore, in celebrating Holy Communion, there is no more salvation (i.e. ultimate saving grace) to be received than in any other meal! This supposedly 'new' paradigm leads to nothing! Indeed, it remains typically Reformed: Holy Communion is no more than strengthening our faith. But this cannot be enough! What is at stake is the question of whether we eat and drink Christ's very flesh and blood in the sacrament! If magic is not the core of the Eucharist, what is? In the Eucharist, a liminal experience takes place in which the boundaries between the domain of God and the domain of human beings meet one another – perhaps they are even mixed and confused. To partake in the Eucharist is to share in an incarnational experience.

And in addition to this, a Lutheran might object: it is this being in, with and under the signs of bread and wine in such a way that we can truly say that bread and wine become the very flesh and blood of our Lord Jesus Christ, which constitutes our assurance of faith! Therefore, if the Lord's Supper is a ritual that is intended to confirm our assurance of faith, this can only be so if the presence of Christ in it radically precedes and is radically independent of our faithful affirmation of it. If Christ is only present in the sacrament when I believe him to be so, on what ground does the certainty of my faith depend?

There are various ways to deal with these objections. Below, I will propose various possible answers, and by relating my own position to these possible answers, I hope to elucidate my position further. A first and preliminary reply to these objections would be: this is a confusion of paradigms. I have made an attempt above to carefully distinguish between the perspective of God and the perspective of human beings, and these objections confuse and combine these perspectives. This is about posing old questions to a new paradigm and that does not make sense. Although this answer would be justified in a certain sense, I do not agree with the reply, because I am of the opinion that one is justified in testing the benefits of a proposed new paradigm in terms of posing the old questions to it and seeing what it has to offer in reply to them. This is also the only way in which people who subscribe to the old paradigm can assess the new one and appreciate its benefits. Therefore, below, I presume that it is useful to ask these questions of the new paradigm and that these objections are fitting and potentially justified.

Another answer might be: yes, from within the old paradigm, which is oriented towards a divine presence in the sacrament that is independent of our faithful response to it, this is indeed a 'Zwinglian' view. One might then follow this path further by stressing that neither Word nor sacrament is intended to communicate saving grace as something that humans can bring about, either on the part of those who administer them or on the part of those who receive them. They are means through which God makes us grow in faith by uniting us more and more with Christ. The sacrament of the Lord's Supper does this in a material way and, in that sense, a bodily manner. In this sense, one can also straightforwardly say that Christ is present in the Lord's Supper in a bodily way, namely as a God-given and promised way to unite us with God. In this way, with Luther, following Augustine, one can say that the real presence of Christ in the sacraments wholly depends on the Word of God's promise which is added to the material signs.[69]

However, a third response to these objections is possible by specifying in more detail what the 'new' paradigm amounts to. Therefore, it is useful to elucidate at this point what I have meant until now when I used the expressions 'from the perspective of God' and 'from the perspective of human beings'. I do not mean that, from a human perspective, we really experience communion with Christ, but from the perspective of God, God does not do anything that God does not do through other means. This would mean that from the perspective of God, Christ is present in the sacrament no more than anywhere else. The distinction between 'from the perspective of God' and 'from the perspective of human beings' has a different meaning in my proposal. To start with the former: by the expression 'from the perspective of God', I mean the ultimate perspective of salvation that is only in God's hands. Phrased differently, by 'perspective of God' I mean the perspective on our life in terms of the question of whether we will be saved or not, using old terminology: regenerative grace. By the expression 'from the perspective of human beings', I mean the question of how people respond to the salvation proclaimed and presented to them in Word and sacrament. Within the paradigm that I have proposed here, one may very well maintain, and I do maintain, that God in Christ is present in the sacrament in a special way and to our salvation. The constitution of our salvation as our union with Christ, however, is not given by the administration of the sacrament. The sacrament is intended to evoke our conscious communion with Christ through the mediation of Christ's presence, towards the fulfilment of God's grace in us through the Holy Spirit. God saves us in two ways: through words, mental guidance to which we respond in affirmation, awe, bewilderment and love for God and other creatures, but also through

---

69. Cf. Martin Luther, 'Large Catechism', in *Triglot Concordia: The Symbolical Books of the Ev. Lutheran Church*, trans. F. Bente and W. H. T. Dau (St. Louis: Concordia, 1921), 733–7.

material signs such as water, bread and wine. Through those two types of means, God restores us to become Christ-formed people.

Related to this, a possible answer to the charge of being 'Zwinglian' could also be: it is not so problematic when this new paradigm is seen as merely 'Zwinglian' because in the recent theology of the sacraments, a view of the sacraments as special means of grace is increasingly criticized anyway. This is especially brought forward by Louis-Marie Chauvet in his influential works on the Eucharist.[70] A way of thinking in which the sacraments are seen as providing us with a kind of 'good' that we receive from a highest being is the product of an ontotheological metaphysics. It turns both God and us into objects instead of interrupting them by means of the sacraments. This view of the sacraments, if interpreted in terms of a physical divine presence among us, indeed turns human beings into magical agents in the sense that they can move things in the divine 'superrealm' and manipulate one's ultimate fate towards one's own benefit. Instead, Chauvet argues, the sacraments must be understood in the context of symbolic performative presence. The church as community of believers performatively re-enacts the narrative of Jesus in the reading of Scripture, the celebration of the sacraments and the life of the community.

Although I sympathize with Chauvet's intentions and try to avoid the danger of 'ontotheology' in various ways in this book, I hesitate to formulate its significance wholly in terms of their performativity. As far as I can see, the Christian community lives from a meeting with a real 'Someone', albeit a real 'Other' at the same time, Someone who radically precedes us as creator of heaven and earth. Thus, we meet God in Christ in a bodily way. This conviction is not done away with in the new 'paradigm' that I seek. God has promised us that if we break bread and pour out the wine in his Name to his remembrance, the bread and wine will be his own flesh and blood. We are invited to hold God to this promise. Indeed, this promise radically precedes our faithful affirmation of it, as Lutheran believers rightly remind us. Our faith is rooted in God who is truly specially, and 'supernaturally' with us in Christ through the sacrament. Precisely in this way, our faith finds rest in God as the only one from whom we can expect salvation, and only in this way, with Luther again, faith is the fulfilment of the first commandment of the Decalogue. Thus also, faith offers praise and thanks to God alone.

8.7 Extra calvinisticum?

Hopefully, the contours of the new paradigm have become clearer in my replies to the charges formulated at the beginning of the previous section. This does not yet

---

70. Louis-Marie Chauvet, *The Sacraments: The Word of God at the Mercy of the Body* (Collegeville, MI: Liturgical, 2001); Louis-Marie Chauvet, *Symbol and Sacrament: A Sacramental Reinterpretation of Christian Existence*, trans. Patrick Madigan (Collegeville, MI: Liturgical, 1995).

solve all problems, however. One is the question of what we mean exactly when we speak about the 'bodily presence' of Christ in the Lord's Supper. In the Reformed tradition, as I have outlined above, the bodily presence of Christ is specifically bound to one place, as our human bodies are as well. How can I speak so easily about the bodily presence of Christ in the Lord's Supper? I have referred various times to Luther in the previous section. Does this mean that I accept some form of Lutheran ubiquity doctrine?

Above, I have already stressed that the so-called 'extra calvinisticum' is primarily motivated by two considerations that indeed closely hang together with the relation between Law and Gospel. The scope of the Gospel is limited by an appeal to the Law in the extra calvinisticum. The danger is that human beings acting in the sacraments would gain power over divine matters, and so the difference between God and human beings would not be strictly maintained. Of course, behind this is a more fundamental Christological concern about mixing up the divine and human natures of Christ, something that the Reformed tradition has always strictly avoided (see Chapter 3). Another danger is that the ubiquity of Christ's body would lead to Christ's ubiquitous presence in the world. This would lead to universalism and contradict the Reformed view of predestination (see Chapter 6).

As I have argued in conversation with Kuyper, this concern about confusing the *opus Dei* and the *opus hominum* does not need to be brought into play twice. Therefore, there is no principal reason to reject the bodily presence of Christ in the Lord's Supper. The question is, however: whose body are we talking about? If we mean by 'bodily presence' the human nature of the risen Christ, we would indeed make the presence of the risen Christ ubiquitous. I do not want to take this step, however. It seems to me that there are reasons not to give up the idea of a concrete locally bound human nature of Christ too easily. I can imagine all sorts of complicated questions about the place of the concrete body of the risen Christ and do not have all the answers to it. Nevertheless, the idea of a concrete locally limited human body of the risen Christ at least takes the concrete humanity of Christ very seriously, and this I see as a good thing, because if Christ has a concrete human body even in his eschatological state, this strongly supports the value of our concrete embodiedness as well. This is a good reason to not give up the *extra calvinisticum* too easily.

If we do not want to give up Christ concrete, locally bound embodiment, the expression 'bodily presence of Christ' in the Lord's Supper must be interpreted in a way that keeps this bodily presence of Christ in place, while giving the 'bodily' presence of Christ in the sacrament another meaning. This does not mean that it is less genuine, however. 'Bodily', as I have argued above, points to the way in which Christ is present in the sacrament, namely in a material way. This way in which Christ is present is opposite to God's presence in the proclamation of the Gospel, although the proclamation of the Gospel certainly has bodily dimensions to it as well. We say that Christ is present in the Lord's Supper in the material objects of bread and wine, and also maintain that, performatively, these material objects are said to become 'flesh and blood' of our Lord Jesus Christ. Thus, a bodily performative event occurs in the sacrament in which the bodily signs of bread and wine, taken up as they are into our bodies, are inextricably bound to the body and blood of Christ, such that, as the *Belgic Confession* has it, 'in the meantime we err not when we say that what is eaten and drunk by us is the proper and natural body and the proper blood of Christ'.[71] Moreover, this bodily performative event is also fundamentally a communal event within the community of faith that is in a very realistic sense the 'body and blood' of Christ, the locus of his ongoing salvific presence through the Spirit. Although, on a linguistic level, the meaning of 'bodily' in the sacrament differs from the meaning of 'bodily' when applied to the risen Christ in heaven, we can nevertheless speak about the deep reality of Christ's bodily presence in the sacrament and in the celebrating community. Through the proclamation of the Gospel and the celebration of the sacraments, the community of faith more and more becomes a Christ-like 'mystical' body, as Augustine liked to call it, one *totus Christus*.[72]

---

71. Philip Schaff, *The Creeds of Christendom*, Bibliotheca Symbolica Ecclesiæ Universalis (New York: Harper & Brothers, 1882), III, 430.

72. Tarsicius J. van Bavel, 'The "Christus Totus" Idea: A Forgotten Aspect of Augustine's Spirituality', in *Studies in Patristic Christology*, ed. Thomas Finan and Vincent Twomey (Dublin: Four Courts, 1998), 84–94.

Chapter 9

LAW AND GOSPEL AS A KEY TO THE THEOLOGY OF THE RELIGIONS

9.1 Introduction

In recent decades, the theology of the religions seems to have been decreasing in relevance. After interreligious dialogue came to replace the theology of the religions in the 1990s and 2000s, the form of engagement with the religions in Christian theology that really seems to be booming nowadays is Scriptural Reasoning and Comparative Theology.[1] To the extent that something like a theology of the religions still exists, it is dominated by Trinitarian theology.[2] There are no doubt various reasons for this trend, but the dead end which the theology of the religions seems now to have reached may be explained in part by the demise of a specific typology, namely that of the distinction between exclusivism, inclusivism and pluralism (and, perhaps, also naturalism[3]). By now, much has been advanced against this typology,[4] and new variants have been developed aiming to overcome the problems associated with the three established types of theologies of religion. Nevertheless, anyone who seeks to address questions pertaining to the theology

---

1. Francis X. Clooney, *Comparative Theology: Deep Learning across Religious Borders* (Malden, MA: Wiley-Blackwell, 2010).

2. E.g. Gavin D'Costa, *The Meeting of Religions and the Trinity* (Maryknoll, NY: Orbis, 2000); S. Mark Heim, *The Depth of the Riches: A Trinitarian Theology of Religious Ends* (Grand Rapids, MI: Eerdmans, 2001); Veli-Matti Kärkkäinen, *Trinity and Religious Pluralism: The Doctrine of the Trinity in Christian Theology of Religions* (Aldershot: Ashgate, 2004); Gerald R. McDermott and Harold A. Netland, *A Trinitarian Theology of Religions: An Evangelical Proposal* (Oxford: Oxford University Press, 2014).

3. Friedrich Hermanni, 'Der unbekannte Gott: Plädoyer für eine inklusivistische Religionstheologie', in *Wahrheitsansprüche der Weltreligionen: Konturen gegenwärtiger Religionstheologie*, ed. Christian Danz and Friedrich Hermanni (Neukirchen-Vluyn: Neukirchener, 2006), 149–69.

4. Perry Schmidt-Leukel, 'Exclusivism, Inclusivism, Pluralism: The Tripolar Typology – Clarified and Reaffirmed', in *The Myth of Religious Superiority: Multifaith Explorations of Religious Pluralism*, ed. Paul F. Knitter (Maryknoll, NY: Orbis, 2005), 13–27.

of religions is still more or less forced to relate to that typology for locating their own position.[5]

In this chapter, I aim to go one step further in order to move beyond the current typology. The first step will be to bring clearer focus to the contours of the current paradigm. Paradigms may change as soon as we start to realize that they are a paradigm, and this happens when the presuppositions under which the discussion had once been undertaken no longer appear self-evident to us. In a first move, I will argue that the current paradigm of the theology of the religions shares the tacit assumption of religious traditions as sources of religious truth, as sources of information about the world and the reality of God and our ultimate destiny, as sources which are then either compatible or incompatible with each other. I do this in conversation with the theology of the religions and ecumenism defended by a group of German Lutheran theologians, among them Eilert Herms, Wilfried Härle and, most notably, Christoph Schwöbel. Schwöbel has already pushed the discussion regarding the theology of religions ahead by interpreting it in terms of a Lutheran doctrine of grace. As we have seen, the Lutheran doctrine of grace is very closely related to the distinction between Law and Gospel. I will argue, however, that Schwöbel does not take the Law-Gospel distinction seriously enough in his theology of religions, because he continues to stand in the Enlightenment paradigm of religions as world-views, as boxes containing truth claims.

Therefore, in a second move, I will try to show that the Reformation understanding of Law and Gospel must lead to a denial of such a common presupposition concerning religions as boxes of truth claims, since it turns the Gospel into the Law. Subsequently, I will argue for the importance of the distinct roles of Law and Gospel in the theology of religions, elaborating on what this means for the practice of interreligious dialogue and the communication of the Gospel to non-Christians.

9.2 Religions as sources of knowledge and truth

As announced above, I am defending the thesis that the three commonly distinguished types of theologies of the religions – that is, exclusivism, inclusivism and pluralism – share the common tacit assumption that religious traditions are primarily sources of knowledge about God, the ultimate, the world and salvation. A religion makes certain claims about states of affairs on the basis of its sources, its sources of revelation.

Since this thesis can be made plausible for the classic scheme with relative ease, I will make no exhaustive argument for it. A look at a concise formulation of the typology reveals that the various types are distinguished according to the

---

5. Cf. e.g. Marianne Moyaert, *Fragile Identities: Towards a Theology of Interreligious Hospitality* (Amsterdam: Rodopi, 2011).

diverging ways in which they deal with the truth claims of religious traditions.[6] Exclusivists believe in the truth of their own tradition in an exclusive way, while inclusivists see traces of truth in other traditions, and pluralists deny every religion a sufficient level of truth concerning God or the ultimate on the ground that the reality of the Real escapes our human knowledge. Furthermore, pluralists view religious traditions as being primarily oriented towards truth claims, precisely by denying each and every religion an exclusive truth claim. Summarizing, we can say that theology of religion has traditionally been oriented towards truth in religions. This comes to pithy expression in the title to a German collection of essays edited by Christian Danz and Friedrich Hermanni, which translates as: *Truth Claims in the World Religions: Contours of a Contemporary Theology of Religion.*[7]

In recent years, pluralism in particular has been subjected to fierce criticism for evaluating the concrete religious traditions from a standpoint that is itself an absolute standpoint, not only creating a new pluralist absolutist religion but also being self-referentially incoherent for denying existing traditions something it relies on for its own credibility.[8] Over against pluralism, various theologians have in particular developed new forms of inclusivism aiming to overcome the foremost weakness of inclucivism, namely its tendency to see religions other than one's own as inferior or even to construe adherents of other religions as anonymous members of one's own tradition.[9]

In this chapter, I only have space to address a single recent revision of inclucivism in greater detail. Some have called it a new Tübinger School of theology of religions, although it also has many links to Heidelberg. The principal proponents of this revision are the German Lutheran theologians Christoph Schwöbel, Eilert Herms and Wilfried Härle, who themselves speak of a *Pluralismus aus Glauben*, a pluralism from faith. I will deal somewhat more extensively with Schwöbel, my own former teacher, since he will be an important conversation partner in the rest of the chapter.

While Schwöbel works with the classic typology, he at the same time turns it on its head by combining elements from a pluralist point of view with a form of inclusivism or even exclusivism. Methodologically, for Schwöbel, pluralism – the fact that there are many religious traditions and that this must continue to

---

6. Christian Danz and Friedrich Hermanni, eds, *Wahrheitsansprüche der Weltreligionen: Konturen gegenwärtiger Religionstheologie* (Neukirchen-Vluyn: Neukirchener, 2006), introduction.

7. Ibid.

8. Gavin D'Costa, *Christian Uniqueness Reconsidered: The Myth of a Pluralistic Theology of Religions* (Maryknoll, NY: Orbis, 1990).

9. For another example not discussed below, see Lieven Boeve, 'Theological Truth, Particularity and Incarnation: Engaging Religious Plurality and Radical Hermeneutics', in *Orthodoxy, Process and Product*, ed. Mathijs Lamberigts, Lieven Boeve and Terrence Merrigan, BETL 227 (Leuven: Peeters, 2009), 323–48, who argues from a Roman Catholic perspective.

be so – is not based on general philosophical or relativistic grounds but is to be derived from the kernel of the Christian theological understanding of God and reality.[10] In this, Schwöbel follows the trend in the theology of religions initiated by Gavin d'Costa's influential collection of essays, to which he himself contributed, which fundamentally questioned the type of pluralism advocated by John Hick.[11] A theology of religions cannot function in an empty space, outside of a particular religious tradition, and therefore, given that the Tübingen theologians are Christian theologians, they develop it from the perspective of a Christian understanding of God and reality. They do so on the basis of the Lutheran doctrine of justification and grace, developing an argument which aims to avoid the traditional problems of exclusivism and inclusivism – namely the fundamental reduction of other religions to one's own tradition and the resulting inability to engage in genuine interreligious dialogue.[12]

If, so Schwöbel argues, Christian faith is a witness to God's Trinitarian acts in creation, salvation and redemption, then this faith in God as Father, Son and Spirit can only be understood as a work of God's grace in and towards us. That we believe in God through Jesus Christ is never a matter of our own merit, but always the work of God, who justifies us as sinners in Jesus Christ. The truth to which we confess ourselves is always a truth that is not in our own possession, and therefore we can never use it as a ground to call other religions false.[13] Faith is always an *opus Dei* and can never become an *opus hominum*. Therefore, we can only gratefully receive this faith. On the basis of our own Christian understanding of God and reality, we can also expect God's grace-filled acts in other religions, and we will be able to discern these acts through the grace of the Spirit.[14]

The main thrust of the argument, we could say, is twofold: first, Schwöbel aims to develop the theology of religions from the core of his own confessional Christian tradition. Second, he wants to do this in a way that makes believers as respectful of, and as careful towards, adherents of other religions and confessions as possible, precisely because such respect is rooted in the kernel of their religious commitment. This is why he can call his view a form of 'pluralism', albeit one 'from faith'.

One might finally ask how this view of the theology of religions relates to my thesis that contemporary theologies of religions understand religions as being

---

10. Christoph Schwöbel, *Christlicher Glaube im Pluralismus. Studien zu einer Theologie der Kultur* (Tübingen: Mohr Siebeck, 2003), 188–93.

11. Cf. Christoph Schwöbel, 'Particularity, Universality, and the Religions: Toward a Christian Theology of Religions', in *Christian Uniqueness Reconsidered: The Myth of a Pluralistic Theology of Religions*, ed. Gavin D'Costa (Maryknoll, NY: Orbis, 1990), 30–47, which is the third fundamental essay, together with those by Rowan Williams and Gavin D'Costa, in this collection.

12. Schwöbel, *Christlicher Glaube im Pluralismus*, 189–90.

13. Ibid., 193–201.

14. Ibid., 201–5.

oriented towards knowledge and truth. Insofar as the answer to this question does not follow naturally from my account of this position, a quotation from Schwöbel may serve to confirm that the primary orientation of religion is indeed towards its truth:

> The specific characteristic of Christian faith is that it combines the disconcerting particularity of the perspective of faith with universal truth claims about the universality of God. This implies that the whole of reality is seen as determined by God's creative, reconciling, and saving agency in such a way that God's action is the condition for the possibility of all natural processes and all human activity.[15]

9.3 The Law and Gospel distinction as a critical instrument in theology

So far, we have seen how religions come into view in contemporary theologies of religions insofar as they are oriented towards truth. In other words, the concept of revelation determines how theologians of religions deal with religion. Insofar as theologies of the religions are developed from the perspective of the self-understanding of the Christian faith, one could say that they are developed on the basis of the Gospel. God has definitively revealed Godself in Jesus Christ, meaning that a theology of religions must be developed in terms of this final revelation. Moreover, it is indeed the person of Christ who is the cornerstone of the Christian debate concerning an exclusivist, inclusivist or pluralist response to the theology of religions.

In this light, we have discovered a close connection between the content of the Christian faith and its understanding of God and reality on the one hand, and the criterion on the basis of which other religions are evaluated on the other. In these theologies of religions, the content and criterion of theology coincide. In some, like the 'pluralism from faith' option, for example, this even represents the explicit aim of the argument, since the method that directs the theology of religions or theology of ecumenism should not be a Fremdkörper vis-à-vis Christian theology, but an integral part of it.

---

15. Schwöbel, 'Particularity, Universality, and the Religions'; translated into German as Schwöbel, *Christlicher Glaube im Pluralismus*, 146:

> Das spezifische Charakteristikum des christlichen Glaubens besteht darin, daß es die irritierende Partikularität der Perspektive des Glaubens mit universalen Wahrheitsansprüchen über die Universalität Gottes verbindet. Diese Auffassung beinhaltet die Überzeugung, daß das Ganze der Wirklichkeit als durch Gottes schöpferisches, versöhnendes und vollendendes Handeln bestimmt gedacht werden muß, und zwar auf solche Weise, daß Gottes Handeln die Bedingung der Möglichkeit aller natürlichen Prozesse wie auch des menschlichen Handelns ist.

Although I fundamentally agree with this position and this chapter is even an application of it, I do draw different conclusions when I argue that the core of the Christian faith cannot be understood in terms of the Gospel alone, but in terms of the interplay between Law and Gospel. Furthermore, this leads to a view of the Christian religion, at least, in which the idea of religion as a set of truth claims is interrupted and reconfigured from an internal theological perspective. In other words, I would like to radicalize the position of Schwöbel and others by reflecting more theologically on what Christianity is as a religion, while they still seem to remain in the predominantly Enlightenment paradigm of religion as a set of truth claims.

I have various reasons for doing so, one of which is practical and contextual. As far as I can see, the concept of pluralism from faith does not go as far as it should to account for the differences between religious traditions, nor does it manage to overcome the problem of traditional inclusivism. As to the first, pluralism from faith still understands non-Christian religious traditions as being primarily concerned with truth, a truth that is revealed. However, in this regard, the pluralism from faith view still seems to interpret other religious traditions from a Christian perspective. It is no coincidence, for example, that it is precisely Christianity that is so concerned with truth. This has to do with the fact that it is a faith tradition in which the historical reality of the life of Jesus has salvific significance. For this reason, there is a lot at stake with the kind of historical reality it is, and how we speak about this reality. In other religious traditions, however, 'truth' is often not of primary significance, since they are more concerned with appropriate behavior than with 'truth'. Reducing these traditions to sets of truth claims does not do justice to the genuine differences between Christianity and other traditions.

Furthermore, the problems of traditional inclusivism do not seem to be sufficiently overcome because, even though the pluralist from faith sees the truth that is revealed to her as a gift that should never lead to the condemnation of the convictions of others, it still sees its own received truth as the truth – and so one wonders about the extent to which the pluralist from faith opens up their own tradition to others. Is not, in the end, the pluralist from faith an exclusivist or, at best, a traditional inclusivist?

A third objection can be derived from the idea that the content and criterion of theology coincide. This turns theology into a circular endeavour. The question of whether Christian theology is true is answered in terms of an appeal to Christian theology rather than to an external criterion. Christians are right in what they believe, because they are right. That does not seem a very convincing criterion for theology.

The above, however, are still quite general objections. In this chapter, I intend to dig deeper and to radicalize the pluralism of faith tradition from the kernel of its own conviction, namely the Reformation doctrine of grace, faith versus works, Law versus Gospel. Such, we could say, is the Ground and object of faith according to a Protestant understanding of Christian faith.[16] The specific form of my argument on the basis of the Law-Gospel distinction will perhaps be more

16. Cf. the paradigmatic collection of essays, published together with a group of scholars from the Lateran Pontifical University: Eilert Herms and Lubomír Žák, eds, *Grund und*

typical for the Reformed tradition than it is for the Lutheran, but there still is much common ground between them.

As we have argued multiple times in this book, the theology of the Reformation is characterized by a strong distinction between Law and Gospel. Eilert Herms summarizes Luther's view of Law and Gospel as follows: the Law tells us what we should do, and the Gospel tells us what God has done, is doing and will do for us in Jesus Christ.[17] The law commands and obliges, whereas the Gospel gives, promises, proclaims, without asking or obliging. If we apply this decisive distinction to the question of the criterion of theology (or, more precisely, the theology of religions), the Gospel cannot be the criterion for theology. This is because a criterion is something that demands something, namely conformity to it.

This rather rigid line of reasoning can be discussed in philosophical terms as well. From the analytic philosophical tradition, we may draw the insight that truth claims always have a deontic character. This means that if someone is confronted with a true proposition, substantiated with a sufficient number of grounds that make the truth of the proposition transparent to the reader, the reader is epistemologically obliged to accept the truth of the proposition. Otherwise, people would be irrational in their convictions. Whoever claims to speak the truth commands others to acknowledge this truth, and thus a theology appealing to truth belongs, theologically formulated, to the domain of the Law. Therefore, if theology makes truth claims, it has a lawlike nature. Hence, if the message of the Gospel is construed as a truth claim, it is turned into a Law. In earlier chapters we already saw that classical Reformed theologians such as Voetius, but also the Tübingen theologians, cannot accept this because the Law-Gospel distinction implies a strict distinction between *opus Dei* and *opus hominum*.

Maybe this feels like a rather abstract argument, but I do not think it is. If the Gospel means 'good news', pure promise, then it witnesses to salvation in Jesus Christ, but it need not necessarily claim to possess the ultimate truth about the whole of reality. One might summarize the core message of the Gospel with a quotation from the Gospel of Matthew: 'Come to me, all you who are weary and burdened, and I will give you rest' (11.29; NIV). Or, with the Gospel of John: 'I am the bread of life. Whoever comes to me will never go hungry, and whoever believes in me will never be thirsty' (6.35). Such formulations have an entirely different ring to them than this: 'We are right, Jesus Christ indeed definitively reveals who God is.' As soon as these two formulations of the substance of the Gospel are juxtaposed, one can see the structural differences between them. 'Come to me' sounds like a promising invitation, but 'I am a Christian, who by the grace of God knows about the true nature of God and the whole of reality' sounds more like the beginning and end of a polemic that leaves no true room for dialogue. This

---

Gegenstand des Glaubens nach römisch-katholischer und evangelisch-lutherischer Lehre. Theologische Studien (Tübingen: Mohr Siebeck, 2008).

17. Eilert Herms, *Phänomene des Glaubens: Beiträge zur Fundamentaltheologie* (Tübingen: Mohr Siebeck, 2006), 379–80.

is all the more so when we realize that the truth claim of the Christian faith in the pluralism from faith account of theology of religions is construed as an all-encompassing truth claim, a theory of everything so to speak.[18]

What emerges if we develop the theology of the religions in terms of the interplay between Law and Gospel? While we might attempt to say many things abstractly, the plausibility of a theology of religions and of interreligious dialogue depends to a significant extent on the question of practical feasibility. For this reason, I would like to illustrate the role of the Law in the theology of the religions and the alternative kind of common ground (see below) that it offers through a fictional conversation of interreligious dialogue in which adherents of different religions are in conversation with each other and in which the first commandment of the Decalogue implicitly and explicitly plays a role.

What I imagine is the style of dialogue in which I have often been involved during my international experience in Germany and Belgium. These are not overly politically correct conversations, nor are they the kind that take place in committees in search of a consensus. On the contrary, they are quite often conversations in which one shares much mutual faith and respect, but due in part to such mutual confidence, all kinds of prejudices and mutual misunderstandings are expressed outright. At the same time, they are conversations in which the authenticity of the other's faith commitment is, mutually, never called into question.

I therefore imagine a Lutheran, a Reformed, a Muslim and a Jew who have become acquainted, with confidence and friendship growing over time. They have also come to know the religious and confessional traditions of the others to some extent. No specific preparation was undertaken for a dogmatic dispute, but one day a conversation takes place, occasioned by the rather practical question of whether it would be possible to pray together.[19] The rather liberal Jew could imagine this possibility, but the Lutheran immediately asks: 'To whom then should we pray?' The Muslim proposes: 'To God in general? After all, the Arabic word *Allah* means "God", and Christians and Jews believe in God, so why could we not pray to God in general? We are all monotheists, so why not?' The Lutheran, however, knows his sources and immediately replies: 'According to my tradition, you cannot pray to God in general. I pray only to the Father of our Lord Jesus Christ. There is no other God and in the event there should be another God, one can only fear that God, and not trust him in faith.' The Reformed conversation partner, who got just too much Barthianism during his religious education to properly understand the history of his confessional tradition, affirms: 'There is no God in general. God can only be known in Jesus Christ.' The Muslim replies with a heavy sigh: 'I have never

---

18. Cf. Christoph Schwöbel, 'Die Trinitätslehre als Rahmentheorie des christlichen Glaubens. Vier Thesen zur Bedeutung der Trinität in der christlichen Dogmatik', in *Gott in Beziehung: Studien zur Dogmatik* (Tübingen: Mohr Siebeck, 2002), 25–51.

19. Cf. several contributions on prayer in the following volume: Marianne Moyaert and Joris Geldhof, *Ritual Participation and Interreligious Dialogue: Boundaries, Transgressions and Innovations* (London: Bloomsbury, 2016).

really managed to understand that. Mohammed had a point: God cannot have a son. One cannot pray to a human being such as Jesus. One can pray to God, but not to Jesus. Jesus is a prophet, even a very important one, but he is not God, and so to pray to Jesus would be idolatry. A human being who would be God? This is impossible!'

The Lutheran, who has already done some reading in systematic theology, replies: 'No, no, no, you just don't understand it right. We don't call the human being Jesus "God" nor do we not worship a human being. This was why something like a two-nature Christology developed in Christianity. If we worshiped a human being, that would indeed be idolatry, but the Christian tradition has attached great importance to a proper distinction between the divinity and the humanity of Jesus, even though they cannot be separated from each other. So, if we pray to Jesus, we do not pray to a human being, but to God.'

'This sounds pretty complicated', the Muslim replies with another sigh. 'With us, all of this has been thought through much more clearly: one God, and Mohammed is his prophet. Clear and easy!' 'I'm not so sure', the Reformed replies. 'What I've never understood in your tradition is why Muslims place such weight on their monotheism and iconoclasm, but still oblige every Muslim to go to Mecca and to walk around the Kaaba. Only Allah is God, no one dares to make images, nor are any images found in mosques (only letter-like figures), and yet that black stone is almost as important as God!'

'And what about you?', the Muslim replies with some irritation. 'What about that Bible of yours?! Every time we meet, you carry it with you, and you want to answer every religious question on its basis. Infallible it is! Could it also not be an idol?'

So far, the Jew has not said anything. She had listened silently, but now she says with a sigh: 'Why do you argue so much? I thought we were friends?' 'Of course we are', the others reply, 'but even then we can argue in a friendly way.' 'I still don't understand why believers have to fight so much with one another', the Jew says. 'For example, why do Christians, who have the Old Testament, believe in a Jew, call God love, more than we Jews have ever done, and still kill six million Jews in the name of European high culture. This is utterly incomprehensible! So stop your fighting!' Silence. After a few minutes, the Lutheran begins the conversation again: 'You're right, this is horrendous! Christians should never have done that!' The Jew replies, sharply, 'But you keep on fighting! And it cannot be that easy, anyway! Centuries of Jewish persecution by Christians must have something to do with the kernel of their faith! I think it must be related to your faith in Jesus Christ. You just think that you can speak the final word about God and world because God became human! This idea of the incarnation is terribly dangerous!'

And so the conversation goes on … What can we conclude on the basis of this conversation for our attempt to use the Law-Gospel distinction as a critical instrument for a theology of religions? A few remarks:

1 Properly distinguishing between Law and Gospel in the theology of religions, distinguishing between what the Law demands and the Gospel promises, did

not lead to relativism or pluralism. The participants in the conversation were not forced to leave their own faith tradition before they could engage in the discussion. The conversation was between and within the confessions, truth claims were constantly at stake, but the truth claim of one did not rule out the truth claim of the other.
2 There was more than just a friendly exchange of confessions to the various religious traditions. There were arguments, and there was criticism in the light of a common critical instrument.
3 The first commandment of the Decalogue was constantly in play, albeit often implicitly. From the perspective of the classical theological tradition, one might say that the Decalogue was present in the discussion as natural law, as a frame of reference accessible to all participants, without having to agree on it ahead of time.
4 The critical role of the Law with respect to religious truth claims was equally critical towards Christianity as it was towards Islam, although it was not so towards Judaism.

In this approach to the theology of religions, the Law receives a primary role in providing a common critical point of reference for theology of religions. Theology of religions as an ongoing conversation is primarily a critique of the domestication of God. A typical consequence of traditional theology of religions is that a conversation between traditions is primarily developed in terms of commonalities and differences between religious convictions. Along the same lines, but as a flipside of the same paradigm, newer theologies of religions tends to turn away from similarities and commonalities and focus on genuine differences between various traditions. While both approaches have their merits, they share the common limitation of discussing the relationships between religions as relationships between mutually exclusive, inclusive or compatible boxes of religious truths. In the model for theology of religions that I am proposing here, I would like to highlight how different religious traditions differ not only by their statements of faith (which is basically a typically Christian approach to religion) but also by the prescriptive aspects of their tradition, while they at the same time share important concerns about the domestication of God. This yields a new way for looking at commonalities between traditions. These commonalities are critical concerns rather than positive statements of faith.

9.4 Religion as truth and the nature of the Gospel as promise

Up to now, we have focused on how the Law-Gospel distinction could function in a new way in the theology of religions. The emphasis was on the role of the Law as a common critical instrument between the religions. This, however, raises the question of how in this theology of religions, if it is a Christian one, the *proprium* of the Christian faith could be communicated. If a theology of religions is not going to abandon the core of its religious tradition, what would it have to say as the core of this message, as the sum of the Gospel? Formulated otherwise, how should a Christian theology of the religions speak about Jesus Christ, the Trinity and the love of God if the primary status of such speech is not to claim that this is the truth about God but its principal intention is to invite and witness to a truth that is not ours? To elucidate this, I would like to introduce another aspect of the Law-Gospel distinction, which is bound up with a characteristic structural difference between the classical Lutheran and Reformed traditions.

In Chapter 2, as well as in later chapters, I largely presupposed that the distinction between Law and Gospel as I drew it from Melanchthon and Voetius belonged to the common Lutheran and Reformed heritage. In both, the Law is said to have the nature of a commandment and the Gospel is said to be a promise. In a certain respect, however, this was an oversimplification. For this reason, I would like to suggest that it is no coincidence that the Lutheran theology of religions, and in particular the Tübingen view of ecumenism and the theology of religions, has developed so powerfully in the direction of an all-encompassing understanding of truth and reality. The reason, or so it seems to me, is its firm rooting in the classical Lutheran doctrine of grace, the so-called notion of the 'Alleinwirksamkeit Gottes'.[20] This doctrine understands God's grace and God's acts in a broader sense in such a way that it sees it permeating all of reality and as a matter of fact. Here only a minor part is left to human freedom and to the instrumental role of faith in the economy of salvation. We saw a trace of this when we discussed the differences between the definitions of Law and Gospel in Voetius on the one hand, and (the early) Melanchthon on the other.

If we look at Voetius' definitions again, we find him saying that the Gospel 'refers to, announces, signifies to us, what Christ has done for us, and what God promises in Christ, what he wants to do, and what he will do'.[21] That sounds good, one might say, it sounds biblical. However, if we compare it to a classical Lutheran definition, we see a marked difference between them. In the very first sentences of his commentary on the Gospel of John from 1523, secretly given to a publisher by Luther, Melanchthon offers the following definition:

> What the difference is between Law and Gospel, has been said elsewhere [namely in the *Loci Communes* of 1521, MW]. Now, it suffices to maintain that the 'Law' is the things prescribed to be done, while the Gospel is the remission of sins and the gift of the Holy Spirit through Christ.[22]

---

20. See e.g. Bengt Hägglund, 'De Providentia. Zur Gotteslehre im frühen Luthertum', *Zeitschrift für Theologie und Kirche* 83, no. 3 (1986): 356–69, http://www.jstor.org/stable/23584950.

21. Gisbertus Voetius, *D. Gysberti Voetii Selectarum Disputationum Fasciculus*, ed. Abraham Kuyper (Amstelodami: Wormser, 1887), 348: 'refert, nuntiat, significat nobis, quid Christus pro nobis fecerit, quidque Deus in Christo promittat, quid facere velit, & facturus sit.'

22. Philipp Melanchthon, *Annotationes in Iohannem* (Nürnberg, 1523), 3r: 'Quid intersit inter Legem et Evangelium, alias dictum est. Nunc satis est monere legem esse quae

Here we see a difference, one that only became stronger once Lutheranism progressed in its development. Voetius sees the Gospel as the speaking about, witnessing to and proclaiming of what Christ has done, is doing and will do. The Gospel is the communication about and of the work of Christ. Melanchthon, however, simply says: 'The Gospel is the remission of sins and the gift of the Holy Spirit through Christ.' In Voetius, the Gospel is a communicative event that is as such not yet the fulfilment of what it communicates. For Voetius, the forgiveness of sins of which Melanchthon speaks is the outcome of the communicative dynamics of the Gospel proclaiming and promising it, and faith embracing Christ as preached in the Gospel. The Reformed tradition rejects universalism in the proclamation of the Gospel,[23] because the fulfilment of God's promises is restricted to the elect. Therefore, the subject matter of the preaching of the Gospel cannot be the *fact* of our being saved but must be the *possibility* of us being saved through faith in Christ proclaimed by the Gospel. The classical Lutheran theologians of the sixteenth century would deny universalism, because, ultimately, only the believer participates in the salvation which Christ has accomplished, but they at the same time affirm the universal scope of the preaching of the Gospel.

This has ramifications for the nature of the proclamation of the Gospel. If the message of the Gospel has a universalist structure, and this is true for modern Lutheranism even more so than for Luther or Melanchthon, then the Gospel takes the form of a proposition. In that case, the Gospel has the character of a truth claim: the fact of the redemption of the world. If the Gospel is not interpreted in a universalist manner, as is the case in Voetius, the Gospel has a dynamic and communicative character as a promise that only becomes a reality once it is embraced in faith.

Analytic philosophy can help us at this point again. As has been noted, Vincent Brümmer, following J. L. Austin's *How to Do Things with Words?*,[24] distinguished between 'constatives' (propositions) and 'commissives' (promises).[25] If the Gospel has the structure of a truth claim, as an announcement of a fact, it has the nature of a constative or proposition: you have been saved. This is a promise as well, but because of the absolute nature of the promise, it has the structure of a proposition. In Christ, God has once and for all taken away the sins of the world. In the classic Reformed tradition, the Gospel takes the nature of a commissive, of a promise.

---

praescribit facienda, Evangelium esse remissione peccatorum & donationem Spiritus sancti per Christum.'

23. Understood here in the sense of the classic pre-modern Reformed tradition that adopted double predestination as one of its identity markers.

24. J. L. Austin, *How to Do Things with Words* (Cambridge, MA: Harvard University Press, 1962).

25. Vincent Brümmer, *Theology and Philosophical Inquiry* (London: Macmillan, 1981), 16–25; see also Maarten Wisse, 'The Meaning of the Authority of the Bible', *Religious Studies* 36 (2000): 473–87.

God promises to save those who entrust themselves to Jesus Christ in faith, and listeners are stimulated, invited and called to do so. They are not confronted with a fact, but with a promise.[26]

How can Jesus Christ be introduced in interreligious dialogues from this Reformed perspective? Not primarily in terms of the announcement of a fact, but in the form of a promise and an invitation. As a Christian believer, I will witness to what can be found in Jesus Christ the saviour and I will, explicitly or implicitly, invite adherents of other religions to embrace Christ as their saviour. I do not claim that my conversation partners have been saved in Christ before they embrace him as he is freely offered to them in faith. This seemingly hesitant approach to the preaching of the Gospel opens up a communicative space in which the dialogue is strengthened rather than weakened.[27]

It is clear that embracing Christ as one's saviour has consequences for one's view of the world and one's understanding of God, but these are not primary. Seeing the world in a certain way is the *consequence* of embracing Christ as one's saviour, but it is not the beginning. If we bring this to bear on issues that we have touched on in the introductory Chapter 1, we can shed some light on the propositional status of Christian faith and theology. My emphasis on the nature of the Gospel as promise and my emphasis on Christian theology as protecting the mystery of God rather than describing the truth about God might lead to the suggestion that I reject the propositional content of the Christian faith and thus of Christian theology. This would be an exaggeration, however. Christian faith and theology has propositional content, even quite extensively and substantially, but this propositional content has an indirect character, embedded as it is in the communicative nature of the Gospel.

For Christian faith, this means that once believers embrace Christ proclaimed in the Gospel, they start the journey of faith as an ever-continuing search for the deep things of God (Eph. 3.11, 18; 1 Cor. 2.10). This search is not a merely intellectual endeavour. It is a search involving the entire body of believers, both individually and communally. Christian theology then, as a second-order discourse that aims to protect the mystery of God proclaimed in the Gospel, reflects accordingly and primarily, in an intellectual way, on the preconditions that need to be met for the Gospel to be true and therefore scrutinizes their propositional content. As such, theology is an endeavour that pursues the believer's search of the deep things of God, but in an intellectual and academic way – faith seeking understanding.

---

26. For a more elaborate account of this point, see Maarten Wisse, 'The Inseparable Bond between Covenant and Predestination: Cocceius and Barth', in *Scholasticism Reformed: Essays in Honour of Willem J. Van Asselt*, ed. Maarten Wisse, Marcel Sarot and Willemien Otten, STAR 14 (Leiden: Brill, 2010), 259–79.

27. For a more elaborate account of this point, see ibid.

BIBLIOGRAPHY

Abrahamse, Jan Martijn. *Ordained Ministry in Free Church Perspective: Retrieving Robert Browne (c. 1550–1633) for Contemporary Ecclesiology*. Studies in Reformed Theology 41. Leiden: Brill, 2020.

Alexander Street Press, ed. *The Digital Library of Classic Protestant Texts*, n.d. https://search.alexanderstreet.com/tcpt.

Allen, Michael. 'Sacraments in the Reformed and Anglican Reformation'. In *The Oxford Handbook of Sacramental Theology*, edited by Hans Boersma and Matthew Levering, 283–98. Oxford: Oxford University Press, 2015.

Aquinas, Thomas. *Summa Theologiae*, n.d.

Asselt, Willem J. van. *The Federal Theology of Johannes Cocceius (1603–1669)*. Leiden: Brill, 2001.

Asselt, Willem J. van, Theo T. J. Pleizier, Pieter L. Rouwendal and Maarten Wisse. *Introduction to Reformed Scholasticism*. Grand Rapids, MI: Reformation Heritage, 2011.

Athanasius. *Contra Arianos*, n.d.

Athanasius. *De incarnatione verbi*, n.d.

Augustine. *Answer to the Pelagians, I*. Edited by John E. Rotelle. Translated by Edmund Hill. *The Works of Saint Augustine: A Translation for the 21st Century 23*. Hyde Park, NY: New City, 1997.

Augustine. *De Civitate Dei*, n.d.

Augustine. *Enchiridion, de Fide, Spe et Charitate*, n.d.

Augustine. *Homilies on the Gospel of John*. Edited by Philip Schaff. Nicene and Post-Nicene Fathers Series I 7. Grand Rapids, MI: Christian Classics Ethereal Library, n.d.

Augustine. *Sermons (94A–147A) on the Old Testament*. Translated by Edmund Hill. The Works of Saint Augustine, III/4. Brooklyn, NY: New City, 1992.

Austin, J. L. *How to Do Things with Words*. Cambridge, MA: Harvard University Press, 1962.

Baars, Arie. *Om Gods verhevenheid en Zijn nabijheid: De Drie-eenheid bij Calvijn*. Kampen: J. H. Kok, 2004.

Barclay, John M. G. *Paul and the Gift*. Grand Rapids, MI: Eerdmans, 2017.

Barth, Karl. *Church Dogmatics*. Translated by Geoffrey William Bromiley and Thomas F. Torrance. Edinburgh: T&T Clark, 1975.

Barth, Karl. 'Das erste Gebot als theologisches Axiom'. In *Gottes Freiheit für den Menschen. Eine Auswahl der Vorträge, Vorreden und kleinen Schriften*, 132–46. Berlin: Evangelische Verl. Anst., 1970.

Barth, Karl. 'Das Wort Gottes als Aufgabe der Theologie'. In *Vorträge und kleinere Arbeiten 1922–1925*, edited by Holger Finze-Michaelsen. Karl Barth-Gesamtausgabe 19, 144–75. Zurich: Theologischer Verlag, 1990.

Barth, Karl. *Der Römerbrief: zweite Fassung, 1922*. Edited by Cornelis van der Kooi and Katja Tolstaja. Karl Barth-Gesamtausgabe 47. Zurich: Theologischer Verlag, 2010.

Barth, Karl. *Die christliche Dogmatik im Entwurf*. Edited by Gerhard Sauter. Karl Barth-Gesamtausgabe 14. Zurich: Theologischer Verlag, 1982.
Barth, Karl. 'Die Grundformen theologischen Denkens'. In *Theologische Fragen und Antworten*, 282–90. Zollikon, Zurich: Evangelischer Verlag, 1957.
Barth, Karl. *Die Kirchliche Dogmatik*. Zollikon, Zurich: Evangelischer Verlag, 1932–70.
Barth, Karl. 'The First Commandment as an Axiom of Theology'. In *The Way of Theology in Karl Barth: Essays and Comments*, edited by H. Martin Rumscheidt, 63–78. Princeton Theological Monographs 8. Allison Park, PA: Pickwick, 1986.
Barth, Karl. *God Is God: zes voordrachten uit 1930–1936*. Translated by Nico T. Bakker. Kampen: J. H. Kok, 2004.
Barth, Karl. 'Gospel and Law'. In *Community, State, and Church: Three Essays*, translated by A. M. Hall, 71–101. Garden City, NY: Doubleday, 1960.
Barth, Karl. *'Unterricht in der christlichen Religion': Zweiter Band*. Edited by Hinrich Stoevesandt. Karl Barth-Gesamtausgabe 20. Zurich: Theologischer Verlag, 1985.
Barth, Karl. *Vorträge Und Kleinere Arbeiten, 1930–1933*. Edited by Michael Beintker, Michael Hüttenhoff and Peter Zocher. Karl Barth-Gesamtausgabe 49. Zurich: Theologischer Verlag, 2013.
Barth, Karl. *Vorträge Und Kleinere Arbeiten, 1934–1935*. Edited by Michael Beintker, Michael Hüttenhoff and Peter Zocher. Karl Barth-Gesamtausgabe 52. Zurich: Theologischer Verlag, 2017.
Barth, Karl. 'The Word of God as the Task of Theology'. In *The Word of God and Theology*, translated by Amy Marga, 171–98. London: T&T Clark International, 2011.
Bavel, Tarsicius J. van. 'The "Christus Totus" Idea: A Forgotten Aspect of Augustine's Spirituality'. In *Studies in Patristic Christology*, edited by Thomas Finan and Vincent Twomey, 84–94. Dublin: Four Courts, 1998.
Bavinck, Herman. 'Calvijn's leer over het Avondmaal'. In *Kennis en Leven: Opstellen en artikelen uit vroegere jaren*, edited by C. B. Bavinck, 165–83. Kampen: J. H. Kok, 1922.
Bavinck, Herman. 'Calvin's Doctrine of the Lord's Supper'. Translated by Nelson D. Kloosterman. *Mid-America Journal of Theology* 19 (2008): 127–42. http://www.mid america.edu/uploads/files/pdf/journal/bavinkkloosterman19.pdf.
Bavinck, Herman. *Gereformeerde Dogmatiek*, 2nd edn. Kampen: J. H. Kok, 1911.
Bavinck, Herman. *Reformed Dogmatics*. Edited by John Bolt. Translated by John Vriend. Grand Rapids, MI: Baker Academic, 2003.
Bayer, Oswald. *Leibliches Wort: Reformation und Neuzeit im Konflikt*. Tübingen: Mohr Siebeck, 1992.
Beek, A. van de. *De kring om de Messias: Israël als volk van de lijdende Heer: Spreken over God 1,2*. Zoetermeer: Meinema, 2002.
Beintker, Michael. 'Der Dialektiker als Dogmatiker'. In *Barth Handbuch*, edited by Michael Beintker, 206–10. Theologen-Handbücher. Tübingen: Mohr Siebeck, 2016.
Beintker, Michael. 'Dialektische Theologie'. In *Barth Handbuch*, edited by Michael Beintker, 200–5. Theologen-Handbücher. Tübingen: Mohr Siebeck, 2016.
Beintker, Michael. 'Resümee'. In *Barth Handbuch*, edited by Michael Beintker, 232–7. Theologen-Handbücher. Tübingen: Mohr Siebeck, 2016.
Belt, Henk van den. *The Authority of Scripture in Reformed Theology: Truth and Trust*. Leiden: Brill, 2008.
Belt, Henk van den. 'The Problematic Character of Sola Scriptura'. In *Sola Scriptura: Biblical and Theological Perspectives on Scripture, Authority and*

Hermeneutics, edited by Hans Burger and Arnold Huijgen, 38–55. Studies in Reformed Theology 32. Leiden: Brill, 2017.

Bergmeier, Roland. *Glaube als Gabe nach Johannes: Religions- und theologiegeschichtliche Studien zum prädestinatianischen Dualismus im vierten Evangelium*. Stuttgart: Kohlhammer, 1980.

Berkhof, Hendrikus. *Christian Faith: An Introduction to the Study of the Faith*. Eugene, OR: Wipf and Stock, 1999.

Berkouwer, Gerrit Cornelis. *De triomf der genade in de theologie van Karl Barth*. Kampen: J. H. Kok, 1954.

Berkouwer, Gerrit Cornelis. *The Sacraments*. Translated by Hugo Bekker. Studies in Dogmatics. Grand Rapids, MI: Eerdmans, 1969.

Billings, J. Todd. *Calvin, Participation, and the Gift: The Activity of Believers in Union with Christ*. Oxford: Oxford University Press, 2009.

Boer, Erik de. *The Genevan School of the Prophets: The Congregations of the Company of Pastors and Its Influence in the 16th Century*. Geneva: Librairie Droz, 2012.

Boeve, Lieven. 'Theological Truth, Particularity and Incarnation: Engaging Religious Plurality and Radical Hermeneutics'. In *Orthodoxy, Process and Product*, edited by Mathijs Lamberigts, Lieven Boeve and Terrence Merrigan, 323–48. BETL 227. Leuven: Peeters, 2009.

Boezelman, Wijnand. *Athanasius' Use of the Gospel of John*. Lewiston, NY: Edwin Mellen, 2019.

Brague, Rémi. *The Law of God: The Philosophical History of an Idea*. Translated by Lydia G. Cochrane. 3rd edn. Chicago: University of Chicago Press, 2008.

Brakel, Wilhelmus à. *The Christian's Reasonable Service*. Edited by Joel R. Beeke. Translated by Bartel Elshout. Ligonier, PA: Soli Deo Gloria, 1999.

Braun, Dietrich. 'Karl Barths Texte zur Barmer Theologischen Erklärung'. *Evangelische Theologie* 45, no. 1 (1985): 81–91.

Breukelman, F. H. *Bijbelse theologie/Dl. IV, 1, De structuur van de heilige leer in de theologie van Calvijn*. Edited by Rinse Reeling Brouwer. Kampen: J. H. Kok, 2003.

Brümmer, Vincent. *Speaking of a Personal God: An Essay in Philosophical Theology*. Cambridge: Cambridge University Press, 1992.

Brümmer, Vincent. *Theology and Philosophical Inquiry*. London: Macmillan, 1981.

Bucer, Martin. *Enarratio in Evangelion Johannis*. Strasbourg, 1528.

Bünker, Michael, and Martin Friedrich, eds. *Gesetz und Evangelium. Eine Studie, auch im Blick auf die Entscheidungsfindung in ethischen Fragen, Ergebnis eines Studienprozesses der Gemeinschaft evangelischer Kirchen in Europa (GEKE)*. Leuenberger Texte 10. Frankfurt am Main: Otto Lembeck, 2007.

Burger, Hans. *Being in Christ: A Biblical and Systematic Investigation in a Reformed Perspective*. Eugene, OR: Wipf and Stock, 2009.

Busch, Eberhard. *Karl Barths Lebenslauf nach seinen Briefen und autobiographischen Texten*, 4th edn. Munich: Kaiser, 1986.

Calvin, John. *Commentarius in Evangelium Ioannis*. Calvini Opera 47, 1892.

Calvin, John. *Institutes (1559)*. Edited by John T. McNeill. Translated by Ford Lewis Battles. Kentucky: Westminster, 1960.

Chauvet, Louis-Marie. *The Sacraments: The Word of God at the Mercy of the Body*. Collegeville, MI: Liturgical, 2001.

Chauvet, Louis-Marie. *Symbol and Sacrament: A Sacramental Reinterpretation of Christian Existence*. Translated by Patrick Madigan. Collegeville, MI: Liturgical, 1995.

Clark, R. Scott. 'Law and Gospel in Early Reformed Orthodoxy: Hermeneutical Conservatism in Olevianus' Commentary on Romans'. In *Church and School in Early Modern Protestantism: Studies in Honor of Richard A. Muller on the Maturation of a Theological Tradition*, edited by Jordan J. Ballor, David S. Sytsma and Jason Zuidema, 307–20. Studies in the History of Christian Traditions 170. Leiden: Brill, 2013.

Clooney, Francis X. *Comparative Theology: Deep Learning Across Religious Borders*. Malden, MA: Wiley-Blackwell, 2010.

Coakley, Sarah. *God, Sexuality and the Self: An Essay 'on the Trinity'*. Cambridge: Cambridge University Press, 2013.

Cortez, Marc. 'What Does It Mean to Call Karl Barth a Christocentric Theologian?' *Scottish Journal of Theology* 60, no. 2 (2007): 127–43.

Crisp, Oliver. *Deviant Calvinism: Broadening Reformed Theology*. Minneapolis, MN: Fortress, 2014.

Cupitt, Don. *Taking Leave of God*. New York: Crossroad, 1981.

Danz, Christian, and Friedrich Hermanni, eds. *Wahrheitsansprüche der Weltreligionen: Konturen gegenwärtiger Religionstheologie*. Neukirchen-Vluyn: Neukirchener, 2006.

D'Costa, Gavin. *Christian Uniqueness Reconsidered: The Myth of a Pluralistic Theology of Religions*. Maryknoll, NY: Orbis, 1990.

D'Costa, Gavin. *The Meeting of Religions and the Trinity*. Maryknoll, NY: Orbis, 2000.

Dekker, Eef. 'Was Arminius a Molinist?' *Sixteenth Century Journal* 27, no. 2 (1996): 337–52. https://doi.org/10.2307/2544137.

Derrida, Jacques, and Maurizio Ferraris. *A Taste for the Secret*. Cambridge: Polity, 2002.

Eagleton, Terry. 'Marxism without Marxism'. In *Ghostly Demarcations: A Symposium on Jacques Derrida's Spectres of Marx*, edited by Michael Sprinker, 83–7. London: Verso, 1999.

Eglinton, James. *Trinity and Organism: Towards a New Reading of Herman Bavinck's Organic Motif*. London: T&T Clark International, 2012.

Enders, Markus, and Rolf Kühn, eds. *Im Anfang war der Logos: Studien zur Rezeptionsgeschichte des Johannesprologs von Antike bis Gegenwart*. Forschungen zur europäischen Geistesgeschichte 11. Freiburg im Breisgau: Herder, 2011.

Erasmus, Desiderius. *Paraphrase on John*. Translated by Jane E. Phillips. New Testament Scholarship 46. Toronto: University of Toronto Press, 1991. http://www.deslibris.ca/ID/417447.

Erasmus, Desiderius. *Paraphrasis in Euangelium Secundum Ioannem*. Basel: Froben, 1523.

Fesko, John V. 'The Doctrine of Scripture in Reformed Orthodoxy'. In *A Companion to Reformed Orthodoxy*, edited by Herman J. Selderhuis, 429–64. Brill's Companions to the Christian Tradition 40. Leiden: Brill, 2013.

Forde, Gerhard O. *The Law-Gospel Debate: An Interpretation of Its Historical Development*. Minneapolis, MN: Fortress, 1969.

Franck, Sebastian. *Das Gott das ainig ain, und höchstes gut, sein almechtigs, wars, lebendigs wort, will, kunst, gesatz, Sun, sinn, Caracter, liecht, leben ... in aller menschen hertz sey: Zeügnuss der hailigen schrifft, der Hayden, alten lerern und vättern*, 1534.

Frei, Hans W. *The Eclipse of Biblical Narrative: A Study in Eighteenth and Nineteenth Century Hermeneutics*. New Haven, CT: Yale University Press, 1974.

Frey, Jörg, and Jens Schröter, eds. *Deutungen des Todes Jesu im Neuen Testament*. Tübingen: Mohr Siebeck, 2005.

Gibson, David. *Reading the Decree: Exegesis, Election and Christology in Calvin and Barth.* T&T Clark Studies in Systematic Theology 4. London: T&T Clark International, 2009.
Gilland, David Andrew. *Law and Gospel in Emil Brunner's Earlier Dialectical Theology.* T&T Clark Studies in Systematic Theology 22. London: Bloomsbury, 2015.
Gleason, Ronald N. 'Calvin and Bavinck on the Lord's Supper'. *Westminster Theological Journal* 45 (1983): 273–303.
Gleason, Ronald N. 'Herman Bavinck's Understanding of John Calvin on the Lord's Supper', 2009. http://www.richardsibbes.com/_hermanbavinck/hermanbavinck.org-Gleason2.pdf.
Gomes, Alan W. 'Faustus Socinus' de Jesu Christo Servatore, Part III: Historical Introduction, Translation and Critical Notes'. Fuller Theological Seminary, 1990.
Greggs, Tom. *Barth, Origen, and Universal Salvation: Restoring Particularity.* Oxford: Oxford University Press, 2009.
Grenz, Stanley J., and Roger E. Olson. *20th Century Theology: God & the World in a Transitional Age.* Downers Grove, IL: InterVarsity, 1992.
Gunton, Colin E. *Becoming and Being: The Doctrine of God in Charles Hartshorne and Karl Barth.* Oxford: Oxford University Press, 1978.
Gutiérrez, Gustavo. *Theology of Liberation: History, Politics, and Salvation.* Translated by John Eagleson. Rev. edn with a new introduction. Maryknoll, NY: Orbis, 2009.
Hägglund, Bengt. 'De providentia. Zur Gotteslehre im frühen Luthertum'. *Zeitschrift für Theologie und Kirche* 83, no. 3 (1986): 356–69. http://www.jstor.org/stable/23584950.
Hanson, Anthony T. *The Prophetic Gospel: Study of John and the Old Testament.* London: T&T Clark, 2006.
Harinck, George. 'Herman Bavinck and Geerhardus Vos'. *Calvin Theological Journal* 45 (2010): 18–31.
Hart, David Bentley. *The New Testament: A Translation.* New Haven, CT: Yale University Press, 2019.
Hart, David Bentley. *That All Shall Be Saved: Heaven, Hell, and Universal Salvation.* New Haven, CT: Yale University Press, 2019.
Haspelmath-Finatti, Dorothea. *Theologia Prima: Liturgische Theologie für den evangelischen Gottesdienst.* Göttingen: Vandenhoeck & Ruprecht, 2014.
Hayden-Roy, Patrick Marshall. *The Inner Word and the Outer World: A Biography of Sebastian Franck.* Renaissance and Baroque Studies and Texts 7. New York: Peter Lang, 1994.
Heeren, Jelmer, and Maarten Wisse. 'Reprioritizing the Lord's Supper among the Reformed'. *Calvin Theological Journal* 54, no. 1 (2019): 91–122.
Heim, S. Mark. *The Depth of the Riches: A Trinitarian Theology of Religious Ends.* Grand Rapids, MI: Eerdmans, 2001.
Hermanni, Friedrich. 'Der unbekannte Gott: Plädoyer für eine inklusivistische Religionstheologie'. In *Wahrheitsansprüche der Weltreligionen: Konturen gegenwärtiger Religionstheologie*, edited by Christian Danz and Friedrich Hermanni, 149–70. Neukirchen-Vluyn: Neukirchener, 2006.
Herms, Eilert. *Phänomene des Glaubens: Beiträge zur Fundamentaltheologie.* Tübingen: Mohr Siebeck, 2006.
Herms, Eilert, and Lubomír Žák, eds. *Grund und Gegenstand des Glaubens nach römisch-katholischer und evangelisch-lutherischer Lehre. Theologische Studien.* Tübingen: Mohr Siebeck, 2008.
Hesselink, I. John. *Calvin's Concept of the Law.* Allison Park, PA: Pickwick, 1992.

Hoffman, Melchior. 'Van der ware hochprachtlichen eynigen Magestadt Gottes und vann der worhaftigen Menschwerdung des ewigen Worttzs und des aller Hochsten, eyn kurtze Zeucknus und Anweissung allen Liebhabern der Ewigen Worheit'. In *Het Woord is vlees geworden: De melchioritisch-menniste incarnatieleer*, edited by Sjouke Voolstra, 227–45. Kampen: J. H. Kok, 1982.

Horton, Michael S. 'Calvin and the Law-Gospel Hermeneutic'. *Pro Ecclesia* 6, no. 1 (2002): 27–42.

Horton, Michael S. 'Calvin on Law and Gospel', 1 September 2009. https://wscal.edu/resource-center/calvin-on-law-and-gospel.

Huber, Wolfgang. '»Keine anderen Götter.« Über die Notwendigkeit theologischer Religionskritiek'. In *Gott, Götter, Götzen: XIV. Europäischer Kongress für Theologie (11.–15. September 2011 in Zürich)*, edited by Christoph Schwöbel, 23–35. Leipzig: Evangelischer Verlagsanstalt, 2013.

Huijgen, Arnold. 'Alone Together: Sola Scriptura and the Other Solas of the Reformation'. In *Sola Scriptura: Biblical and Theological Perspectives on Scripture, Authority and Hermeneutics*, edited by Hans Burger and Arnold Huijgen, 79–104. Studies in Reformed Theology 32. Leiden: Brill, 2017.

Huijgen, Arnold. *Divine Accommodation in John Calvin's Theology: Analysis and Assessment*. Göttingen: Vandenhoeck & Ruprecht, 2011.

Iwand, Hans Joachim. 'Die Barmer These und die Theologie Martin Luthers'. *Evangelische Theologie* 46, no. 3 (1986): 214–31.

Jacobs, Tom. 'Kritiek van de zuivere verlichting: naar een dialectiek van de universaliteit'. Katholieke Universiteit Leuven, 2010.

Janse, Wim. 'Calvin's Eucharistic Theology: Three Dogma-Historical Observations'. In *Calvinus Sacrarum Literarum Interpres: Papers of the International Congress on Calvin Research*, edited by Herman J. Selderhuis, 27–69. Göttingen: Vandenhoeck & Ruprecht, 2008.

Jong, K. W. de. *Ordening van dienst: Achtergronden van en ontwikkelingen in de eredienst van de Gereformeerde Kerken in Nederland*. Baarn: Ten Have, 1996.

Jüngel, Eberhard. *The Doctrine of the Trinity: God's Being Is in Becoming*. Grand Rapids, MI: Eerdmans, 1976.

Kärkkäinen, Veli-Matti. *Trinity and Religious Pluralism: The Doctrine of the Trinity in Christian Theology of Religions*. Aldershot: Ashgate, 2004.

Kilby, Karen. 'Aquinas, the Trinity and the Limits of Understanding'. *International Journal of Systematic Theology* 7, no. 4 (1 October 2005): 414–27. https://doi.org/10.1111/j.1468-2400.2005.00175.x.

Koch, Anton Friedrich. 'Rationalität im Gespräch. Grundlegendes aus philosophischer Perspektive'. In *Rationalität im Gespräch – Rationality in Conversation*, edited by Markus Mühling, 11–22. Marburger Theologische Studien 126. Leipzig: Evangelischer Verlagsanstalt, 2016.

Koch, John D. *The Distinction between Law and Gospel as the Basis and Boundary of Theological Reflection*. Tübingen: Mohr Siebeck, 2016.

Kooi, Cornelis van der. *As in a Mirror: John Calvin and Karl Barth on Knowing God: A Diptych*. Translated by D. H. Mader. Leiden: Brill, 2005.

Kooiman, W. J. *Luther en de Bijbel*, 3rd edn. Baarn: Ten Have, 1977.

Köstenberger, Andreas J. *A Theology of John's Gospel and Letters*. Biblical Theology of the New Testament. Grand Rapids, MI: Zondervan, 2009.

Krötke, Wolf. 'Erwählungslehre'. In *Barth Handbuch*, edited by Michael Beintker, 221–6. Theologen-Handbücher. Tübingen: Mohr Siebeck, 2016.
Kuitert, Harry M. *The Necessity of Faith: Or, without Faith You're as Good as Dead*. Grand Rapids, MI: Eerdmans, 1976.
Kuyper, Abraham. *Dictaten dogmatiek: College-dictaat van een der studenten*. Grand Rapids, MI: J. B. Hulst, 1910.
Kuyper, Abraham. *E voto Dordraceno: Toelichting op den Heidelbergschen Catechismus*. Amsterdam: J. A. Wormser, 1892.
Kuyper, Abraham. *Het werk van den Heiligen Geest*. Amsterdam: Wormser, 1888.
Kuyper, Abraham. *Onze eeredienst*. Kampen: J. H. Kok, 1911.
Leeuw, G. van der. *Liturgiek*. Nijkerk: Callenbach, 1940.
Leeuw, G. van der. *Sacramentstheologie*. Nijkerk: G. F. Callenbach, 1949.
Lindbeck, George A. *The Nature of Doctrine: Religion and Theology in a Postliberal Age*. Philadelphia, PA: Westminster, 1984.
Lombardus, Petrus. *Sententiarum Quattor Libri*, n.d.
Luther, Martin. *D. Martin Luthers Werke*. Weimar, 1883–2009.
Luther, Martin. *Das New Testament yetzund recht grüntlich teutscht*. Basel: Adam Petri, 1522. http://www.e-rara.ch/zuz/content/titleinfo/198933.
Luther, Martin. 'Large Catechism'. In *Triglot Concordia: The Symbolical Books of the Ev. Lutheran Church*, translated by F. Bente and W. H. T. Dau. St. Louis: Concordia, 1921.
Luther, Martin. 'Von der Freiheit eines Christenmenschen'. In *WA*, VII:20–38, n.d.
MacDonald, Gregory. *The Evangelical Universalist*, 2nd edn. Eugene, OR: Cascade, 2012.
McCormack, Bruce L. 'Christonomie'. In *Barth Handbuch*, edited by Michael Beintker, 226–32. Theologen-Handbücher. Tübingen: Mohr Siebeck, 2016.
McCormack, Bruce L. 'Grace and Being: The Role of God's Gracious Election in Karl Barth's Theological Ontology'. In *The Cambridge Companion to Karl Barth*, edited by J. B. Webster, 92–110. Cambridge: Cambridge University Press, 2000.
McCormack, Bruce L. *Karl Barth's Critically Realistic Dialectical Theology: Its Genesis and Development, 1909–1936*. Oxford: Clarendon, 1997.
McDermott, Gerald R., and Harold A. Netland. *A Trinitarian Theology of Religions: An Evangelical Proposal*. Oxford: Oxford University Press, 2014.
McDonald, Suzanne. *Re-imaging Election: Divine Election as Representing God to Others and Others to God*. Grand Rapids, MI: Eerdmans, 2010.
McGrath, Alister E. *Christianity's Dangerous Idea: The Protestant Revolution – a History from the Sixteenth Century to the Twenty-First*. New York: HarperOne, 2007.
Melanchthon, Philipp. *Annotationes in Iohannem*. Nürnberg, 1523.
Melanchthon, Philipp. *Commonplaces: Loci Communes 1521*. Translated by Christian Preus. Saint Louis, MO: Concordia, 2014.
Melanchthon, Philipp. 'Loci Theologici [1521]'. In *Opera Quae Supersunt Omnia*, edited by Karl Bretschneider and Henricus Ernestus Bindseil, vol. XXI. Braunschweig: Schwetske, 1854.
Menken, Maarten J. J. *Old Testament Quotations in the Fourth Gospel: Studies in Textual Form*. Kampen: Kok Pharos, 1996.
Milbank, John. *Being Reconciled: Ontology and Pardon*. Radical Orthodoxy Series. London: Routledge, 2003.
Moyaert, Marianne. *Fragile Identities: Towards a Theology of Interreligious Hospitality*. Amsterdam: Rodopi, 2011.
Moyaert, Marianne, and Joris Geldhof. *Ritual Participation and Interreligious Dialogue: Boundaries, Transgressions and Innovations*. London: Bloomsbury, 2016.

Muller, Richard A. *After Calvin: Studies in the Development of a Theological Tradition.* Oxford: Oxford University Press, 2003.
Muller, Richard A. 'A Note on "Christocentrism" and the Imprudent Use of Such Terminology'. *Westminster Theological Journal* 68 (2006): 253–60.
Muller, Richard A. *Post-Reformation Reformed Dogmatics.* Vols 2, Holy Scripture: The Cognitive Foundation of Theology. Grand Rapids, MI: Baker Academic, 2003.
Owen, John. *Diatriba de Iustitia divina.* Oxford: Thomas Robinson, 1653.
Owen, John. 'Dissertation on Divine Justice'. In *The Works of John Owen*, edited by William H. Goold, 10:482–624. London: Johnstone & Hunter, 1850–5.
Perkins, William. *Works.* London: Legat, 1600. https://archive.org/stream/goldenchain eorde00perk.
Peterson, Paul Silas. *The Early Karl Barth: Historical Contexts and Intellectual Formation, 1905–1935.* Beiträge Zur Historischen Theologie 184. Tübingen: Mohr Siebeck, 2018.
Piper, John. *Desiring God.* Sisters, OR: Multnomah, 2003.
Pollard, Thomas Evan. *Johannine Christology and the Early Church.* Cambridge: Cambridge University Press, 1970.
Ratzinger, Joseph. 'Retrieving the Tradition: Concerning the Notion of Person in Theology'. *Communio* 17 (1990): 439–54.
Reeling Brouwer, Rinse. *Grondvormen van theologische systematiek.* Vught: Skandalon, 2009.
Rosenau, Hartmut. *Allversöhnung: ein transzendentaltheologischer Grundlegungsversuch.* Berlin: W. de Gruyter, 1993.
Ruler, Arnold A. van. *Verzameld werk*, vol. 4A. Zoetermeer: Boekencentrum, 2011.
Saarinen, Risto. *God and the Gift: An Ecumenical Theology of Giving.* Collegeville, MI: Liturgical, 2005.
Sarisky, Darren, ed. *Theologies of Retrieval: An Exploration and Appraisal.* Edinburgh: T&T Clark, 2017.
Schaff, Philip. *The Creeds of Christendom.* Bibliotheca Symbolica Ecclesiæ Universalis. New York: Harper & Brothers, 1882.
Schimansky, Gerd. *Christ ohne Kirche: Rückfrage beim ersten Radikalen der Reformation: Sebastian Franck.* Stuttgart: Radius-Verlag, 1980.
Schmidt-Leukel, Perry. 'Exclusivism, Inclusivism, Pluralism: The Tripolar Typology – Clarified and Reaffirmed'. In *The Myth of Religious Superiority: Multifaith Explorations of Religious Pluralism*, edited by Paul F. Knitter, 13–27. Maryknoll, NY: Orbis, 2005.
Schwöbel, Christoph. *Christlicher Glaube im Pluralismus. Studien zu einer Theologie der Kultur.* Tübingen: Mohr Siebeck, 2003.
Schwöbel, Christoph. 'Die Trinitätslehre als Rahmentheorie des christlichen Glaubens. Vier Thesen zur Bedeutung der Trinität in der christlichen Dogmatik'. In *Gott in Beziehung: Studien zur Dogmatik*, 25–51. Tübingen: Mohr Siebeck, 2002.
Schwöbel, Christoph. 'Einleitung'. In *Gott, Götter, Götzen: XIV. Europäischer Kongress für Theologie (11.–15. September 2011 in Zürich)*, edited by Christoph Schwöbel, 11–20. Leipzig: Evangelischer Verlagsanstalt, 2013.
Schwöbel, Christoph. *Gott im Gespräch: Studien zur theologischen Gegenwartsdeutung.* Tübingen: Mohr Siebeck, 2011.
Schwöbel, Christoph. *Gott in Beziehung. Studien zur Dogmatik.* Tübingen: Mohr Siebeck, 2002.
Schwöbel, Christoph. 'Gottes Ökumene. Über das Verhältnis von Kirchengemeinschaft und Gottesverständnis'. In *Christlicher Glaube im Pluralismus. Studien zu einer Theologie der Kultur*, 107–32. Tübingen: Mohr Siebeck, 2003.

Schwöbel, Christoph. 'Law and Gospel'. In *Religion Past and Present*, edited by Hans Dieter Betz, 4th edn, 3:862–67. Tübingen: Mohr Siebeck, 2006–13.
Schwöbel, Christoph. 'Particularity, Universality, and the Religions: Toward a Christian Theology of Religions'. In *Christian Uniqueness Reconsidered: The Myth of a Pluralistic Theology of Religions*, edited by Gavin D'Costa, 30–47. Maryknoll, NY: Orbis, 1990.
Servetus, Michael. *Christianismi restitutio*, 1790.
Servetus, Michael. *The Restoration of Christianity: An English Translation of Christianismi Restitutio, 1553*. Translated by Marian Hillar and Christopher A. Hoffman. Lewiston, NY: Edwin Mellen, 2007.
Slot, Edward van 't. 'Die christologische Konzentration: Anfang und Durchführung'. *Zeitschrift für Dialektische Theologie* 61, no. 1 (2015): 12–31.
Slot, Edward van 't. *Negativism of Revelation? Bonhoeffer and Barth on Faith and Actualism*. Dogmatik in Der Moderne 12. Tübingen: Mohr Siebeck, 2015.
Socinus, Faustus. *De Jesu Christo Servatore*. Alex Rodecius, 1594.
Sölle, Dorothee. *Suffering*. Twentieth Century Religious Thought. Philadelphia, PA: Fortress, 1975.
Spinoza, Benedictus de. *Complete Works*. Edited by Michael L Morgan. Translated by Samuel Shirley. Indianapolis, IN: Hackett, 2002.
Swain, Scott R. 'Lutheran and Reformed Sacramental Theology: Seventeenth–Nineteenth Centuries'. In *The Oxford Handbook of Sacramental Theology*, edited by Hans Boersma and Matthew Levering, 362–80. Oxford: Oxford University Press, 2015.
Talbott, Thomas. *The Inescapable Love of God*, 2nd edn. Eugene, OR: Wipf and Stock, 2014.
Talbott, Thomas. 'Universalism'. In *The Oxford Handbook of Eschatology*, edited by Jerry L. Walls, 446–61. New York: Oxford University Press, 2010.
Talstra, Eep. *De Éne God is de andere niet: theologie en rolverdeling in Jeremia 5:1–9*. Amsterdam: VU University Press, 2011.
Talstra, Eep. 'Text, Tradition, Theology: The Example of the Book of Joel'. In *Strangers and Pilgrims on Earth: Essays in Honour of Abraham van de Beek*, edited by Ed. A. J. G. van der Borght and Paul van Geest, 309–28. Leiden: Brill, 2012.
Ticciati, Susannah. *A New Apophaticism: Augustine and the Redemption of Signs*. Leiden: Brill, 2015.
Trueman, Carl R. *The Claims of Truth: John Owen's Trinitarian Theology*. Carlisle: Paternoster, 1998.
Tylenda, Joseph N. 'Calvin and Christ's Presence in the Supper—True or Real'. *Scottish Journal of Theology* 27, no. 1 (February 1974): 65–75. https://doi.org/10.1017/S00369 30600059056.
Vanhoozer, Kevin J. 'Analytics, Poetics, and the Mission of Dogmatic Discourse'. In *The Task of Dogmatics: Explorations in Theological Method*, edited by Oliver Crisp and Fred Sanders, 23–48. Grand Rapids, MI: Zondervan, 2017.
Vanhoozer, Kevin J. *The Drama of Doctrine: A Canonical-Linguistic Approach to Christian Theology*. Philadelphia, PA: Westminster John Knox, 2005.
Velema, Willem Hendrik. *De leer van de Heilige Geest bij Abraham Kuyper*. 's Gravenhage: Uitgeverij Van Keulen, 1957.
Voetius, Gisbertus. *D. Gysberti Voetii Selectarum Disputationum Fasciculus*. Edited by Abraham Kuyper. Amstelodami: Wormser, 1887.
Voetius, Gisbertus. *Selectae disputationes theologicae*. Ultrajecti: Johannes à Waesberge, 1648–69.

Voetius, Gisbertus. *Voetius' catechisatie over den Heidelbergschen Catechismus: naar Poudroyen's editie van 1662 op nieuw uitgegeven, bij ons publiek ingeleid, en met enkele aanteekeningen voorzien*. Edited by Abraham Kuyper. Gebroeders Huge, 1891.
Voolstra, Sjouke. *Het Woord is vlees geworden: De melchioritisch-mennisten incarnatieleer*. Kampen: J. H. Kok, 1982.
Webster, John. *Confessing God: Essays in Christian Dogmatics II*. London: T&T Clark, 2005.
Webster, John. 'Principles of Systematic Theology'. *International Journal of Systematic Theology* 11, no. 1 (1 January 2009): 56–71. https://doi.org/10.1111/j.1468-2400.2008.00423.x.
Webster, John. 'Theologies of Retrieval'. In *The Oxford Handbook of Systematic Theology*, edited by Kathryn Tanner, John Webster and Iain Torrance, 583–99. Oxford: Oxford University Press, 2007.
Wengert, Timothy J. *Law and Gospel: Philip Melanchthon's Debate with John Agricola of Eisleben over 'Poenitentia'*. Grand Rapids, MI: Baker, 1997.
Wengert, Timothy J. *Philip Melanchthon's Annotationes in Johannem in Relation to Its Predecessors and Contemporaries*. Geneva: Librairie Droz, 1987.
Wengst, Klaus. 'Der Beitrag der neutestamentlichen Zitate zum Verständnis der Barmer Theologischen Erklärung'. *Theologische Zeitschrift* 41, no. 3 (1985): 295–316.
Westminster Confession of Faith (1646).
Williams, George Huntston. *The Radical Reformation*, 3rd edn. Sixteenth Century Essays & Studies 15. Kirksville, MO: Sixteenth Century Journal, 1992.
Wisse, Maarten. 'Christus in het midden: Identiteit en pluraliteit in het reformatorisch onderwijs'. In *De multiculturele Refo-school*, edited by John Exalto, 215–38. Biblebelt Studies 3. Apeldoorn: Labarum Academic, 2017.
Wisse, Maarten. 'De integratie van theologie en religiewetenschap in Stefan Paas' Vreemdelingen en priesters: De Utrechtse theologische faculteit in de jaren '90'. *Soteria* 35, no. 1 (2018): 19–31.
Wisse, Maarten. 'Doing Theology through Reception Studies: Towards a Post-Postmodern Theological Hermeneutics'. *Nederduits Gereformeerd Theologisch Tijdschrift* 53, no. Supplement 3 (2012): 239–49. https://doi.org/10.5952/53-0-237.
Wisse, Maarten. 'Habitus Fidei: An Essay on the History of a Concept'. *Scottish Journal of Theology* 56, no. 2 (2003): 172–89.
Wisse, Maarten. 'The Inseparable Bond between Covenant and Predestination: Cocceius and Barth'. In *Scholasticism Reformed: Essays in Honour of Willem J. Van Asselt*, edited by Maarten Wisse, Marcel Sarot and Willemien Otten, 259–79. STAR 14. Leiden: Brill, 2010.
Wisse, Maarten. 'The Meaning of the Authority of the Bible'. *Religious Studies* 36 (2000): 473–87.
Wisse, Maarten. *Scripture between Identity and Creativity: A Hermeneutical Theory Building upon Four Interpretations of Job*. Ars Disputandi Supplement Series 1. Utrecht: Ars Disputandi, 2003. http://dspace.library.uu.nl/handle/1874/294105.
Wisse, Maarten. 'Towards a Theological Account of Theology: Reconceptualizing Church History and Systematic Theology'. In *Orthodoxy, Process and Product*, edited by Mathijs Lamberigts, Lieven Boeve and Terrence Merrigan, 351–74. BETL 227. Leuven: Peeters, 2009.
Wisse, Maarten. *Trinitarian Theology beyond Participation: Augustine's de Trinitate and Contemporary Theology*. T&T Clark Studies in Systematic Theology 11. London: T&T Clark International, 2011.

Wisse, Maarten, and Anthony Dupont. '"Nostis qui in schola Christi eruditi estis, Iacob ipsum esse Israel": Sermo 122, In Iohannis euangelium tractatus 7 and the Donatist and Pelagian Controversies'. *Zeitschrift für antikes Christentum* 18, no. 2 (2014): 302–25.

Wisse, Maarten, and Fabian Eikelboom. 'Alle gelovigen zijn gelijk, maar sommigen meer dan anderen: Een verkenning van de relatie tussen avondmaal en ambt'. *Kerk en Theologie* 68, no. 1 (2017): 64–83.

Wisse, Maarten, and Hugo Meijer. 'Pneumatology: Tradition and Renewal'. In *Brill Companion to Reformed Orthodoxy*, edited by Herman J. Selderhuis, 465–518. Leiden: Brill, 2013.

Wisse, Maarten, Bernhard van der Knijff, Pieter Auke van den Berg and Sandra Uijl. 'Promoting Priestly Christianity: The Role of Scripture in Max Thurian's the Eucharistic Memorial'. *Questions Liturgiques/Studies in Liturgy* 101 (2021): 202–20.

Wolf, Ernst. 'Gesetz V. Gesetz und Evangelium, dogmengeschichtlich'. In *Religion in Geschichte und Gegenwart*, edited by Kurt Galling, 2:1519–26. Tübingen: Mohr Siebeck, 1958.

Wollebius, Johannes. *Compendium Theologiae Christianae*, 2nd edn. Amsterdam: Aegidius Janssonius, 1655.

Young, Frances M. 'Christology and Creation'. In *The Myriad Christ: Plurality and the Quest for Unity in Contemporary Christology*, edited by Terrence Merrigan and Jacques Haers, 191–205. BETL 152. Leuven: Peeters, 2000.

Zanchi, Girolamo. *De Religione Christiana Fides = Confession of Christian Religion*. Edited by Luca Baschera and Christian Moser. Leiden: Brill, 2007.

BIBLICAL INDEX

Old Testament

Genesis
32   52

Exodus
33.20   56
24, 33   52

Deuteronomy
29.29   144
30.14   68

Psalms
8.5   59

Proverbs
11.21   144

Isaiah
53.5   154–5

New Testament

Matthew
5.8   28, 56, 59
5.48   40
11.28   102, 103
11.29; NIV   191

John
1.1   63, 66
1.2   66
1.3-4   61, 62
1.3-4; NIV   61–2
1.4   63, 71, 73, 74, 76
1.5   63, 73
1.9   73, 75
1.10-11   63
1.12   63
1.13   73

1.14   62, 63, 64, 71, 74, 75, 102, 103, 105–6, 111
3.16   57
3.36   144
6.35   191
10   87, 90
10.1,9   85, 88
10.30   59
14   60, 87
14.6   53–6, 84, 85, 89–90, 105
14.9   56–8
17.3   63

Acts
17   55

Romans
1   55, 73
1.16   32
1.9   73
1.18   53
2.15   29
3.21-26   24–5, 31
5.20   24
9.13   146
10.8   68

1 Corinthians
6.19   59, 69
5.7f   40

2 Corinthians
3.6   24
5.19   102, 103

Philippians
2.6   58
2.7   59

Hebrews
2.7   59

GENERAL INDEX

Note: Footnotes are indicated by the page number followed by 'n' and the footnote number e.g., 20 n.1 refers to footnote 1 on page 20.

Abrahamse, Jan Martijn 15 n.44
Allen, Michael 166 n.7
Anabaptism 11, 12, 31, 36, 60, 62–4, 66, 71, 73, 74, 77, 119
anthropology 63–4, 155–9, 162
antinomianism 12, 117
anti-Trinitarianism 65
  see also Trinity
Aquinas, Thomas 11, 20, 26
Areopagite, Dionysius 60
Arianism 67
Arminianism 36, 142
Asselt, Willem J. van 36 n.47, n.49, 38 n.55, 117 n.3
assurance of faith 134, 180
  predestination and 147–50
Athanasius 11, 63
atonement, doctrine of 12, 17, 151, 160, 161, 162
  definite 143 n.29
  substitutionary 17, 152–3
Augustine 4, 9, 10, 11, 16, 20, 22–6, 28, 43, 44, 47, 51–4, 55–61, 77, 117, 120, 128, 131, 143, 145, 146 n.33, 181, 184
Austin, J. L. 3, 196
  speech act theory 45
  theory of illocutions 4, 7

Baars, Arie 67 n.53
baptism 67, 70, 71, 174–6, 177
Barclay, John M. G. 7 n.24
Barmen Declaration 84–90, 98, 103, 105, 113
Barth, Karl 1, 3, 6, 16, 22, 33, 38–42, 43–4, 47, 66, 79, 82 n.7, 83 n.8, 80–90, 91–8, 98–110, 111, 113–14, 120, 140–2, 145–6
  actualism 100
  see also Christocentrism
Bavel, Tarsicius J. van 184 n.72
Bavinck, Herman 167–9, 170–2, 174–8
Bayer, Oswald 43 n.66
Beek, A. van de 6
Beeke, Joel R. 144 n.31

Beintker, Michael 81–2 n.4, 84 n.9, 95 n.39
believers 2, 6, 58, 61, 69, 70, 73, 75, 122, 145, 166, 177, 178, 182, 197
Belt, Henk van den 118
Bergmeier, Roland 63 n.42
Berkhof, Hendrikus 6
Berkouwer, Gerrit Cornelis 40, 97, 166 n.4
Bible 1, 3 n.15, 20, 25, 29, 30–1, 40, 44, 46, 56, 60, 69, 86, 90, 114, 120, 123, 124, 132, 139–42, 146, 155–6
Billings, J. Todd 166–7 n.7
Boer, Erik de 72 n.68
Boeve, Lieven 126 n.26, 187 n.9
Boezelman, Wijnand 60 n.34
Bonhoeffer 81 n.4, 136
Brague, Rémi 29 n.25, 56 n.24
Brakel, Wilhelmus à 144 n.31
Braun, Dietrich 90 n.26
Breukelman, F. H. 30 n.28, n30, 34 n.44
Britain 2
Brümmer, Vincent 3, 6, 7, 45, 97 n.44, 160 n.12, 196
Bucer, Martin 60, 64, 65, 72–4, 76 n.83
Bultmann, Rudolf 43 n.66
Bünker, Michael 26 n.15, 41 n.62
Burger, Hans 59 n.33, 118 n.9, 163 n.15, 171 n.30
Busch, Eberhard 85 n.12, 86 n.17, 90

Calvin, John 10, 30–5, 34 n.45, 37, 49, 51, 64, 72–4, 76, 99, 120, 135, 148, 166, 171, 176, 177
Calvinism 135, 138, 182–4
Catechism 85, 86, 119, 120
Chauvet, Louis-Marie 7 n.24, 182
Christ, Jesus 3, 6, 13, 21, 39, 42, 43, 47, 50, 52, 66–7, 73, 75, 93, 95–6, 116, 125–6, 127, 188
Christian 2, 3, 6, 9, 15, 20, 23, 29, 43, 45, 95, 117, 151, 166, 189, 194, 197
  funerals 137
  hedonism 121–2

General Index

and non-Christians 77, 156
   theology 4, 9, 13, 14, 17, 98, 116, 185, 188, 190, 195, 194
   tradition 8, 193
Christianity 4, 9, 17, 19, 20, 21, 23, 54, 127, 132
   classical 52
   history of 23, 40
Christocentrism 16, 17, 19, 42, 44, 47, 48–51, 58, 61, 69, 79, 81 n.4, 110–12
   epistemological 50
   ontological 50
   soteriological 50
Christology 8–11, 47–8, 125 n.23, 165
   'concentration' 79
   radical 64
   and soteriology 11–13
   two-nature 10, 11, 65
Christomonism 81 n.4
Clark, R. Scott 4 n.16, 33
Clooney, Francis X. 185 n.1
Coakley, Sarah 3
Cocceius, Johannes 38, 117
commissives 3, 4, 7, 45, 196
community of faith 2, 7–9, 15
   Christ-confessing 8
confessions 54, 119, 188, 194
   Belgic 35, 184
   Gallican 35
constatives 3, 4, 196
Cortez, Marc 48, 50 n.12, 81 n.2, n.4
Covenant
   New 21, 25, 32, 35, 38
   Old 6, 38, 21
creed
   Chalcedonian 10, 95
   Nicene-Constantinopolitan 10, 60
Crisp, Oliver 2 n.9, 135
Cupitt, Don 2

D'Costa, Gavin 185 n.2, 187 n.8, 188
Danz, Christian 185 n.3, 187
Decalogue 21, 23, 29, 41, 56, 126
   first commandment of 19
   see also Ten Commandments
deification 11, 59, 63
Dekker, Eef 142 n.28
Derrida, Jacques 14 n.41
Deuteronomy 11
Di Medici lords 160
dogmatics 1, 2, 4, 5–6, 8–11, 15, 19, 20, 40, 44, 45, 123, 125
   contemporary 3, 9–10
   critical 3
   elenctic nature 13–14, 40

irenic nature 13
   modern 1, 6, 9
   normative task of 9, 13
   positive 3
   protestant 1
   as 'second act' 7–8
   universalism 138
   verdictive 3
Donatism 57, 70
double predestination 142, 144–7
   classical doctrine of 131–4
Dupont, Anthony 56 n.25, 57 n.27

Eagleton, Terry 14
Ebeling, Gerhard 43 n.66
ecclesiology 165
Eckhart 70
Edwards, Jonathan 121
Eglinton, James 170 n.29
Enders, Markus 61 n.35
enlightenment 4, 19, 39, 42, 122–3
   and postmodernity 5
epistemology 4, 50
Erasmus, Desiderius 49, 62, 63, 64, 66, 68, 73
Eucharist 73, 74, 180, 182
evangelicalism 12, 120
evil 62, 109, 136–7, 141, 156, 159, 161
   see also sin
exclusivism 186–8
expressives 3, 4
externalism 70

faith 1, 2, 11, 101, 127, 181, 182
   in Christ 70, 77, 86, 104–5
   Christian 3, 21, 23, 54, 57, 95, 151, 166, 188–90
   community of 7–8, 64, 170
   see also assurance of faith
Ferraris, Maurizio 14 n.41
Fesko, John V. 117 n.4
Feuerbach, Ludwig 44
Forde, Gerhard O. 40 n.61, 43 n.66
forgiveness 12, 27, 38, 137–40, 159
Franck, Sebastian 67–9, 71, 72, 74, 77
Frei, Hans W. 1, 156 n.10
Frey, Jörg 155 n.8
Friedrich, Martin 26 n.15, 41 n.62

Geldhof, Joris 192 n.19
Gibson, David 48, 80 n.1, 81 n.4
Gilland, David Andrew 42 n.64
Gleason, Ronald N. 171 n.30
God 1, 165
   doctrine of 140

as lord of Florence 160–2
and world 165
Gomes, Alan W. 152 n.4
good
  and evil 161
  see also sin
Gospel of John 16, 47, 49, 51–2, 65, 77, 78, 84, 90, 113, 122, 155, 191, 195
Greggs, Tom 97 n.46, 132 n.1
Grenz, Stanley J. 93 n.35
Gunton, Colin E. 1 n.2
Gutiérrez, Gustavo 8

Hägglund, Bengt 195 n.20
Hanson, Anthony T. 52 n.15
hard universalism 136–42
Harinck, George 170
Härle, Wilfried 186, 187
Hart, David Bentley 132 n.1, 133, 134
Haspelmath-Finatti, Dorothea 15 n.43
Hayden-Roy, Patrick Marshall 67 n.57, 70 n.63
Heeren, Jelmer 165 n.1, n.2
Heidelberg Catechism 120, 151, 168, 171, 174
Heim, S. Mark 185 n.2
Helm, Paul 140
Helvetic Confession of 1536 35
Hermanni, Friedrich 185 n.3, 187
Herms, Eilert 13 n.36, 41 n.63, 186, 187, 190 n.16, 191 n.17
Hesselink, I. John 4 n.16, 33, 35
Hick, John 136, 188
Hill, Edmund 24 n.6, 53 n.17, 54 n.18
Hitler, Adolf 86, 98, 102
Hoffman, Melchior 71–2, 77
Holy Scripture 73
Holy Spirit 10, 26, 29, 34 n.45, 43, 69, 159, 166, 170, 179
Horton, Michael 4 n.16, 33, 34 n.43
Huber, Wolfgang 124 n.22
Huijgen, Arnold 49, 50 n.13, 116 n.12, 118

inclusivism 186–8
Islam 9
Israel 6, 21, 127, 128
Iwand, Hans Joachim 103

Jacobs, Tom 14 n.40
Janse, Wim 166–7
Jews 24, 29, 58, 146, 192–3
  see also Judaism
Johannine prologue 52, 59–61, 64, 113–14
Jong, K. W. de 176 n.62
Judaism 9, 127
  see also Jews

Jüngel, Eberhard 1 n.2, 85 n.12
justice 15–16, 160–2
justification 12

Kärkkäinen, Veli-Matti 185 n.2
Kilby, Karen 10, 11 n.31
Koch, Anton Friedrich 163 n.15
Koch, John D. 43 n.66
Kooi, Cornelis van der 93 n.36, 166, 167 n.9, 171 n.33
Kooiman, W. J. 117 n.6
Köstenberger, Andreas J. 52 n.16, 59 n.33
Krötke, Wolf 81 n.4
Kühn, Rolf 61 n.35
Kuitert, Harry M. 2 n.5
Kuyper, Abraham 17, 21 n.2, 36 n.51, 119, 165–76, 178–83, 195 n.21

Law and gospel 4–6, 8, 9, 13, 16, 19, 20–1, 38, 39–46, 47, 77, 124–7, 131, 162–3, 168, 189–94
law of nature (*lex naturalis*) 29
Leeuw, G. van der 166
legalism 70
Lindbeck, George A. 1
Liturgical Movement 166
Lombardus, Petrus 26 n.11
Lord's Supper 165–6, 168–70
Luther, Martin 4, 11–12, 13 n.36, 22, 23–4, 26, 28, 30, 32–3, 36, 41, 45, 72, 74–7, 86, 92, 99, 100–1, 103, 117, 119, 126, 131, 161 n.13, 169, 175, 179, 181 n.69, 182–3, 191, 193, 195, 196
Lutheranism 29, 33–4, 40–1, 74, 75 n.77, n.79, 76 n.82, n.83, n.84, 119

MacDonald, Gregory 132 n.1, n.2, 133, 136, 137 n.13, 138, 139, 140–2
Maury, Pierre 81
McCormack, Bruce L. 48, 80 n.1, 81 n.3, 82, 100 n.54
McDermott, Gerald R. 185 n.2
McDonald, Suzanne 97 n.46
McGrath, Alister E. 119 n.11
Meijer, Hugo 34 n.45, 167
Melanchthon, Philip 20, 21, 22, 23, 25, 26–30, 32–5, 36, 37, 38, 41, 43, 44–6, 131, 195 n.22, 196
Menken, Maarten J. J. 52 n.15
Milbank, John 62, 66
Montanism 70
Moyaert, Marianne 186 n.5, 192 n.19
Muller, Richard A. 34 n.43, 48–9, 52, 56, 118

Muslim 192–3
  see *also* Islam

neo-Calvinism 167–8
new law 26
Netland, Harold A. 185 n.2
Neuprotestantismus 100
Nietzsche, Friedrich 44
non-Christians 23, 55–6, 67, 77, 156, 190

Olevianus, Caspar 36
Olson, Roger E. 93 n.35
open theism 142
optimistic anthropology 64
Owen, John 12, 17, 151–8, 161, 162, 163

pantheism 67
paradigm, epistemological 4
particularism 51, 143
Pauline/Paul 35, 53
Pelagianism 24, 57, 70
Perkins, William 148
Peterson, Paul Silas 86 n.16
Piper, John 121–2
pluralism 186–8
pneumatology 165
Pollard, Thomas Evan 60 n.34
post-Marxist
  philosophical frame 125
  power analysis 44
predestinarianism 136, 145
predestination 131–4, 144–7
  and assurance of faith 147–50
promises 196
propositions 1, 3, 4, 99, 109, 149, 196
protestantism 12
purification 88
Puritanism 12–13

Ratzinger, Joseph 65
realism 4
Reeling Brouwer, Rinse 30 n.28, n.30, 84 n.9, 86 n.15
Reformation 11–12, 16, 22, 28, 43, 44, 46, 47, 59–61, 65, 70, 72, 115, 116, 117, 125
Reformed orthodoxy 134
religions
  as sources of knowledge 186–9
  as truth 194–7
revelation, in Jesus Christ 2, 6, 13, 37, 39, 42, 44, 19, 99, 101, 106, 108, 109, 112, 116, 127–8, 138–9, 189
Rosenau, Hartmut 132 n.1

Ruler, Arnold A. van 96
Rutherford, Samuel 154

Saarinen, Risto 7 n.24
salvation 8, 9, 11, 17, 33, 44, 64, 133, 168
  in Christ 23, 57, 59, 68
  free offer of 21, 23, 29
  promise of 21
sanctification 12
Sarisky, Darren 19 n.1
Schaff, Philip 54 n.18, 85 n.13, 184 n.71
Schimansky, Gerd 69
Schmidt-Leukel, Perry 185 n.4
scholastic theology
  Reformed 4, 36–8
  medieval 26
  see *also* theology
scholasticism *see* scholastic theology
Schröter, Jens 155 n.8
Schwöbel, Christoph 10, 117 n.6, 124 n.22, 151, 162 n.13, 186–90
Scriptural Reasoning 185
Scripture 2, 8, 12, 25, 28–9, 38, 43, 69, 71, 73, 118, 136, 122–3, 125 n.23
  doctrine of 16, 115
  in dogmatics 19
  management 123
  in theology 10
Selderhuis, Herman J. 34 n.45, 117 n.4, 167 n.8, n.10
Servetus, Michael 10, 11, 31, 36, 50 n.14, 60, 65–7, 68 n.60, 70–4, 77
Simons, Menno 11, 71–2, 74, 77
sin 17, 24, 66, 71, 104, 158, 159
  see *also* evil
Slot, Edward van 't 81 n.4, 82, 94, 97 n.46, 100 n.54
Socinianism 117
Socinus, Faustus 12, 17, 36, 151–8, 157–8, 160–2
sola scriptura 115, 122, 128–30
  and Law and Gospel 124–7
  meaning of 116–20
  positive affirmation of 127–8
  principle of 16, 115, 119
Sölle, Dorothee 132 n.3
soteriology 11, 23, 41, 49, 132, 136
  Christology and 11–13
Spinoza, Benedictus de 115
substitutionary atonement 17, 152–8
Swain, Scott R. 166–7 n.7

Talbott, Thomas 133, 134
Talstra, Eep 129 n.28

Tanner, Kathryn 19 n.1
Tauler, Johannes 68 n.60
Ten Commandments 21
  role in believer's life 29
  see also Decalogue
Testament
  New 5, 10, 11, 12, 20, 27–8, 32, 35, 37, 52, 56, 122
  Old 5, 10, 11, 12, 20, 27–8, 32, 35, 37, 52, 122
theology 1, 2–3, 4, 8, 10, 13, 17, 22–3, 28, 30–1, 40, 47, 60, 62, 64, 115, 119, 133, 178, 185, 165–8, 189–94
  Christian 4, 9, 13, 14, 17, 98, 116, 185, 188, 190, 195, 194
  'Christocentric' 49
  classical Reformed 38
  comparative 185
  contemporary systematic 2
  federal 34, 37
  feminist 132
  medieval scholastic 26
  modern 48, 123
  natural 34, 42, 54, 73, 79
  philosophical 3–4
  pre-modern 48, 49
  protestant 40, 123
  Reformation 22, 28, 38
  Reformed 126
  of retrieval 19 n.1
  Roman Catholic 36, 119
  medieval 26
  systematic 2–3, 19, 22, 44, 115, 132, 165
  Trinitarian 17, 51, 185
Ticciati, Susannah 149 n.39
Torrance, Iain 19 n.1
tota scriptura 117, 122
totus Christus 184
transcendence 127
tribalization 14
Trinity 128, 168, 169, 171, 185, 188
  doctrine of the 10–11
  see also anti-Trinitarianism

Trueman, Carl R. 155 n.9
Turrettin, Francis 38
Tylenda, Joseph N. 166–7 n.7

United States 4
universalism 51, 133
  hard 136–42
  'hopeful' 146 n.32
  soft 142–4
Ursinus, Zacharius 36

Vanhoozer, Kevin J. 2, 3
Velema, Willem Hendrik 167 n.12
Virgin Mary 66
Voetius, Gisbertus 5, 20, 21 n.2, 36, 37, 38, 117, 119, 191, 195–6
Voolstra, Sjouke 71 n.64, n.66, n.67

Webster, John 2, 19 n.1, 80 n.1
Wengert, Timothy J. 30 n.29, 73 n.69, 74 n.76
Wengst, Klaus 88 n.19, 90
Westminster Confession of Faith (1646) 147 n.34, 149 n.40, 176 n.66
Williams, George Huntston 71 n.65
Wisse, Maarten 3 n.15, 5 n.17, 9 n.26, 10 n.30, 13 n.35, 14 n.38, 15 n.42, n.45, 22 n.5, 28 n.22, 34 n.45, 48 n.1, 54 n.19, 56 n.25, 57 n.26, 58 n.30, 62 n.37, 95 n.41, 96 n.43, 97 n.47, 98 n.48, 104 n.62, 117 n.3, 121 n.15, 123 n.18, 124 n.20, 126 n.25, 143 n.30, 148 n.36, 165 n.1, n.2, 167 n.10, 174 n.54, 178 n.68, 196 n.25, 197 n.27
Witsius, Herman 38
Wittgenstein, Ludwig 3
Wolf, Ernst 26 n.15
Wollebius, Johannes 134 n.9

Young, Frances M. 61 n.36

Žák, Lubomír 190 n.16
Zanchi, Girolamo 36, 178 n.67
zwinglianism 165, 166, 173, 180–2

www.ingramcontent.com/pod-product-compliance
Lightning Source LLC
Chambersburg PA
CBHW062222300426
44115CB00012BA/2173